On the Old Plaza

Also by Catharine Savage Brosman

POETRY
Watering (1972)
Abiding Winter (1983) [chapbook]
Journeying from Canyon de Chelly (1990)
Passages (1996)
The Swimmer and Other Poems (2000) [chapbook].
Places in Mind (2000)
Petroglyphs: Poems and Prose (2003) [chapbook].
The Muscled Truce (2003)
Range of Light (2007)
Breakwater (2009)
Trees in a Park (2010) [chapbook]
Under the Pergola (2011)
On the North Slope (2012)

CREATIVE PROSE
The Shimmering Maya and Other Essays (1994)
Finding Higher Ground (2003)

CRITICISM
André Gide: l'évolution de sa pensée religieuse (1962)
Malraux, Sartre, and Aragon as Political Novelists (1964)
Roger Martin du Gard (1968)
Jean-Paul Sartre (1983)
Jules Roy (1988)
Art as Testimony: The Work of Jules Roy (1989)
An Annotated Bibliography of Criticism on André Gide, 1973-1988 (1990)
Dictionary of Literary Biography, volumes 65, 72, 83, 119, 123, edited (1988-1992)
Simone de Beauvoir Revisited (1991)
Twentieth-Century French Culture, 1900-1975, edited with an introduction (1995)
Visions of War in France: Fiction, Art, Ideology (1999)
Existential Fiction (2000)
Albert Camus (2000)
Louisiana Creole Literature: A Historical Study (2013)

On the Old Plaza

Poems

Catharine Savage Brosman

MERCER UNIVERSITY PRESS
MACON, GEORGIA

MUP/ P 491 // H 898

Published by Mercer University Press
© 2014 by Mercer University Press
1400 Coleman Avenue
Macon, Georgia 31207

9 8 7 6 5 4 3 2 1

Books published by Mercer University Press are printed on acid-free paper
that meets the requirements of the American National Standard for
Information Sciences—Permanence of Paper for Printed Library Materials.

Interior Art by Ellen Custer

Library of Congress Cataloging-in-Publication Data
Brosman, Catharine Savage, 1934-
  [Poems. Selections]
  On the old plaza : poems / Catharine Savage Brosman.
      pages ; cm
  ISBN 978-0-88146-514-3 (hardback : alk. paper) -- ISBN 0-88146-514-3 (hardback :
alk. paper) -- ISBN 978-0-88146-496-2 (pbk. : alk. paper) -- ISBN 0-88146-496-1
(pbk. : alk. paper)
  I. Title.
  PS3552.R666A6 2014
  811'.54--dc23
                                                              2014023947

To my husband, Patric Savage,
and my daughter, Katherine Brosman Deimling (Kate), and her family;
and in memory of my parents and grandparents

"Style is a question not of technique but of vision."
—Marcel Proust

"The essence of art is human association."
— Carl Andre

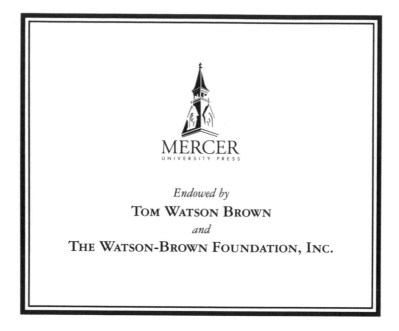

Endowed by
TOM WATSON BROWN
and
THE WATSON-BROWN FOUNDATION, INC.

Contents

Acknowledgments

Grateful acknowledgment is made to the publishers of the following publications, in which the poems mentioned first appeared:

Able Muse: "Birds," "Composition," "Departure," "Edith's Funeral," "For a Singer Who Is Ill," "Sunny," "A Valedictory," "Vermilion Cliffs," "Wilson's Phalarope";

American Life in Poetry (syndicated print column and Internet site): "Cattle Fording Tarryall Creek";

Arkansas Review: A Journal of Delta Studies: "Turtles and Ducks";

Bulletin des Amis d'André Gide: "Gide Misjudges a Manuscript" (with French translation by Jeannine Hayat);

Chronicles: A Magazine of American Culture: "In the Veragua Rain Forest," "On a Disgruntled Poet," "On the Old Plaza, Las Vegas," "To Readers";

First Things: "At Sea," "A Late Summer Idyll," "On a Certain Viennese Doctor," "Smoky Sky";

Měasŭre: "The Dance," "For a Friend Who Hopes to Meet Her Grandfather Among the Shades," "In the Larco Herrera Museum," "Ship's Company";

Modern Age: "Gusty Winds," "On a Ballet by Sir Kenneth MacMillan," "On Alexandrines in English Verse," "Spiraea," "Sunset";

Orbis: "On a Dyspeptic Reviewer";

Quarterly Review: "On an Anonymous Reviewer," "On an Erstwhile Editor, Feminist"; "On an Official, Arrogant";

Sewanee Review: "Degas in New Orleans," "The Empress Eugénie Leaves Paris, 1870," "An Incident After the War," "At Jefferson Barracks Cemetery";

Southern Humanities Review: "In the Public Library";

Southwest Review: "Siegfried-Idyll."

To Readers

Illumined artfully by nature's pains,
new leaves announce intelligence of trees
with verdant murmurs, tracery of veins,
lobes, indentations, glossy verities.

Observe their signs, their waves of plenitude;
read palmate lines, admire pennate green;
feel transpiration through their airy mood—
arboreal pages, marvelous machine.

Though elsewhere dark truths lie—deep, diffident,
in privacy of cells—do not inquire
of roots in earthy commerce what is meant
as leafy head and under-thoughts conspire—

nor ask the composition of the blade
that chisels through the immaterial bone;
the language of substantial sun and shade
is hermeneutic to itself alone.

On the Old Plaza

On the Old Plaza, Las Vegas

—For Patric

Not the town you think when you hear the name,
that gamblers' paradise. No, the *first* Las Vegas,
at the foot of the Sangre de Cristo mountains
in northern New Mexico. Shabby
and disorderly along its fringes, to be sure;
yet it's still got charm, the way it spreads below
the troops of cedar, juniper, and piñon
which escort the range and crowd the mesa;

and the Old Town is styled well, with its plazas
and adobe buildings, churches, ancient trees.
So here we are, in the saloon at the Plaza Hotel,
dating from the 1880s, brought up to date
a bit, though not too much. Conversation
is in Spanish. Why visit Mexico? This is closer;
no one greets us with a sub-machine gun
(as in León airport when I went there last), and we

can drink the water, eat the lettuce, put ice
in our cocktails. Kidnapping is quite unlikely, too.
Moreover, we can have New Mexican cuisine.
New, I stress, with blue corn enchiladas,
surely the most flavorful, and sweet green chile
sauce. This is an arty town, as well—
lots of galleries, with paintings, pueblo pottery,
and native jewelry. We're only passing through,

an honorable one-night stand. No matter;
we can stuff a week of happiness into a day,
years into weeks, making up for time
lost foolishly, and knowing how to look, taste, touch—
returning, as it were, from surgery
or illness, recovery amazing, as if we'd never
been apart. Today we saw fine boulders, wavy
as a choppy lake, and here's a smooth adobe wall,

in terra-cotta hue. Just feel this fine wool textile
from the hands of "Two Gray Hills"; admire
the square, its arbors. What good wine, local, too!
Now, Darling, take my hand, and hold it well,
putting all your love into that act. Tomorrow
we shall lunch in Carrizozo, down near
the *Malpaís*, under a huisache tree, as in a pergola,
all, even regret, silvered in the sunlight and the shade.

Gusty Winds

Along a Colorado road—we won't forget—
three warning signs: "Gusty winds may exist."
—Or they may *not*. It's wise to hedge your bet.
So far this afternoon, at least, we've missed

them.—Is their being vacuously true,
no more? Perhaps they are unreal, a dream,
kin to imaginary numbers. You
and I may likewise be some clever scheme,

invented for strange ends, and even sane
according to odd rules, yet still unsure
of full existence. Varied, the refrain
returns: "High winds are likely." Is it pure

conjecture? Oh, my love! This is no trap
for mind, no darkling plain. Our lives revolve
around the possible; but still—mishap
or good—we're not a phantasy. Men solve

conundrums of the greatest magnitude—
trace stars, split atoms, and explore the moon—
write poems suitable for every mood,
philosophize, make love. We're opportune;

and as when Dr. Johnson kicked the stone,
affirming the reality of stuff,
we know that we're not looney, nor alone.—
Such highway metaphysics are enough

for now; we'll find a spot beneath the trees,
enjoy our picnic, rest, admire vast skies,
rejecting old suspicions of unease,
wits fresh, inviting currents of surprise.

Spiraea

The name suggests a horrible disease,
or bodily dysfunction. Not at all:
it's just a garden shrub, though quite at ease—
Plain Jane—with finer plants along a wall.

Thin branches spraying, tangled, from the root
fan out in asymmetrical design—
rough, arching canes, which seem irresolute
on principles of ornament and line.

In winter, rickety, the bushes flail
about, and scratch the air, till the regime
of April covers them with buds. A veil
of inflorescence spreads; each long raceme

leaves fragrant offerings for a garden god,
and trumpets spring's implicit reign as feat,
anticipating roses, goldenrod.
Adorned, if common, all are potent, neat—

dark premises of earth, sine qua non,
assigned to flower in appointed ways,
affording both the mineral truth of stone
and immaterial essence of bouquets.

Sierra Grande

Asea, on the high grasslands of the Llano Estacado,
we sail northwest into New Mexico. With us,
a school of clouds, multi-tinted in the early light
(gold, pale salmon, white), noses its way
in the shallow blue. Ahead, hazy notions form
conjectures: a phantom fleet, a harbor?
This can't be ocean, though, since the elevation
changes, troughs and billows rising, ten feet a mile,

toward the far chain of the Sangre de Cristos, soon
visible—sawteeth, snowy tops, nebulous idea.
We reach a roughened patch of igneous rock
and cinders scattered on the range, dregs of magma
marking a vast volcanic field—the cone
of Capulin, others shouldering the horizon,
and the broad shield volcano of Sierra Grande, high
above the plain, lit in post-Impressionistic hues,

blue, green, violet. The French explored this land,
as well as Spanish, naming Des Moines
and Capulin; but there's very little left of history—
hamlets, a few ranches, with cattle, pronghorn,
birds. We'll pass on Capulin, visited years
ago, but wonder if a road might take us to the foot
of the Sierra Grande, up her flanks. It seems, however,
that's the business of a day, or never—the terrain

unwilling, let us say, to be apprehended, at least
by passers-by. No matter: we will see the mountain
from three sides, the illumination turning.
Oh, I'd paint it if I could—the smooth incline,
as fitting thought, tonsured above the juniper
and piñon at its brow; mottled hide; cold lava
flowing down the dormant vent of time.
What's that among dark rocks—late-fallen sandstone

scree? No—a stillness that's alive, then movement.
It's a herd of pronghorns, in desert camouflage,
great eyes gazing, seizing almost the circumference—
a cluster with a fawn, two bucks, stern, alert,
grazing in the accidental traces of earth's fiery core,
which ignores us now by somnolence, and grants
us creatures mornings of sweet forage and immensity
of beauty, free, immeasurable, as we imagine heaven.

A Late Summer Idyll

We're superannuated now, no doubt.
Impossible to overlook the facts:
age blotches skin, puts muscle tone to rout,
winnows our hair, and gives us cataracts.

Pat's doctors rule. No whisky, beer, or wine;
he should not take long flights nor go abroad;
he eats rat-poison pills (hardly benign).
These wizards saved his life, though; I applaud.

But love is not dependent on a state
of youthful vigor, health, or pulchritude.
Beholders judge of beauty. Even late,
love is a matter of one's temper, mood,

and that imponderable, happy drive,
that draws *one* to another *one*, unique.
We've made our proper idyll: we're alive!
—and married, with a dash of modern chic.

Our time's our pleasure. From the balcony,
we've seen the mountains shimmer in the haze
of mid-September sun; a maple tree
gives shade and verdant murmurings of praise.

The season's shifting slightly; we admire
new currencies of color, which provide
exchange for wit and kindling for love's fire—
artillery of age, old passion's pride.

French Press

—For Nancy McCahren

It's just a simple coffee pot—a glass carafe, a lid,
a plunger with a filter that one presses down
when coarse-ground beans have steeped
a bit in boiling water, darkening. Oh, that aroma!
Lovely! Carefully, I pour the noble brew
for Nancy, Pat, myself. She and I first met
in France, ages ago ("Don't say how long!"),
where in the freezing winter we would sit

in dark cafés, ill-heated, and, with *jus* and grogs
or wine, talk on for hours—the books
devoured, our classes, men, the places
that we wished to visit. Then we went, first Italy—
where cold rain fell at Eastertide in Rome,
but Naples warmed us; Spain at Pentecost.
Summer finally came—then Greece, old Yugoslavia,
Vienna's pride, and more. Oh my, that time

was good! Our lives, just buds, or barely flowering,
have filled out since—roses, also thorns.
The season wanes, but blossoms still hang on,
their petals curling slightly at the edge.—Scented
coffee mingles with the steaming milk;
it's heavenly. Is this a Proustian moment,
odor, feeling, taste? Not quite; but it's two-layered
time, late Colorado summer, sun and wind,

the aspen turning gold, the coin of memory. We chat
as if no years had passed, while all is predicated
on their passing. Pat joins the reminiscing;
Nancy talks by phone with Mick, her lifetime love.
"Do a poem on the *cafetière*," she asks.
Though elegant, its presence, beside ours, is feeble—
force of heart outweighing form, idea,
all need except its own, the long, enduring thirst.

Columbine

A standing order in the forest: look,
as when I was a girl, for columbine.
It likes moist soil, with shade, beside a brook
perhaps, among the aspen, fir, and pine.

Its lovely name recalls the Latin word
for *dove*—those five white petals in its heart,
surrounded by high sepals, dyed and spurred
(thus *aquilegia*, the eagle's part).

Such beauty's often poisonous; they're bane.
Yet larval lepidoptera devour
the leaves, and prudent Indians would fain
consume, as salads, tasty bits of flower.

I'm searching now for Colorado Blue
("Caerulea"), the finest specimen,
with tones of lavender—a stunning hue,
set off by woodsy verdure of a glen.

At this late hour, what may this errand mean?
It's part nostalgia. My memories,
resolved ideally into fields of green,
require refreshment and details to tease

out meaning. My *innamorato*, Pat,
is here, too—Harlequin, a handsome wit.
I'm Columbine, and in my habitat;
not toxic, though—a condiment, to fit

our late romance and spur delight. The pace
is slower now, and at this altitude
we can't hike far; but still, we have the grace
to love these flowers, in a lover's mood.

Smoky Sky

The skies are sick, a feverish, jaundiced gray,
malodorous with foul effluvia,
dissembling skyline and the light of day—
crepuscular, infernal opera.

The pines, our lofty but immobile kin,
more vincible by axe, plague, wind, and fire,
succumb like straw to hot, malicious jinn,
limbs, trunks consumed, the image of desire,

as ashes, smoke, and orange retardant rise
from burning woodlands, billow up, then drift,
and flames, the essence of the enterprise,
break out and climb when wind directions shift.

Assailed by fire, flooded, shaken, whirled
by tourbillon or hurricane, we must
confront in time this elemental world—
definitively when we turn to dust.

If, at the finish, fire, not ice, prevails,
the whole earth vaporized in gaseous blaze,
the trees, expiring, will tell prescient tales—
sunsets of bile, apocalyptic haze.

At the "North Pole" Amusement Park

Who had the idea of putting rides, shops, a picnic pavilion
on a high mountainside part-way up Ute Pass
in Colorado? The place has been there for some fifty years;
yet this is my first visit, not having been a child
during that period, but having children with me this time,
as if I might be one again. The park is almost
miniature—small attractions cramped together, steep paths
threaded through them, ersatz châlets just big enough

for gift displays; and, in keeping with the theme, here's
Santa's house, and the old bearded man himself, idle,
taking the air on a tiny porch. It's cool today,
with rain clouds threatening on all sides, now that July,
the monsoon season, has begun. Fog encroaches. Through
its scrim, we see skinned, blackened hillsides
where the Waldo Canyon conflagration burned last month,
reaching across forests, leaping fire breaks and roads,

shaking its head of wrath among these paltry visions—
cheap diversions and amusement for the latter days.
Two of us decline to try the rides; the others
take a generous sampling; one looks rather greenish later.
Someone's child begins to howl; oh, there he is,
stamping his foot, rivulets of tears on his dusty face.
The father finally slaps him, then purchases a tawdry
trinket, stuffs it in his hand. An old man stumbles, nearly

falls; few seem to care. Beyond the Ferris wheel, blackened
ponderosa bodies raise their limbs in grief, reproachful—
bony burghers of Calais, scorched. Innocence
is gone; the century's a carnival, not of gusto but derision
and misrule. Here's the rain, too late for the forest, washing
out soil. We make our way downhill, among our fellow
revelers—petty simulacra, lice upon the earth. I toss
my ticket in the trash, token of disaffection, broken doll.

Atop the Peak

The summit's massive, roughly contoured, bare—
a great unpolished gem, with flows of scree,
stone outcroppings, cruel sun, inhuman glare.
The tundra's sparse, and not a single tree

prevails against the wind, the thinning air.
Yet what a view! It seems that we can see
six states. Such vastness, though, inspires despair,
space opening inside, the verity

of nothingness too evident. White flowers
cling tightly, tiny beauties in the grass,
ephemera of brilliant alpine hours,

brief witnesses to will. Our shadows pass,
emaciated, on the rocky slope,
then fall away. I touch a bitter hope.

El Morro

It dominates the landscape, solid, dense—
an earth-red monolithic head, a block
of being in the emptiness, immense:
"A'ts'ina"—"place of writings on the rock."

Exploring through New Spain and to the west,
Juan de Oñate wrote here on the stone—
then others, who had stopped to drink and rest,
renowned, or known by signatures alone.

In search of shelter, centuries before,
the Anasazi climbed these cliffs and found
smooth slickrock, potholes holding rain, a store
of wood.—Now halfway up, I look around,

imagining them on the mesa top,
descending, edging with consummate skill
along the ledges, down a rugged drop,
to stalk for game, get seeds, nuts, berries, till

small fields, and carve their petroglyphs: two deer,
a parrot, hands, a spiraled sun, a star
with points, a hunter brandishing his spear—
the fundamental signs of what we are.

Another hiker says, "It's windy, rough!
Turn back!" I can't; I must find what remains
of walls and granaries along the bluff,
see evidence again of history's chains,

which bound the Old Ones to a common fate,
the mind and body's constant *Malpaís*—
dark, igneous heart, yet hopes of bounty, great
and elemental vision of release.

Vermilion Cliffs

Leaving the North Rim of the Canyon, passing by high meadows
and through the Kaibab Forest—Engleman spruce,
blue spruce, aspen, ponderosa pine—we turn eastward
at Jacob's Lake. Having come this way west, to see
the Great Abyss, we reverse perspective, retracing the route
to Bitter Springs, before we turn again, northward. Past
the montane zone, we descend through piñon pine and juniper,
to the dry plateau crossed earlier—risers of Grand Staircase,

stepping into Utah. Chocolate, Vermilion, White, Gray, Pink—
the five escarpments of the Staircase offer a palette
of pastels and deeper, eerie hues: dull, dusty yellow and dark
brown, the blue of manganese, the red, pink, plum,
vermilion of iron oxides, even green (uranium, perhaps),
plus ashy black of badlands and pale mineral shades.
To our left, for thirty miles, Vermilion Cliffs ruffle
along, solemn in their stony majesty, twisting, edging in and out,

painted over by the sun, with House Rock Valley on the right,
level. Wildflowers bid farewell to summer—but chamisa
dots the landscape still with gold, and desert mallow
lingers by the borrow pits, where rain has run off from the road.
At Marble Canyon, near Lees Ferry and the Paria River
confluence, we cross the Colorado on the Navajo Bridge,
turning our backs to waves of blood-colored rock,
but following now new walls of lithic red and orange,

the Echo Cliffs, defining sacred Indian lands. How would one
tell this to the blind—of eye, imagination, spirit? Say
Vermilion Cliffs reach two thousand feet toward the sky,
that the lower strata are Chinle Formation? That petroglyphs
drawn by the Anasazi can be found, along with remnants
of old ranches and fossil prints of dinosaurs? That this very road
once was a Mormon track? Or that this passes understanding—
human time, of course, within our ken, but, even so,

mysterious. Why did the Anasazi leave? Who were they, who
are *we*, any of us? What can *triassic* mean for eyes
that will not see these cliffs a second time (we think), nor,
despite resolve, love beyond these years of our embodied being—
tender, not wishing to be stone, and yet admiring its solidity,
even as it cracks, erodes, breaks, crumbles, tumbles,
turning into scree, then sand, washing away in ten million years,
crimson glow expiring on the blue, red heart gone?

Cattle Fording Tarryall Creek

—For Kate

With measured pace, they move in single file,
dark hides, white faces, plodding through low grass,
then walk into the water, cattle-style,
indifferent to the matter where they pass.

The stream is high, the current swift—good rain,
late snow-melt, cold. Immerging to the flank,
the beasts proceed, a queue, a bovine chain,
impassive, stepping to the farther bank—

continuing their march, as if by word,
down valley to fresh pasture. The elect,
and stragglers, join, and recompose the herd,
both multiple and single, to perfect

impressions of an animated scene,
the creek's meanders, milling cows, and sun.
Well cooled, the cattle graze knee-deep in green.
We leave them to their feed, the painting done.

Edith's Funeral

Illness having readied her, readied Bob, her husband,
too, her leave-taking was not abrupt,
nor unexpected—more a sluggish loss of life,
seepage even, her vitality all drained. So I had time
to book my flight, and there I was, looking out
on the High Plains of the Panhandle,
with their pie-chart fields in varying tones of earth,
then New Mexico, its mountains, brown or nearly black,

snow-mantled, then the southern tier of Colorado.
There's Blue Mesa Reservoir! And the Black Canyon
of the Gunnison, not far from where we camped,
Edith, Bob, and I, one summer. —Just as last June,
at her natal celebration, we'll have gatherings,
some of the same people, the same dogs,
though fewer. The first evening, it's a home-cooked
dinner, lots of wine, mostly budget-priced;

but oaky Kendall-Jackson Chardonnay arrives,
after the cheaper stuff is mostly gone,
and it's like Cana, a small miracle, honoring
long marriage, cultured palates. The next day,
it's Father Mike who does the service at St. Mark's.
In comes a cat, calico, who must be carried out. At least
she is well-groomed, unlike some human fauna,
sporting jeans, athletic shoes, tank-tops, racer-backed,

and shirttails hanging out. A sluttish girl, who danced
(I'm told) in a casino—tattooed, lip-pierced, bosomy—
comes in a baby-doll affair. (I'm in a suit, midnight blue,
severe, and hot.) Ah well: Edith, who once
wore tailored clothes that she designed,
but long since moved to jerseys and loose slacks,
would understand. That evening, after catered
dinner and more wine, we've got pyrotechnics, thanks

to a friend—an impressive send-off in the garden:
sparks, wheels spinning upwards, skyrockets with noise,
smoke, light, in various trajectories, which rise
past clumps of aspen (leaves waving in goodbye),
to burst above the cottonwoods, their remnants drifting
like confetti. So, farewell, bright thought
of eighty years, ruddy heart, brief explosion,
quickening for a moment, silenced now; farewell.

Whistling Ducks

I spied them feeding where a hawthorn hedge
adjoins the water. "Oh, come see!"
Pat brought binoculars. There, at the edge—
a pair, and posing handsomely.

Black-bellied, they are called, a homely name;
but color marks them too—gray face,
pale eye-ring, beak bright red, vermilion flame
on neck, pink legs (not commonplace),

with bold white bands along the wings. Aground,
they waddle, pecking, wide feet spread,
their winsome gooselike profiles nearly round.
—For minutes, orderly, they fed;

then, flushing suddenly, they rose in flight,
insignia plumage on display,
transformed by aerial power, to our delight—
an avian image of blasé.

Green

Passing by a store called "Green"—part
of a pretentious Houston strip mall where I
must shop (driving many miles) if I want shoes—
I see it's got *mobilier,* furnishings, and household
stuff. Thinking that I finally might find
a lamp for one dark corner, in I wander.
A smiling bimbo hands out complimentary water,
packed in "eco-friendly" bottles;

lighting comes, I see, from those new corkscrew
bulbs imposed on us, so "energy efficient,"
expensive, giving off a poisoned glow,
dreadful for the eyes. Signs everywhere
proclaim respect for Mother Earth.
"No bamboo trees were felled or threatened
to produce this chair—it's made from trash."
Thus the panda bears in far-off China will not

be deprived. (Not that bamboo's rare;
the South has lots of it, along with yellow pine,
fast-growing, good for paper pulp.)
Ah, the uses of this world, as Hamlet
would reflect if he were here. Not a week
that weighty envelopes do not arrive
well-stuffed with cards and leaflets begging me
to get on-line, quit doing business by the mail,

to "save the trees"— letters from banks
especially, those public-service institutions
that have built new branches everywhere,
tearing down old buildings, paving
ever more, uprooting greenery, raising atria,
and all of this for clients in the drive-in lane,
or those who bank from home, or certainly aren't
here when we go in; the place is like

a mausoleum. The eco-models "Green" displays
are not attractive: whatever valuable resources
someone saved in manufacture, not much taste
was wasted in the process; furthermore,
it all is heavy, huge, as if for wrestlers—
sofas so deep you are engulfed, thick armrests,
"chaise lounges" (as they're called) broad enough
to make a bed, "home theatres" with seats

for twelve and giant screens set in massive chests.
As for lamps, they're hopeless: vulgar,
"cute." Two pseudo-Second Empire atrocities,
verdigris in hue, show dancers like Toulouse-Lautrec's
(the shades have words in French, with errors,
as you'd guess); or else it's faux-Victorian,
fake brass and heavy fringe; or, just as bad,
contemporary-cold and minimalist—not in price

(for nothing's cheap) nor in dimensions, but appeal,
even if "Bauhaus-style" (the standard claim
along that line); the metal, says the sign,
has been recycled. Bully for you.—
Well, I'll save the cost, the planet: I'll go home
and rearrange the furniture—move two chairs,
inherited, get out an ancient lamp, illuminate
that corner and my mind with patina and memories.

Prosciutto

The others have not chosen half so well:
a mediocre shrimp-and-scallops dish,
the sauce indifferent, in a cockle shell
of plastic, or pale soup with bits of fish.

I fear all foodstuffs that I do not know,
cannot assess from menus, judge by sight.
To taste may be too late. Much is for show
in restaurants. I'm asked if things are right;

when it's my error, how could I explain
that I'm not pleased? And so I choose with care.
Prosciutto is, essentially, plain;
it's shipped intact; there's nothing to prepare.

With well-honed knife, just slice it, then arrange
it artfully—at most, a star, a rose.
No camouflage desired, nothing strange—
just mint and moons of melon, to compose

a modest still life. Here, the ham is curled
to form small horns, a toothsome, neat display:
red iridescent flesh, white edges, pearled.
Garçon! Bring me a glass of Beaujolais,

well suited to the tongue's delights ahead.
Let others order snails or squid in ink;
I'll favor what's familiar. To French bread,
prosciutto, steak, fruit, salad—and to drink!

Turtles and Ducks

For months I've studied turtles, watched
them swimming in the pond below
our high-rise windows, sunning on its banks.
They are a calendar, or a thermometer.
Through meager days, with lots of rain and fog,
winter was discouraging; they spent
their time below the vegetable layers
of the pond, coming up for air, of course,

but avoiding gusts and deluge. The eye of day
was changing its trajectory, however;
they signaled spring, crawling out on sunny
afternoons, facing the rays, changing position
as the shadow of the building turned.
We thought at first there were five turtles, six,
both young ones and mature. Now the large
have grown still larger, and I've counted

nine at least, a family, a "community,"
collecting on the pond edge near young weeds—
their own symposium. I think about
our two bald eagles that survey this territory;
they've got better fare, perhaps,
without a shell. But what is this, quite near
a gathering of turtles? —It's a pair
of whistling-ducks, perhaps the very ones

we saw last month. They're swimming, pink
feet paddling fast. One seems to have debris,
a train of seaweed, clinging to its feathers.
Oh! The train spreads out, divides,
and bobs erratically; it's hatchlings, miniature
things, a wake of downy camouflage.
They swim together, following now one
adult and now another. Is it curiosity

that leads the parents to investigate each nook,
or else their avian pedagogy, a first
tutorial on the world? The turtles pay
no heed to them; the grackles, mockingbirds,
the gardener with his rake are all discreet.
Those eagles come to mind again,
though. Presently, the ducks approach
the edge and settle on the grass; the female

fluffs her wings; the little ones collect.
Soon they're up and out again, the parents
trolling in the shallows, ducklings
following. Mistakes are possible, of course—
an eagle stoops, or stones fall from the sky;
but now, at least, we of our local world
are peaceable and orderly, at home,
with sure instinct for the birds, good sense

for us. It's Walden Pond in a modern mode,
without reclusion, disobedience,
or the anarchy of old Thoreau's philosophy—
a civil pact that circumscribes the possible
as it designs it too, for us, the privileged,
and for dumb creatures, fellows—
pristine wildness honored, sheltered,
woods a cultivated garden, like our minds.

A Dinner at Brennan's

—For David Clinton

This isn't the original, on Royal Street
in New Orleans, where I'd eaten last
some years ago; but a Texas property will do:
the architecture's right; the garden
looks authentic—all moist this evening
with the aftermath of heavy rain, still dripping,
streaking banana leaves and spattering
forged-iron tables. And the menu—well,

it's true Louisiana Creole certainly, familiar,
if updated (nothing stays the same, and chefs
must be "creative"). So we settle in,
with our guest, a Louisiana man, recently
removed to this fair state. First,
a Sazerac, proving that the bar staff knows
its stuff. As starters, gumbo and turtle soup,
served with sherry, in the classic mode;

then, for the men, lamb chops, for me, redfish,
topped with shrimp and oysters
fried deliciously.—You can't *miss* things
while they're here, but you can weigh
and measure them, assaying them for gold.
Now we've got a layered moment,
flavors of years past interleaved with these,
enjoyed nostalgically and on the tongue:

that feeling of the Quarter in the evenings,
as it returns, the moment's seasoning—
ships calling on the river, yellow sky
blanching to the west, the scent of coffee
from Café du Monde, phrases of jazz
through open doors, and, over all, the pearly air,
warm, humid, and substantial;
drinks on a patio, then dinner. Finally,

the streetcar home, the perfume of the motor,
clanging bells, metallic music
as the wheels percuss the rails, under
ancient oaks. —Like these Bananas Foster,
sweet and smooth, impressions run
together, blending—themes from a sonata,
suavely interwoven, yet robust—
full savor of remembrance, crystal hours.

Wilson's Phalarope

Bray's Bayou is well down from springtime drought;
but in the avian breast there must be hope,
and waterfowl in numbers are about—
great egrets, herons, Wilson's phalarope,

black ducks. The phalaropes are new this year,
—large pipers, doubtless driven by the dearth
of pools and currents elsewhere, finding here
fresh ripples, ample fishing, moistened earth.

Perhaps they're in migration, though, en route
from South America; what made them stay?
Their rationality is sure; both brute,
instinctive impulse and experience weigh.

The female's plumage—brown, red streaks, white tail,
mascara—gives a bit of camouflage
in tangled reeds along the banks; the male
is gray, the more discreet of the ménage.

They wade, swim, stir the water with their wings
in nervous motion, plucking bits of food—
frogs, fish, crustaceans—undistinguished things,
disposed, however, nicely for their brood.

Last night, I apprehended rain, in dream.
Dry winds were stilled, the bayou overflowed,
the birds flushed up, and in a stream
of phosphorescence, bodies flashed and glowed.

Then, having fed, the phalaropes took flight,
and soared immaculate against dark sky.
I followed them in thought—winged, feathered light,
brief present, phantasy, and yet reply.

Dressing Gowns

—For Patric, and for Kate,
who likewise admires Diderot

"Le philosophe en robe de chambre"—that's
my morning mode. Like Diderot. Two of us, in fact,
and two dressing gowns— my old plaid flannel,
bought from L.L. Bean back in the early 90s,
which in an English winter served me well,
and Pat's heavy robe, from Neiman-Marcus, worn,
but handsome still. "Complacencies
of the peignoir," wrote Wallace Stevens. He, though,

spoke of Sunday mornings, whereas we two,
long unemployed, by choice, make few distinctions
among days. —Music of a boiling kettle, spoons.
We look at birds, check the calendar,
reconsider (not, however, in the tragic mode) events
of yesterday, plan the afternoon, read, or muse,
talking of books and poems, thinking and exchanging
grand thoughts or modest ones. Two phalaropes

are at the pond this week, feeding, lovely creatures
of late spring; the whistling-ducks have come
again, pecking in the grass, bathing, bobbing
together, living toys; and a newer visitor,
a rail, keen-eyed, properly thin, studies the pool.
All perishable, all condemned, like us. I look away
a moment, and the phalaropes are gone—
leaving perturbation on the water, a commotion

in the trees, and ripples of reflection. —Molecules,
and nothing more—small bits in orbit, Pascal's
microworld, reducible to energy, to waves:
ultimately, we're the stuff of light,
which creates that leafy chiaroscuro pattern
on the grass, small prisms when the sunshine strikes
globules of early mist, and sparkles that you watched
last night, from far and long-extinguished

cosmic fires. Admire, but do not touch! Life
is a gallery of beauty which we cannot own, just visit
on a temporary pass; better not become
too attached. And then that journey elsewhere, by
oneself. But I'm attached to you, and joyfully.
The day grows long in the tooth; *finie, la philosophie!*
Or, philosophy lived out, with energy and love—
mind and muscles, even old ones, in the service of ideal.

Stirrup Cup

—New Orleans, November 2007

I'm leaving now for Texas, to see Pat.
His email bears the caption "Stirrup Cup"—
a lover's toast, a wish, advice—all that.
"Drive well; stop often; keep your ginger up."

—What's this? The interstate is closed, it seems,
because a damaged bridge near Lafayette,
which crosses cypress swamps and Stygian dreams,
has not yet been repaired. I'll have to get

to US 90, take the longer route,
by Morgan City, New Iberia.
My well-planned schedule for today is moot.
No matter; there's no urgency. Hurrah!

In fact, these extra, patient miles afford
more time to study trees, the marshy scene,
trace bayous sloughing down. Should I be bored?
Two egrets, haughty in their plumage, preen;

dark geese lift off in wedges, turn, then set
their compass south. Mine's fixed on love—ideal
(the greater for a current of regret),
transformed by fate into our commonweal,

a lasting pact renewed after long date—
such high romance as moves an angel's heart.
I'll telephone to let Pat know I'm late,
but "stirrupped well," with all my rider's art.

Sunny

In fifty-one, she danced the Charleston, well,
attired in a twenties skirt, with fringe,
belonging to her mother, I suppose—
they had no money for new dresses (*who*
had money then, along the Rio Grande?).
She danced that night with Buddy Macintosh,
unprepossessing, but with lively feet.
He wore a beanie and a raccoon coat,

a hand-me-down from some distinguished man
who'd gone to Princeton. With her fringe and lace,
bedecked with retro necklaces, she charmed
us all, her heels kicked up, her hair awhirl,
as Buddy turned her deftly to the beat.
She went to college in New Mexico,
taught school, and drove a Thunderbird, her prize—
with style, yet with decorum. Many men

in that male world discerned her quality.
She chose one for his goodness, not his means.
Two sons came next. She barely aged, though—danced,
wore open sandals to preserve her toes
from deformation, kept house cleverly,
and made her namesake drink, sun tea, in jars.
She greatly favored green. Through twenty years
of boys and men, her ivy dishes, chipped,

were still in use. One day, not quite by chance
(her husband casually mentioning some vase),
she looked on a high shelf and found new green—
a set of pottery, the choice of love.—
How years evaporate!—like rivulets
that die in desert sands, like rain above
the Organ Mountains, vanishing in air.
In time, she was unwell; her eyes played tricks,

her head ached; long siestas did no good.
She'd watch the evening gold and salmon play
across the sky and wonder if next year
she'd see them still. The illness grew in her,
the poisoned progeny, unnatural,
of her unwilling being. Finally
her thoughts became delusions, flickering,
then darkening, until the sun went out.

Osage Orange

We were at war with Mexico, foreseen,
considering the skirmishes provoked
when, as invited, Anglos crossed the Red
and the Sabine. The Alamo was next,
then Goliad. "Remember" was the oath
at San Jacinto. Texas had become
a free republic, not acknowledged, though,
by Mexico. There followed hot disputes

on where the border lay—the Rio Grande
or the Nueces. Statehood did the rest,
ensuring war would follow. I joined up
with the Missouri Mounted Volunteers,
which Colonel Price, from my home county, raised.
We rode to Santa Fé, where Price—named general
and military governor—put down
an uprising in Taos. Later, word

arrived of Mexicans advancing north.
With orders to remain, instead we left
and reached El Paso, early in the year.
I hadn't seen much save that incident
in Taos—neither glory, injury,
nor death—and hoped for nothing more. But wind—
the constant wind—cold, barren sand,
and treeless hills disheartened me; I wished

for branches, even bare, with latent buds,
and streams that flowed, beneath their ice, to spring.
Though evidence of Mexican intent
was scarce, we crossed the river, riding fast
toward Chihuahua's capital. We met
an enemy detachment carrying
the flag of truce. A treaty had been signed,
the captain claimed. The general would not

believe him. We proceeded, thus, on south,
and occupied the city, then pursued
the Mexicans, who had already fled
to hold and fortify instead the town
of Santa Cruz of Rosales. Demands
by Price for their surrender were refused.
The siege was fierce—bombardment morning-long.
A few of them behind us were dispersed,

and we dismounted for the final act,
as in a theater. —I saw a play
once in St. Louis, some old tragedy:
dramatic cries, with knives and pistols drawn,
two bodies on the stage, dark curtain down.
  —The scene was strangely similar. We crept,
with rifles ready. Streets along the edge
lay emptied, shutters closed, the populace

inside; but near the center tension rose—
presentiments of presence, hints of fear.
The Mexicans fought well, but we prevailed.
Before the plaza fell, I found myself
engaged along a narrow *calle*, and alone
with three—a postscript to the day. One man
reversed direction, disappeared; one fled
another way. The third shot back, then ran,

still trying to reload, into a grove
of Osage orange, thorny, tough.—His blood
seeped slowly into earth, already red,
and tufts of yellowed grass. I felt the cold,
imagining—a flash—the green of spring,
which would not come for him now. In the copse,
I cut, not easily, a supple limb,
its color visible under the bark

where it was slashed, and carved a walking stick,
a twisted column for the anguished crypt
of conscience; knots where I had trimmed the thorns
regarded me—dead eyes, yet seeing far.
I tied it to my rifle, carried it
beside me, back across the Rio Grande
and home. What irony: en route, we learned
that war had ended well before our fight,

the treaty signed by both belligerents,
and ratified by the U.S. while we
rode south. The general may have deserved
his reprimand; he later was discharged
with honor. Since, the cane has served me well—
a morbid trophy of necessity,
yet sturdy pleasure through the fields and woods,
ideals and hard realities conjoined.

For a Friend Who Hopes to Meet Her
Grandfather Among the Shades

—For P. J. T.

Miss Pearl, the operator, put him through—
a local man, remarried to the wife
he'd cast off twice, now courting someone new
—a foolish rake who gambled with his life.

Miss Pearl heard everything, rang up, and told
his wife, who felt fresh outrage, reaching bone.
—Did he feel shame at last? Or simply fold,
conceding he had lost? The telephone

was ready, like the shotgun. "Madam, you
have killed a man," he shouted to Miss Pearl,
hung up, then told his dog goodbye and blew
his brains out. Scores of years have passed; a whirl

of questions lingers. All the rest have died
—one self-inflicted death, disease, old age;
and now you are the only one this side
of Hades who remembers. Spleen or rage,

depression, stoicism: in the hall
of suicides, do Socrates, Woolf, Crane,
the younger Cato, Hemingway, Nerval,
and the anonymous, recall their pain,

extolling or regretting death, too late?
If we, like Dante, could descend to hell,
yet live—or call at least within its gate—
you would inquire, ask if all were well

there in the underworld; instead, you wait,
till you will join the shades, where, in the gloom,
you hope to meet him, speak of love and fate,
old voices breaking in the timeless room.

The Empress Eugénie Leaves Paris, 1870

A crowd had gathered at the Tuileries,
unruly, in a nasty mood. "Long live
the Third Republic! Down with Eugénie,
the Spanish whore! Spit on the emperor,
the traitress! To the guillotine!" Sedan
had fallen to the Prussians and their prince
two days before; the empire was in shreds,
Louis-Napoleon a prisoner.

She feared for honor only. When she heard
the shouting, saw the gates besieged, she knew
she must depart—though for the servants' sake.
The palace joined the Louvre, but a door
was locked. An old valet appeared, and used
his key. No baggage, but a veil. With friends,
she crossed the silent galleries—Greek art,
Egyptian treasure, looted, useless now.

They slipped out to the street unnoticed, found
a cab for her and her attendant, bade
farewell. *Hide first, then reach the Channel.* Help
was crucial. Trusted houses—two—were dark.
Her money gone, she sent away the cab;
they walked, exhausted, to her dentist's home,
a Dr. Evans. She had saved his life
in Turkey once; he was American.

A fellow doctor volunteered his aid.
She had a British passport, genuine,
designed as a precaution by a friend,
for "Mrs. B." and "Doctor C." The trains
were dangerous—they would be watched. By coach
the four drove down the Seine, changed horses, stayed
at miserable inns. A sighting once,
another close escape, the *tricoteuses*

of '93 a spectral thought. They reached
Deauville and a hotel; by Providence,
the dentist's wife was there on holiday.
She helped conceal the empress and her maid
until a vessel could be found. Not French,
of course. An English yachtsman first declined
to aid them, but his wife, less scrupulous,
and pitying, soon interceded. Late

that night, the empress would embark, along
with Dr. Evans and her maid, and gifts
from Mrs. Evans. Two policemen searched
the yacht; by chance, the party had not yet
arrived. They walked through rain and puddles, soaked.
On board, they found dry clothes, a bowl of punch.
They sailed at seven. The seas were rough; a squall
blew up, the yacht went reeling; Eugénie

stood steady through it all. At dusk they glimpsed
the Isle of Wight. At last the wind swung west;
they anchored in Ryde Roads. The British queen
had shown strange kindness to her earlier,
receiving the imperial pair despite
the suspect name *Napoleon*—and though
Victoria's kindred were in Germany.
Thus England meant a haven. —What thick knots

of rivalries and conflicts, what dark blood!
The fires of Europe were set, awaiting time
and flint. The old queen died; the empress lived,
remembering anarchy, the Tuileries
torched, later, by the rabble. Worse might lie
ahead for Prussia, France, her son—new wars,
the fields of glory gone, with only ash
and ossuaries, relics of the dream.

A Vigil

—For Jean Miller

Winds roared across the range—a very gale—
to aggravate and mock the final act
of living, as mortality's old flail,
relentless, threshed fatigue, distress, and racked

him wholly. Just at dawn, the howling ceased;
a softer light pierced through the stormy screen,
and snow began to fall. He died, released
to easing of his limbs and tranquil mien.

So Death, a rowdy and unwelcome guest,
showed late decorum, offering compromise:
for tortured nerves, relief; a lasting rest
for valiant body; for itself, a prize.

An Incident After the War

Three officers arrived—Americans
(at that time occupants)—to check for arms
and ammunition. Heinrich's father met
them, courteously, opening the door.
Inspection was no insult. What good luck,
besides, to live in Essen, in the west,
and not be subject to the Russian gangs,
the Reds, the "liberating" brutes he loathed;

and what relief to have the Nazis gone,
whom he had not supported—dangerous
fanatics, often vile. Their handiwork
lay everywhere—the war, its aftermath
(whole cities gone, starvation, murders, grief,
the disappearances, the guilt). His wife
and he had feared, gone hungry, suffered, crazed
by sirens, bombs, and strafing in the night,

but he had helped a Jew, discreetly, fed
his younger children, and survived. What might
befall them now would be non-sequitur,
a dispensation of new, different gods.
The officers began to search the rooms,
quite formally. The father, questioned, said
he had no weapons stored. Strange, though: as if
by instinct, one lieutenant found a gun—

a service pistol—hidden in a drawer.
"*Mein Gott*," the German murmured, scared, dismayed.
"That pistol was my son's, my Heinrich's, sent
to us after his death. How well aligned
the German mind can be: meticulous,
nay, elegant. My Heinrich died along
the *Ostfront*. There, you know, men were deprived,
shot, captured, executed; armies starved,

surrounded, frozen, brutalized. In short,
for Germans, Stalingrad meant death, defeat.
Yet somehow, bureaucratic forms prevailed;
the pistol was identified, returned.
I had forgotten it—suppressed it, I
suppose—the sign of wasted sacrifice,
disaster of a world half-mad. Excuse
me, please." The officers exchanged a glance,

examining the pistol. "No harm's done,"
the captain said; "I recognize the arm—
a *Hauptmann*'s. It may symbolize both loss
and honor, lacking in this brutal age.
Just keep it out of sight—a souvenir."
He nodded slightly, gave the weapon back,
turned, followed by the others. Twilight fell;
the house felt lonely, silent as a tomb.

The Retriever

Bending down, the man awakes the sleeping dog
and motions to him. Time to go. The door is closed;
they climb into the pickup, the retriever riding
shotgun. Right, left, ahead, he looks, nerves
tingling, eyes still keen, nose picking up the scents.

It's dove season; they're a small shooting party,
the two of them. A light snow has powdered stubble
left from harvest, dusted naked twigs on brush
along the stream, turned weeds in borrow-pits
to jeweled scepters. Here's the field they've favored

for ten years. No need for instructions, save a few
hand signals. Time feels both short and long:
watch, quivering; wait for the shouldered shotgun,
then the sign; retrieve. Hunting's good; birds flush
up against the sky, as if by autumn's order. On

the way home, quiet, till the man whistles scraps
of tune. The dog is dozing, knowing the routine;
he whimpers for a moment, twitches, then is still
again, in voiceless dream. His strength has waned,
vigor ebbing, waves of sound receding into silence;

his legs will fail him soon. Then the man will be
obliged to shoot him also, friend to the last,
turned executioner. The hunter, too, is creaky, old,
and lonely. In the sky, Orion with his dog is out
tonight, treading the galactic fields, snowy, free.

At Jefferson Barracks Cemetery

Three soldiers from the Revolutionary War are buried here,
it's said, having died as old men after 1826,
when this post was founded. At the highest point, one sees
the Mississippi River, eastward through the trees,
but the whole West lay to the other side, the vast Missouri
River and the dark frontier of exploration, trading, suffering;
and men sent out to fight came back sometimes
in coffins, if they were not captured, tortured, burnt

by Indians. And then the war of North and South, dividing
and antagonizing, and the full, bloody reaping
of four summers spilling over, crushed forever in this grass,
Union ruins beside the sad Confederate dead.
Your father lies here too, a son of Eire gassed for America
in the Great War, lingering then for twenty years,
marrying, but losing the alveoli of lungs and life.
—Wandering in squares, we could not find his marker;

until suddenly, you looked across and saw the name "Elvira"
on a stone, with dates—your mother, buried over him. Such
serendipity, among two hundred thousand graves!
It comes from yearning, concentration, need—a pilgrimage
in this case. We turn to see the other side. Yes.
"JOHN S. SAVAGE, MASSACHUSETTS," and his date of death.
As you remembered, fine stone walls wind downward
to a grove, and then the river, farther, deepening the scene,

as if an artist had designed it to create perspective. How far
from Ireland, sacred causes, victories unholy.
We reread the inscriptions, while you entice two bodies
that were persons into momentary being—images—
then think yourself into an empty plot nearby, not wishing
death, but knowing it beforehand as you can. The mind
retreats at last from non-existence. Leaving off
mourning's mantle, we wave goodbye, as with a handkerchief.

A Valedictory

—In memory of A .M. G. B.

Before, he'd thought of killing both: his wife,
himself. With his weak heart and labored breath,
her Alzheimer's, what happiness did life
still promise? Yet he hesitated. Death

decided shortly, taking her one night.
He waited for a sign, unsure, depressed.
The winter he turned ninety, and despite
his friends' attentions, he resolved to wrest

the game from chance. The shot went through his jaw,
his eye, but not his brain. For hours he bled,
until they found him struggling in the maw
of fate, delirious. "I'm dead, I'm dead

already," he declared, as if resigned.
Yet later, though, he smiled. What had he seen,
feared, welcomed in that limbo of the mind?
The nether world, ideal—the shades serene,

discoursing on philosophy and art,
while banqueting and listening to the lyre?
Lithe bodies running and a lively heart
in gardens of affectionate desire,

53

where he would share the chase, and share the kiss?
Instead, did he regret his awful act,
perceiving nothing but a dark abyss
before him, realizing the only pact

with spirit is the body? He survived,
apologized, lived as he could, then left
us. Now, in void or being, he's arrived.
Farewell. We too are absence, and bereft.

Looking for Gravestones

The portents favored us—soft rain toward dawn
over the arid mountains, parched for weeks,
around El Paso, followed, after sunrise,
by a full rainbow arching across the river, plinth
to plinth, striding southeast, signaling our route.
We got off late, however: saying goodbye
to friends is rarely quick; besides, we breakfasted
quite leisurely. We ran along the river for a while,

before it said *adiós*, taking with it all the green,
leaving only desert—yellow, cinder gray,
glassy white. Along the interstate, trucks sped past
legally at 80 mph, as if to flee the desolation. At
Van Horn, we turned off—almost the only travelers.
Time had changed, meanwhile—an hour dropped—
and it was past mid-afternoon when finally
we got a bite, in Marfa. Twenty-six miles more,

and here we are, circling the unkempt cemetery
where I hope to find my parents' stones.
There's no custodian, no other visitor—nothing
but an old directory. There's too much space;
the dead are scattered as if they'd turned
misanthropic in their last retreat. It's hot as Hades,
only thin shade from a few Italian cypresses,
classic verdure for a cemetery, aliens here. Pat

is not well; he dare not leave the cooled air
of the car, blowing valiantly. I wander
where the stones I seek—pink granite—lie (I think)
half-sunken in the sand. Weeds, burnt to straw,
conceal memorials and names, and I walk
with caution, snakes, insects, goat-heads
on my mind, as lonely for a moment as if *I*
were dead, feeling bereft of even the last evidence

of lives that gave me mine. Where is the order
that burial plots deserve, to fit the final order
of eternity? The caliche nearly blinds me.
There are no grounds for grounds like this—
such anonymity, such hasty degradation
into nothingness. We cannot stay; Del Rio
and the next hotel are still two hundred miles away,
along a good but twisting road. "Here is no water

but only rock"—no prism to refract my memories,
merely unearthly hues of soil and dark striations
in the Pecos River canyon, like a Styx.
It's vanity to want to see those graves, to wish
for a return, striving backwards against
the grain of life. I retreat into myself, the wilds.
At 8:00 we reach Del Rio, whipped,
and yet relieved, dry hearts shriven and delivered.

Installation

On the gallery tonight, a blind man studies the stars,
while a mute, beside him, reads astral poetry
aloud. The blind man traces signs and figures
with his hands—a long-handled drinking cup, a chair,

a cross, a crab slipping sideways down sidereal
sands. As farther lights confer, the moon,
just rising, animates vast recesses of darkness.
Liquid sounds of a piano run, break off, then resume;

a dancer in white tulle steps out, moving to melody
she cannot hear. The music shines a moment
more, then turns to shadow; crystals form
on gladioli spears, on the round, suspended notes.

Siegfried-Idyll

Musicians were collected and rehearsed
in Zurich, secretly; Hans Richter took
the lead. With themes composed before and used
in *Siegfried*, later—and especially
its love-*motive*—and bits of cradle-song,
the Master had devised an homage, pure,
serene, to celebrate the natal day
of Cosima (the daughter of Franz Liszt)—

since August of that year his wife—and mark
the recent birth of Siegfried, their third child,
their only son, who bore a hero's name.
The orchestra collected on the stairs
of "Villa Tribschen," facing Lake Lucerne.
If she suspected something was afoot,
she gave no sign, until the music rose
that morning, with its "Peace" motif,

sustained, ethereal, her husband's hands
shaping the sound—even a trumpet. Mad
King Ludwig, was not there, of course;
he'd banished Wagner from Bavaria,
his subjects having protested against
expenditures and eccentricities
of Ludwig's favorite (though the monarch once
sent four musicians to perform quartets

of Beethoven in Wagner's honor). Which,
the visionary artist or the king,
was more the fool? A swan-boat on a lake,
or on a stage; a royal devotee,
or a fanatic, moved to emulate
Greek drama while he mined medieval lore,
the mystic spirit of true Germany?
—Though genius was familiar, Cosima

was touched; such tenderness, such light, for her
alone, below her bedroom, were divine.
Great debts obliged her later to give up
the score, the philter of romance, the jewel
of love. But one can live on memories.
Beyond the *Ring* and *Parsifal*, beyond
Bayreuth and Wagner's death, the *Idyll* held,
supremely, past and future: mysteries

of sacrifice and blood turned into art
so lyrical it makes one weep in awe;
then darkest Europe, heathen conquerors,
redemption and the Grail, a holy quest—
such vast imaginations of one mind
and then another, met by circumstance
but meant as one and joined as for all time—
angelic bands performing at their side.

Carnation, Lily, Lily, Rose

The light, as Sargent wrote to Stevenson, was "paradisiac"
and made one rave with pleasure. He meant
late-summer evening hours at Broadway, in the Cotswolds.
Following the scandal caused in Paris by his canvas
known now as "Portrait of Mme X," he'd left France
for England. London first. On a boat trip on the Thames,
he saw near Pangbourne two small girls lighting
paper lanterns "from rose tree to rose tree." The image

struck him. Broadway was next, a lively artists' colony—
Henry James and Edmond Gosse were residents in '85—
and, in August, Sargent went to live and work there.
He resolved to paint the Pangbourne scene. Conditions,
though, were not ideal—the blossoms, dying
by September, had to be replaced with paper imitations
pinned to branches; his young model, too dark-haired,
he thought, was given a wig; the weather later turned

quite cold. Still, he set up his easel at each day's end.
By good chance, Frederick Barnard, an illustrator,
settled there with his two fair-haired daughters. Seeing
them, Sargent altered his design—two girls
instead of one. He'd wait until a mauvish, dusky glow
infused the scene, then rush to light the lanterns,
have the models pose, and madly paint until the twilight
failed. Two summers were required. An old song

revived that year asked "Have you seen my Flora?" The reply:
"Carnation, Lily, Lily, Rose." So Sargent painted
music, love, a garden, light—an idyll. Oriental lanterns glow,
domesticated stars; the girls, all solemn in their flounced
and ruffled smocks, are flowers also; grasses, dark, profuse,
bend around their feet. We are drawn into the picture,
wondering at such exquisite, shimmering shadings of an hour,
innocence and fragile beauty lit, until the lamps burn out.

Composition

This is not good painting, in which colors, lines,
textures, ought to please—oils, impasto,
spread, swirled, sculpted with a palette knife
to design topography of vision. Not quite
good collage, either; disparate elements, as if random
(postcards, a photograph, scraps of musical score,
yarn, lines of a poem, heteroclitic bits),
do not create a whole, irreducible. The frame itself

is colonized by disarray: burlap stuck on, scratches,
and a blob of paint. Odd, in short, the medium
uncertain, and even Valéry's "beautiful disorder"
visible only by intense imagination. Was this
failure of artistic genius, truly past remedy? Or
some subtle rationale, to the second power
of thought? The awful artifact is hung in the museum
of the mind, however. "Life," it's called.

What purpose can it have, what truth? Here's a gash
—intentional, or accident? And look
below the wound: a second layer, perhaps another.
You can't peel back the canvas; but think by X-rays,
see the strata as a palimpsest, an archive—
flayed body of the past, damaged nerve, muscle, sinew,
flesh unbearable, organic rot. —Is that debris
the half-hour lapse, the phone call left unmade,

which might have kept a love alive? Or foolish whim,
impatience, chance misdirections, or the anger
that destroyed the grounds of meaning?
—(as a painter in despair, or self-destructive,
takes a kitchen knife and madly stabs the canvas,
slashing, ripping). —Strange: as I turn my eyes away,
a curator arrives, identifies the composition,
carefully removes it, taking pains, as if to honor

it. It's old, he says, and out of date; life, strangely,
can be redesigned, eschewing evidence;
layering is multiple, and rich. What's done cannot
quite be undone, but flaws may be disguised,
miscalculations mended, and cross-purposes aligned,
at last, so that the composition is shored up—
shadows and light, proportion, subtle harmony,
principles of beauty after all. We shall be surprised.

Degas in New Orleans

"The sublimity of his mature art is the application
of classical skill and aristocratic taste to modern
and plebeian subjects, often framed with the
off-center casualness of a passing glance."
—Peter Schjeldahl,

—1870 and after

That dreadful war! Degas, a patriot,
aged thirty-six, enlisted in the Guards—
a gesture only (Paris would not be
at risk, they knew; the Prussians would retreat,
the French pursuing them across the Rhine)—
sincere, however. Then Sedan, the fall
of emperor and empire, German gains,
Paris blockaded and besieged, the Loire

campaign, and Paris fallen; winter then,
starvation (rats for sale in sacks, like fish),
disorder, the Commune. Who would not wish
to leave? His mother's family, Creoles, lived
on Esplanade, between the Marigny
and Vieux Carré. They all spoke French; the dress,
the mores pleased him; the great river ran
nearby, a liquid cord to home. He knew,

however, that he had defective sight—
that rifle training in the Guards revealed
his disability, a painter's curse.
Louisiana light, subtropical,
was dangerous, he thought. He stayed indoors,
did portraits and domestic scenes; he liked
dim corridors and doors in *enfilade*
successively receding in the dusk,

or courtyards shaded by profuse displays
of greenery, both sensuous and cool.
His uncle worked in Faubourg Sainte-Marie
in "Factors' Row"; Degas resolved to paint
his offices—the desks and chairs, the clerks,
the cotton brokers in top hats—a scene
of modern life, a bit off-center, caught
as by a glance. His brother, at the left,

inclines beside a window; one man reads
a paper; foregrounded, his uncle cleans
his glasses; cotton samples point to wealth,
the soft, exotic coin of the New World
for European furniture, gems, gowns.
Degas made sketches, studied colors, lines,
and paid his homage to New Orleans. Still,
he feared the southern sun, and finally

returned to France for twenty years of work,
perfecting beauty. "Drawing is one way
of thinking, modelling another." Aged,
he walked the streets of Paris, nearly blind,
alone, remembering banana leaves
in steamy rain, dark doorways, Creole skin,
the casual framing of a moment caught
by eyes become opaque and brilliant thought.

For a Singer Who Is Ill

—For S. K. F.

Yours is the gift of voice, of tone and ear,
the heavenly skills of Saint Cecilia,
by which celestial visions reach us here—
motets, *chansons* and *Lieder*, opera.

And yours is now the burden of disease,
not as the price of beauty—it is free,
if one consents to let the Muses please—
but as a warrant of humanity,

the terrible insignia of the Fall
when harmonies of body, torn apart,
became cacophony and funeral drum,

and led to elegy and mortal art.
You're tied to tubes, infusions, ports. Recall
your song; breathe soundly; let new music come.

Victor Hugo at Hauteville House

"A lunatic," said Jean Cocteau, "who took
himself for Victor Hugo"— striding through
his century, by genius, vigor, fate,
a true colossus, the Napoleon
of letters. He had suffered, though: Eugène,
a brother, had gone raving mad; Adèle,
his wife, pursued a long affair; he fell
in love with Juliette Drouet, all ripe

from roles of passion in his plays. Distress
and self-reproach had followed. Critics called
his drama *Les Burgraves* extravagant.
Then came death of his beloved child
Léopoldine—a girl, a recent bride—
by drowning in the Seine (the boat a tomb,
her skirts stone weights). He, incognito, was
on holiday with his beloved. News

arrived by accident. In haste he left
for Paris, greasing palms to urge on coach
and horses; but it was too late, since she
had been laid out already, then interred.
In '51, Louis-Napoleon,
the president, whom Hugo called "Petit,"
betrayed the constitution by a *coup
d'état*. The poet, who opposed him, chose

to live in exile: Brussels, Jersey next,
at last the lovely isle of Guernesey,
and Hauteville House. The house was ample; he
enlarged it to accommodate his will.
He built a belvedere, a "widow's walk"
of glass, his private refuge, with a flag
he hoisted when he wrote—his vessel's bridge,
commanding contemplation, poetry,

and "Oceano nox." It was the age
of séances. At evening, candles lit,
in awe and silence, everyone sat round,
and summoned those they loved, the dead.
A name; three raps upon the table leg;
a solemn question, then the table turned.
More questions: "Who are you? Reply! Spell out
your answer, please! Léopoldine? My son,

first-born? My love?" —Death tracked him still,
the image of his daughter in the waves,
the dead of revolutions, coups, and those
condemned to garotte, guillotine, or rope—
or hunger. Melancholy stalked Adèle.
The sons, uprooted, ineffectual,
pursued their pastimes born of *ennui*,
while Victor's shadow grew. The younger girl,

besotted with an English officer,
ran off to Nova Scotia. Spurned, she left
next for Barbados. All in vain. A slave
adopted her and took her back to France,
on Hugo's coin. Insane, she was interned.
Hopes gone, Adele departed too—this life—
from stroke. The poet lived and prospered on
his isle, reading the stars. A photograph

portrays him, eyes half-closed as if in dream.
"He's listening to God," the caption reads.
Before Sedan, the empire crumbling, pride
relieved, he left for Belgium, then returned
to Paris—new disorders, but the love
and recognition of the grateful crowds
acclaiming him as theirs, while he sailed on,
with Hauteville House, to immortality.

The Reasonable Aesthete

Ideal
and real
both appeal.

My heart—
apart—
is in art;

my mind
you'll find
with my kind,

where sense
augments
evidence.

A fool
may rule
in art's school;

the sane
contain
logic's pain,

although
we owe
to *le beau*

alone
full-blown
grands frissons.

On a Ballet by Sir Kenneth MacMillan

—Houston Ballet, September 2011

It's Mahler's masterpiece, *Song of the Earth*,
transformed into ballet. The soul of dance
does not respond, alas. Is there a dearth
of music suitable for feet? Mere chance,

as at a raffle, might provide a page
that's better fitted for Terpsichore.
Try Liszt, Chopin, Albéniz, even Cage.
What's more, this work's a clashing pot-pourri,

comprising ancient Chinese poems wrought
in German, sung (two voices, quite drowned out
by cymbals, tam-tam, drum, bass horns—all fraught
with powers of cacophony). Aesthetic doubt

persists: strange choreography, worse style.
Thus "Von der Schönheit" is an ugly scene,
with awkward poses. One can't reconcile
intention with such form. What does it mean?

Nor shall I mention scenery and dress.
That Death should play a role in this, I grant.
Its herald should dance well, though; happiness,
while fleeting, shine. Here, nothing else but scant

display of dancers' skill, stiff movements, grim
impressions, scowls. "Warum? Warum?" Indeed!
Expecting noble gestures and a hymn
to life, we've got contortions. —I concede

great art may spring from disappointment, grief,
but not the dismal swamp. It's all a waste.
The ending brings a palpable relief.
Thus modernism's spirit is disgraced.

Vocation

—In memory of André Gide

As others enter the religious state,
he entered art. Thus *in* the world; not *of*
it, though. The portals of *le beau* are strait;
desire requires sacrifice. Youth, love,

experience, each was channeled to an end
both existential and ideal, with words
consuming life, refigured to transcend
contingency—bejeweled, unearthly birds.

Idolatrous, thus, yet he had the grace
to see how beauty is a parasite
of good, as others suffered in his place,
expedient victims, flotsam in the night

among vast phosphorescent tides. The mark
on him was deep, however, the appeal
peremptory. His vision flashed, a fiery arc—
if scandalous, yet with an angel's seal.

On Alexandrines in English Verse

The French adore the form; there's little rhythm, though:
caesura halfway through; six syllables to go
before another beat. That language lacks the stress
which gives to English speech its accented address.
We rarely get away from our iambic sound,
though trochees, anapests, and dactyls stick around.
No need to stretch the lines. Thus Milton, Dryden, Pope
preferred pentameter. The latter's clever trope

(a wounded snake that drags his slow length through the verse)
displays the glaring truth: the alexandrine's worse
for those of Shakespeare's tongue. (Alas: give writers rope,
and they will hang themselves. A line of lesser scope
might favor good effects.) The dramatist Racine
used twelve-syllabic lines, scene after tragic scene,
but he, of course, was French; and so were Molière
(so witty!), Mallarmé, Vigny, and Baudelaire,

all masters of their art.—In contrast, think of Keats
(much magic), Coleridge, Donne—just four or five clear beats.
(Remember "Kubla Khan"!) And there's this evidence.
The great Paul Valéry (a poet of much sense
and rare, exquisite taste) used for his masterpiece
(the "Cemetery" ode, evoking France and Greece)
a rhythm he had heard emerging in his head—
decasyllabic, strong. Insistently, it led

him on: he would attempt to raise the power of ten
to alexandrines' twelve. A further challenge then:
he would divide the lines four/six or else six/four,
the syllables arranged to honor even more
impressions of expanse through art's economy.
The alexandrine's length can be curtailed, you see,
with little sacrifice. Or so it would appear,
when genius sounds the note. One point arises here:

why whip a dying horse? The alexandrine's flown;
césure, enjambement—such terms almost unknown.
In France, as here, you choose: bad prose or weak free verse—
no form, much sophistry; "postmodern" is a curse.
Hexameters or not, the aim of verbal art
is beauty, sorcery—seducing mind and heart.
From measured English feet to unaccented French,
some demon is on hand: true poetry's a wench.

In the Public Library

No quiet here!—no studious frowns; it's more
like bedlam. Children dart among the stacks
and squeal; bored people lounge about, or pore
through tapes and DVDs on crowded racks,

or scan new fiction—Cromwell, Brown, and Clark
(a dozen copies each). What can they lose?
In short, it is a air-conditioned park,
a beach. Teens chatter, showing off tattoos;

a drifter, drunk or drugged, accosts a pair
of women, muttering a fishwife's word;
he's taken out by guards (by guards!). And where
in all this is the catalogue? Absurd

to ask: on-line, of course. —A harmless drudge
(as per Sam Johnson), I should like to find
four literary books. But this is sludge,
the dregs of culture. Scholars of my kind

will be extinct ere long, good books removed;
we'll read on screens, or else won't read at all.
As everyday experience has proved,
Eden's long gone; this is the newest fall.

Avoiding drunks and dragons, I succeed—
knight-errant—in procuring an array
of unread tomes. The addicts have *their* need:
withdrawal is, I'm glad, still years away.

On a Disgruntled Poet

Annoyed because I had declined
to print his poems—two frail barks,
unseaworthy, I thought—he whined,
included out-of-place remarks

alleging my incompetence,
then added that I was too old
to be an editor. What sense
he may possess should tell him, "Hold

your pen! That's *agism*! You're daft!"
Why burn a useful bridge? Instead,
acknowledge that the poet's craft
is hard, success unsure. Ahead

new chances lie; but talk goes round—
friends, patrons, publishers might hear,
concluding that you've run aground.
Miranda rights for this aren't clear.

Envoi

You're doubtless waiting for my death.
Write on, Sir, but don't hold your breath.

On a Dyspeptic Reviewer

Dyspepsia must be the source
of such distaste—or envy's sting,
like that of hornets. To endorse
the work, at least to say a thing

or so about the poet's art
would have been apt. Quite the reverse:
line after line was picked apart.
One rhyme word vexed the critic; worse,

an image did not meet his test;
he shortly found two foreign terms
that bothered him. Thus with the rest:
he looked within the flesh for worms

to prove corruption. That good wits
should be so used is almost vice,
and foolish also: picking nits,
he may himself acquire lice.

Envoi

Beware: we know that critics' spite,
a boomerang, comes back to bite.

On an Erstwhile Editor, Feminist

The portraits of the men came down—
all those who'd steered that ship of letters;
now captain, she'd achieve renown
by proving women are their betters.

Who wants those vestiges, well dead—
tradition-bound old patriarchs?
Such dregs won't do; new wine instead,
new bottles! Yet, when one embarks

on change, discarding tiller, wheel,
one easily is set adrift.
Her measures did not keep the keel
right steady. Poetry, a gift

of heaven, suffered, as did prose.
Through strange events, she lost her post
(we labor, but the gods dispose).
Belles-lettres do not claim her ghost.

Envoi

Let race, class, gender nurse their bile;
diversity cannot trump style.

Gide Misjudges a Manuscript

—Offices of the *NRF*
Paris, 1912

His eyes had fallen on the page
that limned a bony forehead, bare,
displaying "vertebrae," which age
made prominent, below false hair.

"Absurd, confusing spine and head!"
He leafed along, found strange perfumes,
a sleepless narrator in bed,
or mesmerized by hawthorn blooms.

The sentences dragged their full length
in dense meanderings of thought;
if anything, the writer's strength
was drawing so much out of naught.

"Why bother with this manuscript?—
It's dilettantish," Gide deduced.
"If I accept it, I have slipped."
In fact, the author spurned was Proust.

Envoi

It was a critical mistake.
Reviewers, watch the moves you make.

On an Official, Arrogant

Complacent at the microphone,
you'd say, but hiding nerves, he beams,
coughs, then commences to intone
his packaged words of thanks. It seems,

however, *he's* the gracious man,
and *we* should owe him gratitude
for genius and his global plan,
far-sighted, condescending.—Rude,

in short. "This institute is now
transformed and up-to-date; the ship
sails fair since I've been at the prow."
He rambles on, but makes a slip,

demeaning us, and thus our gift.
He's got our money—awful waste.
We must conclude we've gone adrift.
Such discourse leaves an acid taste.

—We've learned. We are a Texas crowd.
This fellow clearly is a dork.
No more for him; we won't be cowed.
He doesn't know; he's from New York.

Envoi

You're number one right now, no doubt;
A palace coup may throw you out.

On an Anonymous Reviewer

A man? A woman? Quite close-lipped,
at least, invited to assess
a scholar's lengthy manuscript.
It was shot down, without finesse.

"The work, I see, does not succeed
except most literally; such
will not suffice now. As I read,
its flaws grow evident. Too much

historical concern—the worms
of time; too little theory, too;
clear prejudice revealed by terms."
(The context does not count; what's true

depends on dogma, and we must
rewrite the past as it should be.)
"Insensitive in tone, unjust;
two small mistakes in chapter three."

In retrospect, it was naive
to think postmoderns might be fair;
they obviously can't conceive
how *they* are blindly doctrinaire.

Envoi

The wheels of fortune slowly turn;
your book may be the next to burn.

On a Certain Viennese Doctor

Inventing a refined disease
afflicting all the human race,
he took away ideas of ease,
exposed us, left us in disgrace.

We're ego, libido, and id,
with sundry drives—a warring beast—
while Superego keeps the lid
on crime, in principle, at least.

Like Oedipus, though, men would kill
the father-rival, marry Mom;
while girls—hysterical and shrill
Electras—loathe without a qualm

maternal flesh. We're driftwood, brief
phenomena, tossed on the drink—
dark seas of lust, without relief.
To know yourself, go see a shrink.

What good results must be offset—
and soon—by spreading psychic stain;
you're parted from your money, yet
those clever complexes remain.

Envoi

Eschewing gods, we turn to Freud;
we might as well address the void.

A Voyager's Journal

—For Patric

1. Departure

Six ocean-going cruise ships crowd the piers,
all sailing late this afternoon. We're last,
and least, among the thousands in arrears
with pleasure. Skies at noon were overcast,

but, to salute us, changed to *bleu marine*,
before imploding in a cloud of ash,
transpierced by scarlet light and notes of green—
soupçons of melancholy, with panache.

The air is mild. The sea's got patchy froth,
however, and it's swelling, even rough,
with fractured planes—old, sacerdotal cloth.
Perhaps it's molting, having had enough

of ancient skin, and self. It writhes and roils,
but thereby draws me more into the waves—
seductive, mortal danger. We're its spoils,
they say, its progeny, the jewel of caves

where elemental matter moved and churned,
compounded, multiplied—its being caught,
amazingly, for future sense—then turned,
in time, toward shore, and rudiments of thought.

We're swaying, as we enter the Gulf Stream.
What then in the Antarctic latitudes?
I'll give them all my courage, my esteem,
in homage to the world's primordial moods.

2. Before Dinner, in the Lounge

By chance, not knowing yet the layout of the ship,
we've found this little lounge and stopped
a while near the piano, silent now, but promising,
we hope, good music later. People wander through,
en route to bars and restaurants, or at loose ends.
The light's not too severe; the chairs are friendly.
What of our fellow travelers—*simpáticos*?
Each surreptitiously glances at the others walking

past or taking seats; but eyes are cautious, meeting
barely, turning warily aside. It is too soon; we must
scope out our fellows carefully, take note
of gender, age, attire, taste, listen to their speech
(language, foreign accent, tone, and traces
of class origin). Two sculpted lions, almost life-
sized, survey and guard the scene. What fine beasts,
the great cats of the wild! Yet they have suffered

greatly, and caused suffering, since cruelty is king
in the forest, on the savannah (killing rivals
in the gene pool, eating other creatures). Man
invented its refinement, called it evil, then thought
of goodness and atonement. As of music. Here
come two musicians; one goes to the piano
as the other opens a violin case, gets his fiddle,
runs a chamois on it, resins down the bow, tunes up,

and sits. Good cocktail music, bits of pops, an aria
from *Norma*, even Bach and Mozart. One traveler,
exhausted, I suppose, is sleeping, mouth agape,
though not snoring yet. I watch the lions watching us,
and wonder: if they could be free to know us
as we know ourselves, remembering still
their jungle selves, their power, would they forgive us,
join in our awareness, tap their great paws to the beat?

3. At Sea

We stream on color: blue, aquamarine,
dove gray. To look straight down gives vertigo,
but farther out the surface seems serene,
both concentration and reflective flow.

Horizons offer us expanse—confine
us, also. Every wavelet, though unique,
resembles all. The latitudes decline;
there's almost no dusk, southward. In a week,

we'll sail past the equator; Capricorn
lies next. —Around us, vast capacity,
dark mouths of nothingness! The old god's horn
still sounds somewhere, perhaps, beneath the sea.

4. Santa Marta

—On the north coast of Colombia

This is a working port, specializing (so it seems)
in coal, loaded by conveyers from huge piles.
At least a dozen ships are waiting in the roadstead
for a berth at dock. Good: I like such industry.
We sign up for a tour, city and surroundings.
The tour guide drives me crazy, though—not a moment
without babble, and in broken English. What I'd like
to know (tonnage per year, the universities),

he doesn't say, but keeps up his patter—jokes,
insinuating comments. We visit, past the outskirts,
Quinta de San Pedro Alejandrino, a colonial estate—
large park and villa, a sugar mill once, and distillery.
The trees are marvels: palms—trunks smooth, fronds
thick—and vast acacias, with spreading limbs
bending to the ground and cactuses adorning them.
Strange birds call; iguanas dart among the ferns

and lilies; here's a coral hedge. No botany, though;
we're shown history—the room where Simón Bolívar,
who'd taken cold in Bogatá, last breathed, and a huge
monument, a cavern. We're treated to another lecture,
seeming endless. People wander, paying no attention;
finally, as we're about to leave, Pat, thinking
of the fine acoustics, opens into song. He means
no sacrilege; it's just *élan vital*, music asserting life.

5. Ship's Company

This ship holds fourteen hundred, give or take
a few. On deck, in the buffet and bar,
not *one* we'd wish to know. So, *my* mistake,
in thinking that, for traveling this far—

with money, thus—these passengers have taste?
Of course! —We've got a bottle of champagne
(a gift) but haven't opened it: a waste
to share it with these boors. Oh, why complain?

I wonder, though, if I'm too civilized.
But now, we've met the cruise consultant, Dutch,
who's gracious, cultured, chic; and I've revised
my judgment, thanks to her—not really much,

however, since the others don't improve.—
We'll set a small buffet, with wine, designed
for three: ten thousand years of arts behoove
us, legacies of manners, style, and mind.

6. In the Veragua Rain Forest

It's Costa Rica, before Panama,
and then the western coast. Puerto Limón
is mangy, but relieved with towering palms,
shrubs, flowers, everywhere. A guide arrives,

quite prolix, a performer; we're her crowd,
and captive. We are shown the countryside—
looking like Mexico—before we reach
a park. By crowded cable car, we slip

through tangled vines and trees, their feet
concealed in valleys and their heads in sky.
We glimpse some howling monkeys, hear their screams.
No birds, alas. A center for research

displays live snakes, dried butterflies, toads, frogs.
Since that's the route, we must inspect them all.
Nocturnal species live in ersatz night,
where paths are slippery; banana leaves

assault me in the dark; elephant ears,
enormous, almost block the way. I can't
see anything—no frogs, no guide, who's left
us here. Pat nearly stumbles, but goes on.

I reach for him, find nothing, almost trip
myself. Quite blind, I grope around—and touch
plate glass; I could have walked right through it. Now,
we're out, at last. Not OSHA standards!—more

a fun house filled with obstacles, a trap
for the unwary. Well, they're fixed in mind,
guide, jungle, and elusive frogs: distress
is sharp, and marks more deeply than delight.

7. Birds

One seems to follow us. It circles, dives,
arcs high, returns, displays its plumage—white,
soft brown, and gray. If I had many lives,
I'd be a bird once, fabulous in flight,

enjoying currents, feeding from the swell.
This one—a painter's tactic to relieve
unaltered blue—keeps pace alongside well,
and I imagine giving it reprieve

from solitude. And now another sort
(wide wings—a *W*— long bill, forked tail)
collects around us, as we near a port—
the famous frigate birds, which plunge and sail

with grace, but, kleptoparasitic, steal
from other birds, tormenting them, and strip
their catch. What signals, though!—the old appeal
of sea lanes, legendary bird and ship.

8. On the Central Pacific Coast

Nearing land, north of the isthmus and Costa Rica,
we are greeted by volcanoes—first, a chain
in Nicaragua, far enough from shore to look
pale lavender, like distant mountains in New Mexico,
and yet appearing close. The nearest
is the largest, broadly conic, regular as if designed
by hand. All dormant, clearly, though
one can imagine hovering wisps of cloud as vapors

from a kettle boiling underground, or breath of dark,
telluric goddesses. The slopes, chameleons, change
color as the day advances, disappearing finally
in haze. Now, as we approach Puerto Quetzal,
we're greeted by twin cones, symmetrical—
harbor sentinels—and then a sibling. They'll be bright
throughout the day, friendly—like the natives
and the thatched huts built for tourists, clean,

amazingly, without a scrap of trash. Crossing
the footbridge from the dock, over a narrow sea arm,
I find a grove of trees, magnificent:
traveler's palms, their fronds flattened, like a fan;
lofty coconut palms, their fruit bright green; flowering
flamboyant trees, orange, magenta, red. All this
could be destroyed if Vulcan fired up his forge—
as when on Guadeloupe la Grande Soufrière, restless,

spat up flames and smoke, and lava streams devoured
the sugarcane. I think of Saint-John Perse,
and how the Leger family, ruined, fled to France— he,
an erstwhile Robinson loath to be rescued, missing
his island forever. Poetry was born of ash and exile
then, as it is born now beneath great palms of love
fanning us, mid currents from the sea, and the volcanoes
tranquil, blue, serene—no ruins yet, no ruins.

9. The Dance

Each night, we listen to the string quartet—
a standard European repertoire.
This evening, though, is different—a set
of tangos, beautifully played. The star

is not the first violinist—though she's skilled,
magnetic—but a dancer, who appears
at once, and takes the floor, as if he'd willed
the scene. It's like ballet; one sees and hears

as with one sense. His partner is his wife,
attired in a handkerchief-hemmed frock.
Their steps are beautiful, proclaiming life
remade as order. They draw closer, almost lock

their feet flirtatiously, then turn aside,
yet move as one, a whirling, rhythmic square.
Their little boy is watching them, with pride.
A paralyzed old man wheels up his chair

and gazes, doubtless marveling that youth
endures, while his is gone forever. How
we cover nature!—raw, unpleasant truth
disguised by roses, music, love—the slough

of mortal being hidden for a while.
The paralytic, icon of regret,
begins to doze; the dancers show their style
again. Last year, an opera singer met

his end here, where he'd sought a late reprieve
from loneliness. He sang once, a romance,
inviting joy. He did not want to leave.
Death waited through the last step of the dance.

10. Guayaquil

We take a bus into town, passing through the port,
industrial zones, and dusty neighborhoods.
Nothing's very old—pirates in the past,
and many fires. The center teems—packed streets,
little shops, huge stores, hotels, cafés, with open doors,
displays and tables, so that inside and out
flow in a single space. We get off by the cathedral,
of Gothic revival style, plain but well-proportioned,

it too with portals wide. People crisscross the *parvis*,
linger, enter, leave—prayers, like errands,
done. In "Iguana Park," the statue honors Bolívar;
but the rest is fauna, very much alive: turtles
in a well-kept basin, many pigeons, and iguanas
everywhere—on walkways, on the grass and in the trees,
feeding on lettuce, sleeping, staring from large,
lateral eyes as we stare at them—gargoyles absent

from the church, latter-day reminders of primeval
times and rampant ancestors. One iguana
moves toward us; another tourist bends down,
cautiously, and it lets itself be photographed, admired,
touched. A young policeman—truncheon,
paratrooper's boots, keen gaze and Indian nose—
keeps watch. The better class of vendor manages,
or is permitted, to remain, but one poor woman—

babe suspended from her breast and trinkets
of the poorest quality—must go. We are, as usual,
voyeurs, not vicious or perverted, simply here,
both out of place and welcomed. Tonight,
the ship will sail along the Guayas River, past unearthly
mangrove tangles, to the sea. I feel the ages looking
out—looking *through* me, as by kin,
attended by an angel and the visionary beasts.

11. Orchids

Their kin are on display in Guayaquil:
wild blossoms wound on trees beside a road,
combining loveliness with the appeal
of things exotic; then, a different mode,

commercial specimens in open sheds,
for sale abroad especially. In rows
of hundreds, they bud out and raise their heads,
all taking a demure yet charming pose

to show off faces to advantage. Cream,
dark violet, lavender, pure white, cerise,
with subtle stripes and freckles: all a scheme
of nature's, merely, yet designed to please

their philofloral fans. And thus I praise
the shipboard staff whose wherewithal and taste
provide us orchids, colorful arrays,
as table ornaments—erotic, chaste

alike. The leaves are few; the spindly stems
require tutors; but each artful bloom
gives compensation, as expensive gems
seduce us by the value they assume.

Slim torso, shadowed eyes: coquettish skills,
withal; one winks, one smiles, as if to talk.
You'd think the world, afflicted by its ills,
would take more time for pleasure on the stalk.

12. Catacombs

—In Lima

At noon, we watched the changing of the guard
before the presidential palace, with salutes, drum rolls,
and goose-stepping troops. The square was packed;
yet this goes on each day. We've studied
the cathedral, sun yellow, Pat climbing shakily
up steps without a single railing. We have walked
now to the monastery, San Francisco. Pat
can go no farther; he finds a bench and waits, while I

proceed, marveling, into the church, the cloister—friable,
often shaken by the tremors, then rebuilt, old frescoes
visible still—and an exquisite garden, bright
in its array of bougainvillea and hibiscus. Now
the group is led into the catacombs—many doorways,
low, and twisted passages, uneven walls,
and steps and thresholds more like mountainsides
than work of man. One hollow room leads to another

till we reach the ossuaries. What we see is shank-bones
only, bins and bins of shank-bones, browned,
arranged with some concern for order, even patterns
often. The remains of tens of thousands lie here,
women, children, men, and monks, of course. Where
the other bones are kept we are not told.
No mummies, unlike Guanajuato; and no crania.
The shanks seem long, as though these people—Indians,

a few Spaniards—had expressed the urgency of labor
in their legs. I think of Pat's long shins,
carrying him around the tennis court for sixty years.
If there's any power left in me, past
death, I shall love his bones eternally, join mine
to his by dint of thought, sprinkle my dust,
make figures of our remnants, as we traced
our tangent circles, and wait for the admiring crowds.

13. In the Larco Herrera Museum

We saw the heart of Lima yesterday—
the ancient square, cathedral, balconies
of wood as in Seville, the catacombs,
the San Francisco monastery, all
colonial, rebuilt from time to time
because of earthquakes. This house, elegant,
was raised on pre-Columbian remains,
a palimpsest, thus. Shelves of pots, preserved

and classified, in diverse shapes—beasts, plants,
sun, crescent moon, and human images—
attest to old arts of the sacred, born
of immemorial fires, flourishing,
then dying out, to be transformed again.
The owls delight me—penetrating eyes,
well-feathered wings. There's silver, too, and gold
interred too deeply for the conquerors,

or incidental pieces judged too small.
Erotica attract attention most.
It's not just living human beings portrayed;
the dead are likewise shown enthralled, their gaze
intense, their organs magnified, as though
proclaiming potency beyond the grave.
The very gods know love here; they spill out
their seed and blood, inseminating earth.

All fertile—heaven, underworld, and men.
What does this have to do with us? Not much,
yet everything. These deities, are they
now dead, or do they linger in the sky
of South America, resigned and mute,
or wounded—or rejoicing, vigilant,
as faces turn to them in awe and fear—
the same fantastic urge, the old desire?

14. Casa Luna, Lima

We went to town again today—another tour—to see
two houses, typical, it's said. First, an old
colonial seat, near the cathedral, that has survived
the devastating *sismos* and daily wear of centuries.
But we are dropped off much too far away;
Pat declines to walk; I must imagine it. Next,
a 1950s residence, Bauhaus-style, called "Casa Luna,"
where the coach stops at the gate. The Luna family

welcomes us, showing off the patio, the house,
their antique furniture and art, *nacimientos*
collected from Peru and Europe—scenes on wood
or cloth, carved figures, stone or wooden, or made
of plaster, often gem-incrusted, with the Child
always at the center, saints or animals
as observers, angels, perhaps, holy light radiating,
and inscriptions in many languages. A grand piano

draws my eye; someone says it might be played.
I speak for Pat, and soon we hear the notes
of Satie's *Gnossienne* no. 1. Conversation ceases;
French doors open; sounds circulate among
banana trees, the brilliant birds of paradise,
the bougainvillea, to a gazebo where the others,
startled momentarily, put down their cocktail glasses
filled with famous Lima Pisco sours. Unaccustomed

to such urbane visitors as we (we're dressed
quite tastefully, disdaining oversized athletic shoes
and shorts, and, unlike many tourists, do not gape
or cackle in loud voice), the hosts are pleased
and thank us warmly for the music. The visit gives
its tone of taste and lightness (the house is of pale
stucco, the music slides smoothly over one's mind)
to the city and the day. At six, the ship departs,

rounding huge freighters at the dock, slipping past
the breakwaters. Farther out, we see the fishing fleet,
at anchor, like a Dufy painting—dozens of boats,
blue, red, yellow, white, lit by the setting sun,
its cape spread golden on the sea, serene, the men,
after hauling in their nets, at rest or mending
things, their presence glowing as with its own tone,
its own imperative, *pescadores* of their lives, and ours.

15. Robinson Crusoe Island

Chileans called it Más-a-Terra—more
toward land—until the archipelago
was rebaptized, in order to restore
cachet and lend it literary glow.

What other island bears an honored name
from English fiction? I don't know enough
to say there's none. Still, reasonable fame
would reach my ears. Perhaps, near Greece, some rough

formation rising in the wine-dark sea
commemorates a name from epic war;
and Polynesian isles, past memory,
recall forgotten gods who ruled their shore.

That is, however, legend; this is fact.
One Juan Fernández, lost en route
to Lima from Cape Horn, by fortune tacked
and found a lava island, trees, some fruit.

Surrounded, though, by barren cliffs and hills,
their rugged summits scratching at the sky,
he saw each landing as a test of wills—
refreshment, or a different way to die.

Then others came, anonymous or known,
got water, hunted goats, repaired their sails,
left traces scattered in debris and bone
and, later, in romantic seamen's tales.

Thus Selkirk, a percipient, dour Scot,
who spoke his mind on shipboard and defied
his captain, was rebuked and left to rot—
and think—for years, alone and ill-supplied.

Defoe's imagination did the rest,
creating not one man but two, that he
might mirror solitude—as both the test
and ransom of our human frailty.

And Stevenson, a dreamer of the sea,
may likewise have conceived of such an isle
for simple old Ben Gunn—epitome
of those marooned, their folly and their guile.

Dark shadows gathered on the shore compose
a threnody; I picture empty caves,
and somewhere in my mind a conch shell blows
as rising wind churns up the spumy waves.

16. Saint-Exupéry's Winds

Having run into great floes of krill and therefore
changed our route, first sailing west, then veering back,
we're late, by eighteen hours, in reaching port
at Punta Arenas, on the north shore of the Strait of Magellan.
With snowy foreheads, shoulders of stone, flanks
darkly wooded, the southern Andes stride like gods
and breathe cold air on us. Still, the sunlight sparkles
on the water's blue, the weeds, the gaudy reds and yellows

of the roofs—fair summer spectacle for latitudes
below the 50th parallel south. Ah, but there is something else:
great winds, and costly. For a little fee of twenty grand,
the tugs that get the ship into position dockside
must remain all day to push us constantly against the wharf,
lest moorings break. Even then, the vessel tosses,
angrily, you'd say, and stirs up furious waters
as it heaves.—Waiting to go ashore, we line up near

the gangway, while the sailors try to steady it against
the waves and troughs. Pat stands with me, in his Guinness
jacket. Now the queue begins to move. Going down
the shifting steps, I clutch the handrail. Pat should be
behind me; yet he doesn't come. Someone says
he turned around, through prudence, but wants me to go on.
All right; I want to see Magellan Square and St. John's Church,
with services in English still, and, most of all,

the square named after Saint-Exupéry, who flew down here
with Aéropostale, from Buenos Ayres (as he wrote)
to Patagonia and back, part of the new routes he opened.
Shaken by the wind, I manage to climb in a bus.
The vehicle is hammered from both sides. At the town center
it stops beneath disheveled palm trees, fronds like broom straw,
near the statue of the great Portuguese. Vendors
at their stalls are few; the wind is steady now, it's said, at fifty,

gusting to the strength of low-grade hurricanes. No wonder
I make headway awkwardly around the plaza, to admire
fine buildings—hotels, clubs, and banks—erected
by the French and British. Ropes arranged for windy days
along the walkways are not out. Where's St. John's?
—On another street. I dare not go that far. Neither will I see
the plaza where the characters from *Le Petit Prince*
greet children of all ages. But at least I understand the winds

that St-Ex endured, trying to take off, or, worse, to land—
whirled, blown back, low on fuel perhaps, the field in sight,
unreachable. He did not crash, however. Accidents
came later, at sea south of Marseilles, in the Sahara, then
his final wreck, off Toulon, in wartime, serving
France.—I'm whipped back to a bus, which lurches
to the port. What violent connections to the world!—tumults
of air and sea, eddies of war on all sides—but knots of meaning.

17. In Antarctica

Cruising in seas of the Antarctic Peninsula,
we're almost stilled between two icebergs,
tabular. They are no threat to us, we're told
(visibility being adequate); they're like tigers
in a zoo, to be admired—not domesticated,
but, if we keep our distance, safe enough.
I think of how my mother said, "It is not I;
it cannot be," as she and my father sailed

for the first time to England from America.
Yet it *was* she, and she looked at things
according to *her* vantage point, aspectually,
her scribal voice the same. What surrounds
us fits accounts, but somehow it is altered
by the observer—Heisenberg for travelers,
the foreignness arising from co-presence.
We've seen a leopard seal stretched out—

an odalisque—on floating ice, and penguins
waddling on their ledges, diving, surfacing;
we've taken note of glaciers, dark crevasses,
floes; we've passed high, barren cliffs, quite
vertical, and the peaks behind them, sharp
as awls, permanently masked in white, now
freshened (snowflakes have begun to swirl
around us, rejoining quickly fellow molecules

on drifting ice or in deep troughs). It's cold,
of course, but we go out on deck, wrapped up
in three layers, to look for birds—perhaps
a cormorant—oh, there!—buzzing blue ice,
or the gray-headed albatross, of great wings.
I plane with them against the iron sky, soar
toward rocks, plunge into the choppy sea.
The wind assaults my lungs, though, settling

in them with cathartic force; the waves swell
toward the ship as if asserting claims on us.
No warmth touches me but blood and love,
no channels, no recourse, and narrow chance,
only a dreaded end, that "distinguished thing"
which, alone, can separate us—one, stricken,
while the other is laid out, icy, as on the stone,
the mind forsaken and the flame of body out.

18. Tango

It's an ambitious program we've concocted
for ourselves: four hours of touring (bus and foot),
starting at nine; then lunch, siesta, dressing
for the evening, a quick drink, another visit into town.
Can we manage? But we *must*. From girlhood
on, as I studied Spanish, I have thought
of Buenos Aires as a city to my liking—cosmopolitan,
almost European, but with New World flavor,

yet not far in miles from vast grazing lands
like those I knew, nor in spirit. Now we're moored
in the wide estuary of the Río de la Plata, looking out
at an imposing skyline, ready to study the city
in three dimensions, partake of its delights. Lovers
may be disappointed, upon closer inspection;
I am not. Here, with colonial remnants,
are the authentic designs of France: Second Empire,

wide tree-lined avenues, ornate façades and doors,
the famous opera house, even work by Le Corbusier
(Victoria Ocampo's residence). Here are German,
French, Italian names; statues, parks, squares
in the continental mode, but also native trees—palms
and jacarandas—this is South America! The accent
is particular, lots of *j* and *ch* sounds. Separated
in the bus, Pat and I exchange quick mental messages

of admiration, knowing well each other's mind.
To top off the sense of strangeness blended
with familiarity, we're taken to a working district
called "La Boca," which resembles sections
of New Orleans, the houses and tin roofs painted
in bright colors, with tramway tracks, defunct,
and markets on the cobbled streets—artists, stalls,
cafés. Oh, my! We've got the cream of *la bohème*

with the savor of three continents. Riches enough,
one would say; but the Café de los Angelitos—
in a listed building—still awaits us, offering Malbec,
bife de chorizo, a sweet *postre*, and a tango show.
Tourist entertainments are quite often
crude—glare, vulgar music, flimsy sequined jackets,
feathers, cheap simulacra of traditions. This, however,
is true art—a history of the celebrated *paso*, set out

via dance by a small troupe in period costumes,
with enchanting choreography, rare taste,
and formal, cool eroticism, controlled but sensual,
one toe moving smartly up a trouser leg—
just short of the *risqué*. Can I honor better
my young self, crossing years, like this broad estuary
where we'll sail off tomorrow, taking a city
with us, squaring, as in the tango, circles of desire?

19. Land's End

On port side, sipping my first coffee, suddenly I glimpse
an enormous rock breaching the water,
then another, as we move; we're coming in
to Land's End at Cabo San Lucas. They're mastodons,
relics of the ages. The early sun discloses fissures,
smooth façades. They're wrapped in a vast scarf
of water, blinding; and the sky's pale linen cloth,
an alba, slips around each eminence. Now,

veering, we see the archway wrought by time—the great,
magic passage, from one sea to another—
Cortez here; beyond, the Pacific. Small beaches
fringe the waves, and a narrow strip of sand
between two rocks separates the waters as it joins them.
This is the journey's end, nearly. —The last time
I went to Mexico, I vowed not to return:
sub-machine guns pointed at me in the airport seemed

excessive, and I'd like to drink the local water, eat
a piece of fruit without much thought. But I'm not *there*,
just in the port. This place is likely safe, anyhow:
with golf clubs, restaurants, elite hotels,
surely they can keep from making visitors quite ill.
Yet I'm unhappy in the artifice of tourist villages,
resorts; even Puerto Quetzal, *muy simpático*,
still is not quite right. Beauty, yes, and authenticity,

whatever that may mean; that's what I want; evidence
of struggle, failure, overcoming—the suffering flesh
of history—and sacrifice (oh, those murals
at the Temple of the Moon, the ritualized killings,
with the heads of victims held up for the crowd!
—the price paid to be human). Farewell; I cannot truly
travel out of time, nor would I wish to.
Many lives are torture. I'll go into San Lucas, after all.

20. Sunset

It's like a watery canvas by Monet,
ashimmer: "Coucher de soleil en mer."
The skies are overcast, pearl-white and gray;
clouds gather distantly, a dark affair,

not promising. But in a narrow rift
vermilion thought—a bit of melon rind,
a note of orange—appears. More strata lift;
mist parts; the flaming orb, our cosmic mind,

displays itself in brilliant red, entire.
Rays, gold and roseate, invest the sea,
incendiary, in a wake of fire.
All is suspended, until, suddenly,

the sun, devoured, collapses, sinks, becomes
a remnant—but designing as it dies
bouquets of roses and chrysanthemums,
expanding in a glorious reprise.

Notes

The quotation by Carl Andre, known as a minimalist sculptor, comes from Calvin Tompkins's profile on him in the *New Yorker*, 5 December 2011, p. 66.

"On the Old Plaza, Las Vegas." The term *Malpaís* (which appears also in "El Morro") refers to vast lava fields in western and south-central New Mexico.

"Gusty Winds." When James Boswell observed that George Berkeley's idealism could not be refuted, Samuel Johnson replied: "I refute it *thus*," and kicked a stone.

"Sierra Grande." The Ratón-Clayton volcanic field, containing Capulin National Monument (with a road to the summit), Sierra Grande, and more than a hundred additional cones, is in the northeast corner of New Mexico. Sierra Grande, at 8,723' (and some 2,000' above the surrounding terrain), is the easternmost location of the United States above 8,000'.

"French Press." *Jus* ('juice') is French slang for 'coffee.'

"Columbine." The columbine plant, especially the roots and seeds, produces cardiogenic toxins, fatal under some circumstances. Columbine and Harlequin (or Colombina and Arlecchino), characters from the Commedia dell'Arte, are perennial lovers, paralleling the couple of *innamorati* whom they attend. Their garments are bright and multicolored, and they are pictured sometimes with fancy headdresses. While known for his antics, Harlequin is not just a clown; he is resourceful, agile, quick of mind and step.

"El Morro." "A'ts'ina" is the Zuni name for El Morro. The Anasazi ("Ancient Ones") settled on cliff sides and mesa tops on the Colorado Plateau late in the first millennium A.D., spread out additionally early in the second millenium, then left some 150 or 200 years later. Juan de Oñate (1550-1626), named governor of northern New Spain, was charged with exploring the territory and spreading Christianity there. Even by the measures of the age, his treatment of the Ácoma Indians after incidents at their pueblo (1598) was very harsh, with hundreds put to death and hundreds more mutilated; the mention of him here is not to be viewed as homage.

"Stirrup Cup." Readers of *Breakwater* (Mercer University Press, 2009) will recall that my husband, Patric Savage, and I had married in the distant past, but were divorced. We remarried in 2008. Hence the expression of regret.

"The Empress Eugénie Leaves Paris, 1870." Details of the empress's flight come from David Duff, *Eugenie and Napoleon* (New York: Morrow, 1978).

"Looking for Gravestones." The quotation toward the end is from *The Waste Land* in T. S. Eliot, *The Complete Poems and Plays* (New York: Harcourt Brace, 1952), p. 47.

"Siegfried-Idyll." The original title given to this composition (1870), as translated, was "Triebschen Idyll with Fidi's Birdsong and Orange Sunrise," but the piece is much better known under the title assigned in 1878 when Wagner reworked his composition before the score was sold. Certain details here come from Adolphe Jullien, *Richard Wagner* (1892; trans. Florence Percival Hall, rpt. Neptune, NJ: Paganiniana Publications, 1981). The son, Siegfried Wagner, was born in June 1869.

"Carnation, Lily, Lily, Rose." This painting, by John Singer Sargent, was displayed at the Royal Academy in 1887. It was a critical success. At the insistence of the Academy president, Sir Frederick Leighton, it was subsequently purchased, through a bequest, for the Tate Gallery, now Tate Britain. The song in question, "The Wreath," is by the British composer Joseph Mazzinghi (1765-1844).

"Composition." A statement by Clementine Ponce (1912-2013), a Santa Fe artist, is pertinent to this poem. "When you are young, others paint pictures for you; but the wonderful thing about the canvas is that each one of us has the ability to paint over the old pictures. There is no limit to the changes we can make or the help we can ask for to make the canvas beautiful—a picture of our life." Clementine, whom I had the good fortune to know, was honored as a Living Treasure of Santa Fe in 2002; the statement appears on the organization's web site, where I found it by chance some time after composing the poem.

"Degas in New Orleans." The statement by Peter Schjeldahl comes from the *New Yorker*, 17 Oct. 2011, pp. 94-95. The Faubourg Sainte-Marie, now called the Central Business District, across Canal Street from the French Quarter, was the American business section. For additional information on the 1873 painting described here, see Marilyn R. Brown, *Degas and the Business of Art: A Cotton Office in New Orleans* (University Park: Pennsylvania State University Press, 1994).

"Victor Hugo at Hauteville House." Certain details in this poem come from Timothy Raser's article on Hugo in *Dictionary of Literary Biography*, volume 119. "Oceano nox" is the title of a poem from *Les Rayons et les ombres* (1840). It alludes to death at sea (some three years before Léopoldine's drowning). "Reading the stars" is an oblique allusion to *Chatteron*, a play by Alfred de Vigny, at one time Hugo's friend; the eponymous central character, based on the British poet of that name, tells his detractor that such is the poet's task.

"Gide Misjudges a Manuscript." The incident is documented in a letter Gide wrote to Proust in January 1914. See Marcel Proust, *Lettres à André Gide* (Neuchâtel and Paris: Ides et Calendes, 1949), pp. 9-11. The phrase "dragged their full length" is a modified borrowing from Alexander Pope.

"A Voyager's Journal." This series is based on two sea journeys on Holland America Line ships, with port calls in the Caribbean, Central America, South America, and Mexico and a visit to Antarctic waters. One voyage ended in San Diego—hence the penultimate poem, set near Cabo San Lucas, in Baja California. These travels were undertaken with the permission of Pat's doctors, who acknowledged the good medical care provided on shipboard and in many foreign cities. (See "A Late Summer Idyll.")

"On the Central Pacific Coast." The poet Saint-John Perse (1887-1975), also a distinguished diplomat, was born Alexis Saint-Leger Leger on his family's island, part of Guadeloupe. Two years after the destructive earthquake and eruption of the Grande Soufrière in 1897, the family returned to France. He had great difficulty in adjusting to the climate and to urban life. His series of short prose poems, *Images à Crusoé*, suggests, through Defoe's famous character as he is imagined after his return home, some of the poet's own nostalgia for his island.

"Saint-Exupéry's Winds." In 1929 Antoine de Saint-Exupéry was appointed by the Compagnie Générale Aéropostale to extend the company's routes by a subsidiary through southern South America. He died on a military reconnaissance mission on 31 July 1944. It was long assumed that his plane had been shot down south of Nice. In 2000 the wreckage of an aircraft identified as his was discovered in the sea near Toulon.

"In Antarctica." It was Henry James who called death a "distinguished thing."

"Land's End." The Temple of the Moon is outside Trujillo, Peru. It is currently undergoing excavation and conservation.

CONTROLLING WHITE-COLLAR CRIME

Design and Audit for Systems Security

John M. Carroll

Professor
Computer Science Department
University of Western Ontario
London, Ontario, Canada

ν

BUTTERWORTH PUBLISHERS
Boston • London

Library of Congress Cataloging in Publication Data

Carroll, John Millar.
   Controlling white-collar crime.

   Bibliography: p.
   Includes index.
   1. White collar crimes—Prevention.
I. Title.
HV6652.C35 1982   364.1'68   82–12938
ISBN 0–409–95065–3

Published by Butterworth Publishers
10 Tower Office Park
Woburn, MA 01801

10 9 8 7 6 5 4 3 2 1

Printed in the United States of America

To Billie, my Wonder Woman,
and
Lisa, Michelle, Kristina, Talena and Kathy,
our Security Directors of the future.

CONTENTS

PREFACE

This book focuses upon the kinds of white-collar theft that causes serious financial loss to business enterprises. The perpetrators may be customers or vendors but are usually employees, and the thefts are accomplished by:

1. Forging documents.
2. Falsifying business records.
3. Falsely pretending authority over assets.
4. Fraudulently establishing claims to assets.

The threat is serious. White-collar crime has already forced one retail chain into bankruptcy. It will get worse for the following reasons:

1. The computer makes it possible for more people to get their hands on corporate assets. It's what New York-based consultant Bob Courtney calls the democratization of white-collar crime.
2. Business organizations are changing so fast that a serious theft possibility can be overlooked in the shuffle.
3. More people are tempted to steal these days.
4. Hard economic times provide them with an excuse.

The principal defenses against white-collar crime are controls over systems. By controls we mean accounting checks and balances. By systems we mean sets of procedures that handle things like receivables, payables, inventory, payroll and fixed assets. The major thrust of this book is to tell how to design controls into asset management systems, both manual and computerized, that will increase their resistance to fraud, forgery, falsification, and false pretences.

The techniques described range from traditional ones that businessmen have used since the Hanseatic merchants introduced modern bookkeeping, to safeguards that take advantage of the technical capabilities afforded by modern computers and data-base management systems.

It discusses as well, how to audit systems to see that these protective mechanisms are in place and performing their intended function, and also discusses the investigatory steps to take when, despite best efforts, a loss due to theft occurs.

This book is directed in the first instance at security specialists, both self-employed and company employed, who are responsible for probing security weaknesses, investigating losses, and apprehending perpetrators. However, the complexities of modern business systems, both manual and automated, dictate that systems analysts and designers, auditors, and accountants must also play major roles in the protection of assets. Indeed, some of the methodology presented has evolved from teaching third-year university courses in systems analysis and data-base management systems to computer science students just as some of the examples have been taken from the practice of industrial engineering specializing in the design of information systems.

In short, the purpose of this book is to demonstrate how to:

1. Recognize the structure and ingredients of a secure business system.
2. Understand how auditors go about disguising the security of business systems and why their reports may sometimes be misleading.
3. Zero-in on the weak points of systems to apprehend attempted theft.
4. Investigate reported losses efficiently by knowing which documents to examine and which employees to interrogate.
5. Prove job-related opportunity once you have identified a suspect with means and motivation.

It is a truism that eternal vigilance is the only real safeguard against loss arising from the dishonesty of employees, customers and vendors. Nevertheless, business systems designed with security, integrity, deterrence, and auditability in mind create an environment hostile to the white-collar criminal in which the vigilence of security specialists can be most constructively focused.

ACKNOWLEDGEMENTS

Successful defense against white-collar crime requires a team approach. It is not enough to be only a security specialist, a computer scientist, an auditor, or an accountant.

——I was fortunate, as a neophyte industrial engineer with a wartime background in communications security, to start my professional life in 1952 concurrently with the emergence of the computer from the laboratory. My involvement with computers grew with the industry from writing about them, to using them, to teaching engineering students about them, to full time teaching and research in a university Computer Science Department.

However, the security side of the problem was never so neatly packaged, and my experience over the years came from having the privilege of working with many fine organizations and individuals whom I would like to thank. First there was the Canada Council, who in 1969 sponsored my study of the confidentiality of university student records; The Defence Research Board of Canada; the Privacy and Computers Task Force of the Canadian Departments of Justice and Communications; Superintendent Frank Fedor and the Royal Canadian Mounted Police; The National Association of Convenience Stores; Skip Farber and the International Security Conference; Alain Hassounes and the Professional Development Institute; Colin Venning and the Ontario Trucking Association; Ron Minion of Base-Fort Patrol Ltd.; Dave Harding and The Safety and Security Technology program at Ohio University; the Food Marketing Institute; the Bank Administration Institute; the Forest City Chapter of the Institute of Internal Auditors; Jim Driver and the Ontario Police College; Ted Hayes and the London Police Department; the Wisconsin Bankers Association; Jerry Lobel and Honeywell Information Systems; Bill Sniher and the Royal Bank of Canada; Roy Whitsed and

Computer Data; Jim Finch and Colin Rous of Cerberus Inc; Jack Bologna of
George Odiorne Associates; the Southwestern Ontario region of the Associa-
tion for Systems Management; Bob Wilk and the International Association
for Computer Systems Security; the Canadian Information Processing
Society; the Data Management Association of Canada; John O'Mara and the
Computer Security Institute; the Business Department of Fanshawe College;
Tim Schabeck of Practical Management Consulting Inc.; the Canadian
Certified General Accountants' Association who sponsored my study of
computer fraud; the National Science and Engineering Research Council of
Canada who sponsor my technical research under grant #A7132; and other
friends and clients who have to remain nameless because of ongoing
investigations.

And Billie who not only typed the manuscript but did much of the
research.

John M. Carroll
Lobo, Ontario, Canada
1982

Chapter 1

WHITE COLLAR CRIME AND THE LAW

White-collar crime is difficult to define. It is commonly thought of as a non-violent theft committed by persons of relatively high socio-economic status in the conduct of their usual and lawful occupations. The usual breakdown of white-collar crime focuses in on: (1) who was victimized; (2) what instrument was used; (3) what the subject matter was; and (4) the relationship between victim and perpetrator.

The victims can be consumers, governments or companies. This book will focus on crimes in which companies are victimized.

The instruments of white-collar crime include false advertising, mail, telecommunications, personal solicitation, games of chance, forged or stolen documents, counterfeit money, and altered records. For the most part, this book will examine situations in which company records and accounts, whether maintained manually or by computer, are unlawfully manipulated either to facilitate theft or to cover it up.

The subject matter of white-collar crime includes gold and silver bullion, precious stones, real estate, stocks and bonds, vehicles, bank transactions, works of art, and merchandise. This book will be concerned with losses due to theft of company assets, whatever they may be, and will concentrate upon theft that takes place at the points where a business is most vulnerable: cash receipts, payroll, inventory, accounts payable, and accounts receivable.

Inasmuch as white-collar crime is generally accomplished by deceit or diversion, the perpetrator often has a close relationship with the victim whether it is a spouse, relative, in-law, friend, employee, employer, customer, client, supplier or vendor. This book will look principally at villains among employees, but will also pay critical attention to the criminal actions of customers, clients, suppliers and vendors.

Since white collar crime is so hard to define, it is understandably hard to estimate the amount of money lost annually because of it. In 1976, the U.S. Department of Commerce estimated that crime against business cost victims $40 billion a year. The declining value of the dollar surely must have pushed that figure to $60 billion, or more, by 1982. We must keep in mind that all white-collar crime is not directed against business, nor is all crime against business classified as white-collar crime. But just as bank embezzlement runs ahead of bank robbery, by nearly a ten-to-one margin, so too do the proceeds of white-collar crime exceed those from robbery or burglary. It would seem reasonable to estimate the current loss due to white-collar crime against business at $55 billion a year, with dishonest employees taking, by far, the largest portion.

White-collar crime is hard to prosecute because the victim may not realize he has been taken until it is too late for anything to be done about it. Indeed, he may never know he has been victimized. Moreover, because of a close relationship between victim and perpetrator, the victim may be reluctant to identify a suspect or give evidence against him. Also, because a substantial loss may be involved, the victim may be more interested in pursuing restitution than in seeing the guilty party punished.

Historically, the law has been slow to react to the challenge of white-collar crime. It may well be that white-collar criminals have been more imaginative than the lawmakers. More likely, the failure of the legal system to recognize white-collar crime, until recent times, is a reflection of the fact that human nature reacts more strongly to an external assault than an internal one, especially an internal assault that reveals the victim to have been gullible, careless, venal—or perhaps all three.

COMMON-LAW ROOTS

The laws defining white-collar crime are derived from two common-law offenses: larceny, or non-violent theft, and forgery. Until the nineteenth century larceny was a felony for which thieves were hanged. Forgery was originally a misdemeanor. After a sound flogging, the offender was set free to walk away or be carried home by his friends. The reason why these offenses were treated differently in the middle ages is explained by the sociology of the times.

Larceny is defined as the unlawful act of taking and carrying away another's personal property with intent to permanently deprive him of it. It was deemed all good things came from the king and personal property, even if in possession of a fellow peasant, was part of the royal bounty. An offense against personal property struck at the heart of the feudal oath, and for that reason the offender's life had to be forfeited.

Forgery was another matter. It was defined as knowingly making a false document either to the prejudice of anyone, or to induce someone to do, or refrain from doing, something. In medieval times priests, but few others could read and write. Moreover, the business community was relatively small and, in many countries, inconsequential. However, as time passed, more and more people learned to read and write. As business documents assumed increasing importance in the community, so too did society come to regard the crime of forgery as a more heinous act.

During the Renaissance, forgery was upgraded to a felony with the penalty eventually set: a hanging without benefit of clergy. In an age in which most people were still concerned about where their immortal souls would spend eternity, hanging without benefit of clergy ranked in severity somewhere between hanging in chains (the penalty for piracy) and drawing and quartering (the penalty of high treason).

Forgery does not only deal with false documents. It also comprehends altering a genuine document with intent to defraud, either by omitting any material part, or making an addition or erasure.

In some jurisdictions it is important to distinguish between the act of forgery and the offense of forgery. The act of forgery includes three offenses: forgery itself, uttering forged documents, and possessing the instruments of forgery.

The offense of uttering is committed when a person, knowing a document is forged, uses it as if it were genuine.

The offense of possessing the instruments of forgery takes several forms. It is an offense to knowingly and unlawfully make or possess government forms or the paper stock upon which they are printed. It is also an offense to make or possess other material with which to commit forgery — stamps, inks, printing presses and the like.

The definition of the act of forgery and of the offenses comprising it were refined over the centuries by legal precedent so as to get the errant penman coming and going. How well these definitions will hold up in the computer age may well be another matter.

THE DEVELOPMENT OF STATUTORY LAW

Over the years there has been a lot of juridical tinkering with the common-law concept of larceny.

In court, it was not always easy to establish the four cardinal points of

✳ larceny: (1) unlawful taking; (2) carrying away; (3) personal property (as contrasted with real or intangible property); and (4) intent. Even with the effective investigatory tools that existed in the middle ages: the rack, thumbscrews, and the press room, larceny was difficult to prove.

For example, if Jack Peasant was told to take his Lordship's horse into town for a shoeing and kept on riding, there was no trespassory taking and the indictment would fail. For this reason and others, during the reign of Henry VIII (1509–1547), a new statutory offense was defined, larceny by bailee or criminal conversion. This new law well and truly settled the hash of the peripatetic peasant. Even today, car rental agencies can thank Bluff King Hal for their means of legal recourse when one of their clients fails to return a vehicle.

However, the onrush of commerce raised additional complications. As commercial enterprises grew and flourished, it became the norm for the proprietor of a business to delegate the buying and selling of goods to hired managers. What was the owner to do when an unfaithful steward skimmed off the profits of an enterprise for his own benefit? Clearly a new law was required. During the reign of George III (1760–1820), the offense of larceny by servant or clerk, or embezzlement, was defined.

Several loopholes still remained. What was to be done when someone, by subterfuge, willingly induced another to part with personal property? This eventuality was accommodated by defining another statutory offense, larceny by trick or artifice, also known as False Pretenses. A person was deemed to violate this law when he obtained the personal property of another by knowingly misrepresenting a matter of fact, either present or past.

Over the years, several important legal presumptions have grown up around the concept of false Pretenses, to wit:

- Negotiating a worthless check,
- Obtaining credit by a false pretense or fraud,
- Making a false statement in writing, with respect to financial condition with intent and for the purpose of procuring personal property, money, credit, or discount, and
- Using the mails to transmit letters to defraud the public, or to obtain money under false pretenses.

The most glaring shortcomings in the concept of false pretenses are that the offense comprehends only personal property; real estate and important rights and immunities are not recognized; and that the requirement exists that the misrepresentation deal with a matter of fact, past or present. This requirement makes false pretenses an ineffective net with which to catch the bucket-shop operator who avers, contrary to fact, that a particular stock is certain to double in value overnight.

Today, the statute of frauds is the chief weapon in the fight against white-collar crime. It is of comparatively recent origin, dating back only to the nineteenth century. This statute was drawn broadly, and even today a policeman's rule of thumb is: "When in doubt, charge fraud."

A person commits fraud who, by deceit, induces the public or any person to part with any property, money, or valuable security. There are at least seven specific offenses associated with the concept of fraud. This specification of offenses does not exclude other acts; rather it enhances the effectiveness of the criminal justice system in dealing with frequently encountered situations. These specific offenses are:

1. Fraudulently obtaining food and lodging (hotel and motel skips).
2. Fraudulently obtaining transportation.
3. Fraudulently pretending witchcraft.
4. Fraudulently (im)personating any person, living or dead, in order to: (1) gain advantage, (2) obtain property, or (3) cause disadvantage.
5. Stealing, forging, possessing or using a credit card unlawfully, or knowingly using a cancelled credit card.
6. With intent to defraud, affecting the public market price of stocks, shares, or merchandise.
7. Falsifying an employment record (for example, a time card).

Of course, nearly all jurisdictions have specific laws against impersonating a police officer, using a false passport, and other offenses against the credibility of the state as represented by its officers or legal instruments.

BUSINESS CRIME TODAY

The twentieth century has witnessed a dramatic redefinition of white-collar crime. For example, bribery had historically applied only to officials. This concept has now been extended to embrace all types of commercial misdeeds including kickbacks and unauthorized commissions.

Election fraud is now a coherent offense whereas, only decades ago, widespread buying of votes was considered to be the norm in many otherwise democratic countries.

The motto of the marketplace was *caveat emptor;* let the buyer beware. Today there are veritable legions of officials dedicated to protecting the consumer. Truth in advertising, labeling, and lending have all become the subjects of law. Truth is one of the watchwords of our age.

Fairness is another good word. We now have Fair Employment Practice, Fair Banking Practice, and Fair Credit Reporting. Concepts like these were lifted out of the precincts of chancery and ecclesiastic courts and became part and parcel of the legal fabric of our times.

In the matter of computer-based crime, the inadequacy of the traditional concepts of fraud, forgery, and false pretenses has become increasingly evident to laymen and jurists alike. Several states, led by the State of Florida, have passed legislation specific to this point.

At the Federal level, the most comprehensive approach to the control of computer-based crime is exemplified by a bill first introduced by Senator Abraham Ribicoff (D/CT) and subsequently reintroduced several times in the United States Senate, but not as yet passed. The so-called Ribicoff Bill would specifically protect computers, computer systems and networks, and the programs and data in computer systems from intentional, unauthorized access, alteration, damage or destruction by people. It would do so by defining these actions as federal crimes.

The Ribicoff Bill also defines the crime of accessing computers, computer systems, and computer networks by false or fraudulent pretenses for purposes of fraud or to obtain money, property or service. The sweeping nature of this proposed law, and its possible intrusion into the realm of states rights, may be the reason why it has not yet been passed.

As civilization becomes increasingly more complex, crime becomes more complex. The law, dedicated to precedent and to sober second thought, has always lagged behind societal and technological changes. But sooner or later, the law will catch up.

In viewing history, the horse-stealing peasant of the Dark Ages may be thought of as the philosophical progenitor of the present-day computer thief as he fiddles a terminal.

It is hard to say which direction the law is heading. In July 1980, the Supreme Court of Canada struck down "Telecommunications Theft" as a weapon with which to fight theft of computing service from remote terminals. The Court said that if Parliament had intended the computer to be regarded as a telecommunications device, it would have said so explicitly. Need we be reminded that "wire fraud" is the FBI's favorite weapon against computer crime, and there is at least one case in the process of appeal to the Supreme Court. One result of the Canadian decision was that subsequent to July 1980, two persons who stole millions of dollars worth of government information from a remote computer were convicted only of the theft of $26 worth of computer time - petty theft, and their first offense at that. They were given probation.

There have been attempts to link trade secret thefts with "misappropriation" of personal information. Such linkage would, in effect, put an Equifax investigator, who questions a subject's neighbor, in the same category as someone who sells high technology for making advanced silicon chips to the Soviet Union via a complex network of U.S., Canadian and Western European dupes, shills and cutouts.

The law sometimes tends to sleep; then it overreacts. Consider the U.S. Foreign Corrupt Practices Act of 1977. This act is of concern to you, even if you are not corrupt and do no foreign business at all. It applies to nearly all publicly owned corporations and compels them to institute "reasonable" accounting safeguards to account for diversion or disposition of company assets, operating on the theory that if you don't know where your money is going, there is a chance someone might be using it to buy-off a sheik, or two.

The Electronic Funds Transfer Act leans heavily in the direction of consumer protection, so much so that banks now stand a considerable risk of being victimized by unscrupulous consumers who choose to fraudulently disavow transfers of their funds by use of bank debit cards at unattended automatic teller machines. A bank that tries to protect itself against this kind of loss by careful customer selection, stands a chance of running afoul of the Fair Credit Reporting Act. Even keeping track of how often a depositor has cried "theft" under questionable circumstances could invite trouble for the bank under the terms of the Right to Financial Privacy Act.

As a consultant, the saddest thing I have had to do is to tell a client who thinks he has caught a white-collar thief that it is useless to prosecute, and that he would be wiser to cut his losses, take his lumps and quietly dump the guy—but to beef up his internal security so it doesn't happen again. And I'm not one to suffer the accusation of Pollyannaism gladly!

The fact is that when the evidence of a theft is lodged within a computer, or heaven forbid, has been erased electronically, it is hard to introduce it to substantiate charges. Therefore, someone can steal $24 million and then turn around and sue you for another $2 million if you even suggest he is a thief. This has happened!

Modern white-collar criminals are a highly mobile breed. They move easily from one company to another, from one country to another, and employers assume a heavy personal risk if they take it on themselves to tell another prospective employer about prior bad experiences with a job applicant.

European laws are particularly severe in this regard. Exchange of information about white-collar crooks among companies, or even keeping a file of prior adverse events could lead to a company being kicked out of some Western European countries. Conversely, international borders mean nothing to white-collar crooks. They cross and recross with impunity.

Your only protection is to control and document, and control and document some more. The security director has to learn to play the game of electronic "paperwork" or he will be left fishing electric drillmotors out of the lunchboxes of blue-collar workers while the white-collar criminal takes a million dollars out the front door.

The fight against white-collar crime must include prevention and detection as well as prosecution. The security director has a role to play in each phase but he should not work alone.

Prevention of white-collar crime requires that the security director work with the personnel manager to see that only honest and reliable employees are hired. He may have primary responsibility for pre-employment screening which can include checking references, making police and credit checks where permitted, initiating background investigations, and in some cases, participating in pre-employment interviews.

The security director can also help prevent white-collar crime by working with the manager of systems design to see that new or revised information processing systems have built-in controls and safeguards against dishonesty. He should participate in the review of plans for systems and critiques of system performance. His participation may entail working as a member of systems design teams.

To play an effective role in the detection of white-collar crime, the security director must become aware of apparent weaknesses in accounting controls, perceived irregularities in information processing and unexplained shortages of valuable company assets. To do so, he will have to work closely with the internal auditor, the data-processing-manager and those in charge of assets, such as the manager of inventory.

In cases of serious white-collar crime, the decision of whether or not to prosecute should rest with top management. However, the chief executive officer should have the benefit of the best advice he can get. His advisors, in such an affair, should include at least the security director, the internal auditor and the company's legal counsel. The decision should ultimately turn on whether or not it is possible to prove criminal conduct by one or more individuals.

A word of caution is appropriate here. As a person of high status, it is reasonable to assume that the suspect will be fully aware of his rights. In this regard, it is well to remember that only a court, by due process of law, has the right to label a person a criminal. To otherwise suggest the same constitutes slander if done orally, or libel if done in writing. The former can lead to civil action; the latter act may, in itself, be criminal.

It might be wise to look at this hypothetical situation in which a security director finds himself working for a company that is shot through with corruption and everybody, from the president on down to the janitor, is involved in criminal acts. In such a situation, there is only one course of action the security director can follow: resign immediately, and lay any personal knowledge he has of criminal acts before the district attorney. Anything else would leave him open to possible charges of conspiracy, obstruction of justice, or misprision of felonies.

Chapter 2

ROLE OF THE SECURITY DIRECTOR IN DESIGNING CONTROLS

A prudent security director is instinctively alert to the possibility that thieves may break in and steal valuable company assets. To thwart their attempts he surrounds the perimeter of company property with a fence, installs appropriate locks on doors and may station guards at entrances. He sets up badging systems to prevent unauthorized persons from breaching company security by subterfuge, and routinely works with the personnel officer to prevent criminals from joining the company.

However, the most dangerous thief may already be on the inside. He may even occupy a high position of trust and responsibility. This is the white-collar criminal.

The white-collar criminal frequently handles company money, or other valuable assets, as part of his job. He may be able to divert it to his own use, and he can often cover his thefts so they remain undetected for a long time, perhaps forever. A white-collar criminal sufficiently well-placed can plunge a company literally into bankruptcy.

The purpose of this book is to focus attention on the white-collar criminal, expose his methods, and show how security professionals, in concert with other company officials, can prevent white-collar crime or at least increase the chances of detecting it before it does irreparable damage to the company.

The white-collar criminal works in a make-believe world in which valuable assets are represented by pieces of paper, entries in books or, more commonly today, by electronic impulses stored within a computer.

Indeed, we are witnessing the democratization of white-collar crime. Formerly, only a handful of employees, usually those highly trusted with many years of service, could make entries in sensitive manual accounting records; now any person with access to a computer terminal can do so. Many of these people have been with the company only a short time and, nominally, may have duties that would not suggest that they have any control over company assets.

To prevent improper use of company assets, it is necessary to establish control over them. Control is established by accounting. This means that a permanent record must be made of all money or other assets acquired by the company and of all money or other assets relinquished by it. The difference between these figures is, obviously, the net worth or the value of assets possessed by the company.

The existence of an accounting system implies accountability. It is a basic truth that every person is accountable to someone else. Employees are accountable to managers. Managers are accountable to the owners, usually shareholders as represented by an elected board of directors. Partners are accountable to each other, and owners are accountable to various levels of government to see that taxes are paid and legal commitments honored. One of these commitments is the obligation to pay employees' salaries and wages. Thus, the cycle of accountability comes full circle.

The breach of trust implicit in white-collar crime can adversely affect the interests of fellow employees, managers, shareholders, consumers, vendors, and the public at large. Sometimes white-collar criminals try to rationalize their crimes by saying that stealing from a corporation doesn't hurt anybody. This is untrue. The fact is, that to a greater or lesser degree, it hurts everybody.

A security director can be excused for feeling uneasy about coming to grips with white-collar crime. He may never have had to deal with accounting records before, to say nothing of computer programs. That's an understandable feeling; but it works two ways. The company accountant or data processing director may never have had to confront a real, live criminal before.

There are a great many company professionals who play, or should play, a role in fighting white-collar crime. If they are to do so effectively, they have to understand each other's jobs. There is nothing strange about this for the security director. He is used to working with plant engineers and architects to see that new or renovated premises are safe and secure. The principles of accounting systems designs are no more mysterious than the provisions of building codes.

One reason why white-collar crime flourishes is that the specifics of fighting it fall between the normal responsibilities of several specialists. In some situations, it might well be the security director who can bring an awareness of loss-prevention into planning and thereby strengthen the company's defenses against white-collar crime.

OTHER PLAYERS

In the first instance, it is an accountant who sets up a company's books. Accounting is a profession steeped in tradition, and its methods incorporate many principles that any security director would recognize as valid: separation of duties, division of responsibility, and maintenance of an audit trail, that is, a recallable record of transactions involving valuable assets. The usual criticism of a particular system is that the books do not reflect the special needs of a company, given that they were designed to suit the needs of a whole class of companies; or that over time, their structure has evolved into a degraded system in which traditional safeguards have inadvertently become weakened.

A company's accounting department might be properly called a bookkeeping department. Its various subdivisions like payroll, accounts receivable, accounts payable and so on are responsible for making day-to-day entries reflecting the on-going activity of the company. These entries are made in accordance with established procedures.

Procedures are established by systems analysts. More often than not they report to the director of data-processing. Usually, they have come up through the ranks of computer programmers and may know little, or nothing, about either accounting or security. Their primary objective is to keep data moving, or as they put it, improve throughput. This is why situations arise in which accounting controls may be routinely bypassed or non-existent.

The auditors are usually thought of as being the first line of defense against white-collar crime. This is not true. Auditors, by the very nature of their work, tend to arrive on the scene only after the crime has been committed. Sometimes too long after.

There are two principal types of auditor, the external and the internal. The external auditor is a self-employed professional, usually a certified public accountant. His responsibility is to the shareholders of a corporation and the public at large. His duty is to determine, for the benefit of present or future owners, whether the company's books of account fairly represent the actual value of the company as of a particular calendar date, usually that of the annual meeting of shareholders. External auditors may choose to comment on weaknesses in accounting controls; they may discover shortages or discrepancies between the reported and actual values of assets; in very rare instances they may even unmask white-collar criminals, but these are not their primary duties.

The auditor most likely to catch a crook is the internal auditor. The internal auditor works for the managers of a company. He has wide-ranging responsibilities one of which is to determine whether accounting controls and procedures are adequate and being implemented properly. However, the internal auditor's mandate extends to fighting all kinds of waste and inefficiency. He may become so occupied within other jobs that he does not get around to finding the loophole in some accounting control that a white-collar criminal has exploited. Curiously, the crime-fighting expertise of the internal auditor may not be brought to bear even when new accounting systems and procedures are being devised.

Many internal auditors believe that it is essential for them to remain independent of the systems design process so they will be in a position to comment critically on the adequacy of the system once it has been installed. By that time, some white-collar criminal may already have exploited the weakness in question.

The security director, on the other hand, need not feel any more inhibitions about involving himself in the design of systems and procedures than he does in commenting on the placement of doors and windows in a new building. Afterwards, if the internal auditor chooses to point out some weakness the security director has overlooked, the company will only benefit and this will be no skin off the security director's nose.

The design of a new or modified data-processing system is usually a team effort. For example, in designing a payroll system the team might be chaired by a systems analyst from the data-processing department, but would most likely include representatives from the personnel, timekeeping, wage-salary-benefits administration, and payroll departments. A representative from security should be on the team as well. To be effective, the security representative should understand the function of the system and the steps in its design and implementation.

In general, the design team backs into its task. It starts with the reports that management requires and the documents needed to implement the system and then works toward the input. In a payroll system, these outputs and inputs might include the federal tax table, personnel files, special pay sheets, statement of hours worked by each employee, payroll files, pay statements, pay checks with stubs, and a report of errors and exceptions.

The controlling document for the system is the data dictionary. For every data item that is encountered on system documents and reports, an entry must be made in the data dictionary. This entry includes:

1. Type of field. In data-processing jargon, the term *field* is used to signify a number, or one or more closely related words. For example, EMPLOYEE NAME, EMPLOYEE NUMBER, HOURLY RATE, or DEPARTMENT DESIGNATION.
2. Maximum length of the field in characters.
3. Source of the data.
4. Destinations of the data.
5. Where the data is stored—that is, in which files does it reside?
6. Who may change the data and at what times, or how is the data calculated? For example:

$$\text{OVERTIME PAY} = \text{HOURS WORKED (over 40)} \times$$
$$\text{HOURLY RATE} \times 1.5.$$

7. Validation rules such as, "hours worked cannot be less than 0 or greater than 80."

FIELD TYPES

Figure 2.1 illustrates some conventions used to show field types on input and output document formats. The numeral 9 stands for "any number" when used to describe a field (see top left-hand). The letter X stands for an alphanumeric character. The letter B stands for an embedded blank, (one that does not occur at the beginning nor at end of a field). These conventions are illustrated in the top right-hand example. The letter Z stands for "zero suppress." When used at the beginning or end of a numeric field, it means that if the numeral zero occurs in that character position, a blank will be substituted for it (middle left-hand example).

A string of dollar signs ($$...) denotes a floating dollar sign. In such a field, the dollar sign will always appear immediately to the left of the highest order numeric character. A dollar sign followed by a string of asterisks ($**...) denotes dollar protection. The dollar sign will always be placed in the leftmost character position of the field and the intervening character positions, to the left of the first numeric character, will be filled with asterisks. This is a way to protect the figures amount field of a check from the efforts of manual forgers trying to unlawfully raise the value of the check. The middle and lower right-hand examples show floating dollar signs, and dollar protection, respectively.

The validation of data has great significance to security and there are many safeguards that can be built into a system to detect errors and fraud. Implementation of safeguards requires extra data-processing, so however, it is important that security voices its concern to counteract arguments for improved efficiency, at the expense of protection of company assets.

9 = Numeric
X = Alphanumeric
Z = Zero suppress
* = Dollar protection
B = Embedded blank
$ = Floating dollar sign
. = Decimal point

								9	9	9	9
								0	0	3	2
								4	0	6	9
									10		

								X	X	B	9	9
								A	B		3	2
								B	6		0	4
								3	0		5	0

								Z	9	9	9
									9	8	7
									4	6	2	5

						$	$	$	$	9	.	9	9
									$	4	9	.	5	0
							$	6	8	9	0	.	0	0
									$	0	.	5	0

						X	X	X	X	X	X
							J	O	N	E	S
						W	I	L	S	O	N

						$	*	*	*	.	9	9
						$	*	*	8	.	5	0
						$	1	6	8	.	3	5
						$	*	8	5	.	0	0

Figure 2.1.   Field symbols

After creating the data dictionary, the team makes up the formats for the input and output documents. Today, these may not be "documents" in the conventional sense. They may only be screen display formats for cathode-ray tubes, possibly with blinking locations into which operators are instructed to type input data. Nevertheless, it must be possible, given the data dictionary entries and access to locations where input and output records are stored, to trace any item of output data back to the items of input data from which it was created.

This is called following the audit trail. It is an essential step in investigating allegations of fraud. The security representative on the systems design team has to make sure that data, making up parts of the audit trail, is retained long enough so that frauds can be successfully investigated within a reasonable time period. This time period will have to be selected to reflect company policy, common sense on the part of the security specialist, and in some cases, the applicable statutes of limitations.

The very nature of data-processing means that some input data items will be combined to create new ones. This is sometimes referred to as programming logic. The design team may set forth these steps in a decision table, although there are other ways to do it.

As an example, consider one step in payroll preparation, namely the computation of regular and overtime pay. The relevant input items are:

Type of employee—allowable values are "salaried" or "hourly."
Rate of pay   —basic hourly rate in dollars and cents.
Hours worked   —in hours to the nearest tenth.

The relevant output items are:

Overtime pay (OVT)—at time and a half of regular pay.
Regular pay (REG).
Message 1   —Investigate: unauthorized overtime.
Message 2   —Investigate: unauthorized absence.

The decision table is used to graphically set forth all possible conditions that can occur and the corresponding actions to be taken.

Conditions	ACTIONS	REG = WAGE x 40	REG = WAGE x 40	REG = WAGE x 40	REG = WAGE x 40, MSG 2	REG = WAGE x 40, OVT = WAGE x 15 MSG 1	REG = WAGE x 40, OVT = WAGE x (HOURS - 40) x 1.5	REG = WAGE x 40	REG = WAGE x HOURS, MSG 2
Type "salaried"		•	•	•	•	X	X	X	X
"hourly"		X	X	X	X	•	•	•	•
Hours greater than 80		•	X	X	X	•	X	X	X
equal or less than 80 and greater than 40		X	•	X	X	X	•	X	X
equal to 40		X	X	•	X	X	X	•	X
less than 40		X	X	X	•	X	X	X	•

Code: • means "true"; X means "false"

Notice that an attempt has been made to see that all possible combinations of circumstances have been addressed specifically.

You can readily see that this decision table implements three management rules:

1. Salaried workers shall not receive overtime.
2. No overtime shall be authorized in excess of 40 hours (80 hours in all).
3. Employees who work less than 40 hours have to give reasons for an absence.

However, an alert security representative should also be able to spot two loopholes.

1. If operators can input *negative* hours for workers who do not work for some reason, their "negative pay," which might be suppressed at the time checks are issued, could be used to offset fraudulent entries inserted when checks are printed and cover up theft inasmuch as the totals would come out as expected.
2. The second loophole would be that a salaried employee putting in as much as 40 hours of overtime might well be using that time to perpetrate unlawful activities.

For these reasons, the security representative might want to recommend that error, or warning, messages be printed if the system is to detect entry of a negative value for "hours worked"; or an entry signifying that a salaried employee has worked more than 80 (or possibly some lesser value) hours.

After preparing decision tables, the systems design team will move on to drawing up flow charts which will be used by computer programmers, who write instructions for the computers, to carry out the processing of data. The team will also create test decks of dummy data that will be run and these results can be compared with the precalculated results to ensure that the system is working correctly. We'll discuss these steps later.

This introduction to systems analysis is intended to show that security officers can play as important a role in the creation of paperwork systems as they now do in the design of physical facilities. Indeed, they must contribute their special expertise in this area if companies are ever to protect against the very substantial losses that can be caused by white-collar theft.

There are, however, alternatives to being left out of the systems design process on one hand, or actually participating in it on the other. In one large chemical company, the security director is a member of a management committee which must review and approve all plans for new or revised information systems. It is known as the security and safety review panel. If the security director is satisfied with the presentation made by the systems design team, his involvement in the design process can cease at that point. Otherwise, he can interject critical comments and establish specific requirements. In special cases, he may choose to become directly involved in the process.

In this company, internal audit stays clear of the design process and performs a review function once a system is in place. Relations between security and internal audit are close. Security is kept advised of the findings of internal auditors and is asked to participate in their investigations whenever a suggestion of dishonesty arises.

Chapter 3

ACCOUNTING SYSTEMS: A SECURITY PERSPECTIVE

The first line of defense against business fraud is a sound accounting practice; accounting practice is based upon the concept of double-entry bookkeeping.

DOUBLE-ENTRY BOOKKEEPING

Double-entry bookkeeping is a security measure that dates back at least 500 years. It is a specification of the principle of separation of duties.

In the double-entry system, every business transaction such as buying inventory, selling merchandise, paying bills, collecting accounts, paying wages, paying taxes, borrowing money, etc., generates two bookkeeping entries. One of these must be a debit to one account, the other must be a credit to another account. Ideally, the accounts should be set up so that different employees handle the accounts whose entries tend to offset each other.

Periodically, the debits and credits are added up to determine whether or not they do, indeed, offset each other. This is called taking a trial balance, or balancing the books. Balancing the books is a function usually assigned to a third employee who is highly trusted.

The Audit Trail

Should an imbalance be discovered during the balancing procedures, another traditional safeguard, that of the audit trail, comes into play. The idea behind the audit trail is that every transaction must be evidenced by one or more source documents.

Payments can, for example, be evidenced by vouchers that authorize the issue of a check; check stubs, carbon copies of checks, and ultimately by cancelled checks returned by the bank.

Cash receipts can be evidenced by receipt stubs, carbon copies of receipts, cash-register tapes, memos of cash-register totals and ultimately by the testimony of the payer backed up by the original of the receipt.

Sales of goods or services must be backed up by copies of sales invoices issued to customers. Purchases of goods or services must be backed by purchase orders and purchase invoices (bills) received from vendors.

These source documents provide the information necessary to record transactions in a journal. The entries recorded in the journal (*i.e.,* "day" book or chronological record of transactions) in turn provide the information necessary to record the debits and credits in the proper accounts. These accounts collectively make up the ledger, or book of accounts.

The principle of separation of duties persists in respect of the audit trail. Different employees should be assigned to handle different kinds of source documents, make different kinds of journal entries, and ultimately to initiate different kinds of ledger entries.

Debits and Credits

The basic equation of accounting is:

$$ASSETS = LIABILITIES + OWNER'S\ EQUITY$$

For example, if I start a business with $2,000 of my own money and $1,000 borrowed from the bank, on the first day, the financial position of the business would be:

Assets		=	Liabilities	+	Owner's Equity
Investment	+ Bank Loan	=	Bank Loan	+	My Stake in the Business
$2,000	+ $1,000	=	$1,000	+	$2,000

Owner's Equity.   Thereafter, in the course of business, we will spend money and we will make money. Money spent is called an expense. Money gained is called income or revenue. The different ways money can be spent, or made, gives rise to different kinds of expense and income accounts. These accounts can be regarded as temporary equity accounts.

At year's end (or at the end of whatever the accounting period may be), the difference between income and expense is determined, this is called profit (or loss if it is a negative quantity). It is then added to (or subtracted from) the owner's stake in the business.

An increase in the owner's equity is called a credit and is recorded in the right-hand column of the accounting statement or book. Since income is a temporary equity account, an increase in income is also called a credit. Conversely, decreases in owner's equity or income are called debits. They are recorded in the left-hand column of an accounting book. Because expenses diminish income from business, and ultimately the owner's equity, a *decrease* in expense is regarded as a credit while an *increase* in expense is regarded as a debit.

Assets and Liabilities. The other side of the basic accounting equation consists of the sum of assets and liabilities. To uphold the principle that books of account must balance, the offsetting entries in asset and liability accounts must have exactly the opposite arithmetic signs from the corresponding entries in equity accounts (and hence expense and income accounts as well).

For this reason, an increase in an asset is called a debit and an increase in a liability is called a credit even though at first brush this may seem contrary to an intuitive perception. Conversely, a decrease in the value of an asset is regarded as a credit while a decrease in the value of a liability is regarded as a debit.

The Chart of Accounts

In conformity with these basic principles, it becomes possible to set up a business-wide chart of accounts. There are at least five different kinds of accounts. It is common practice to number these accounts in a manner which provides a clue as to the kind of account under consideration. For example: asset accounts (100 to 199); liability accounts (200 to 299); equity accounts (300 to 399); income accounts (400 to 499); and expense accounts (500 to 599). Every conceivable business transaction will result in a debit or debits to one or more accounts and offsetting credit or credits to one or more different accounts. The result must, of course, be that debits equal credits when summed over all accounts.

Journalizing Transactions

Much accounting practice consists of deciding what transactions affect which accounts. For example:

1. Investment in the business
   dr *Cash*   cr *Owner's Equity*
2. Paying the rent
   dr *Rent Expense*   cr *Cash*
3. Making a cash sale
   dr *Cash*   cr *Sales*
                                      cr *Sales Tax Payable*
4. Paying wages
   dr *Salary Expense*   cr *Cash*
                                      cr *Employee Income Tax Payable*
                                      cr *Social Security Tax Payable*
                                      cr *Unemployment Insurance Tax
                                          Payable*
5. Buying office furniture
   dr *Office Furniture*   cr *Accounts Payable*
6. Paying a bill
   dr *Accounts Payable*   cr *Cash*
7. Sale on account
   dr *Accounts Receivable*   cr *Sales*
                                      cr *Sales Tax Payable*
8. Collecting a bill
   dr *Cash*   cr *Accounts Receivable*
9. Paying taxes
   dr *Employee Income Tax Payable*   cr *Cash*
   dr *Social Security Tax Payable*
   dr *Unemployment Insurance Tax
       Payable*
10. Purchasing office supplies
    dr *Office Supplies Expense*   cr *Accounts Payable*
11. Taking a discount
    dr *Cash*   cr *Accounts Payable*
12. "Capitalizing" a debt
    dr *Accounts Payable*   cr *Notes Payable*

Because there must be offsetting debit and credit journal entries for every business transaction, the journal may be proved simply by adding up the debit and credit columns for each page.

Posting Transactions

After the journal has been proven, the entries may be posted, or transferred to the ledger.

The ledger has one page devoted to each account. The debits and credits are entered in each account along with a cross reference to the offsetting entries in other accounts. Cross references are also made to the originating journal entries.

The Trial Balance

At the end of each accounting period, a trial balance is struck to prove that the equality between debits and credits has been maintained throughout the journalizing and posting processes.

Profit and Loss Statement

The first financial statement to be prepared after the trial balance is struck is the income statement, also called the profit-and-loss statement. It is made up of the balance from the income and expense accounts over the accounting period in question. The balances of the expense accounts are shown only as debits (positive; or negative for reversals), and the balances of the income accounts are shown only as credits (positive; or negative).

Balance Sheet

Next, the balance sheet is prepared. It is made up from the balances of the asset accounts and the balances of the liability and equity accounts. At this time, the profit (net income) for the accounting period is transferred to the owner's equity account, less withdrawals, if any.

The asset account totals are shown on the left as debits only; the liabilities and equity (net worth) account totals are shown on the right as credits only. In other words, these balances may be negative.

The balance sheet provides a snapshot of the financial condition of the company at the end of the accounting period under consideration. Financial statements are legal documents that establish the value of a business. They are vitally important to prospective purchasers, investors and lenders. Customers contemplating a long-term relationship with a company as well as vendors deciding upon the conditions of sale for their products may be interested in financial statements. The government uses them to establish certain tax liabilities; in lawsuits, unions and plaintiffs use them to assess the ability of a company to pay awards or damages.

Appraising the worth of a company by analyzing its financial statement is both a science and an art. Moreover, the way a statement is interpreted is highly dependent upon the interests of the prospective buyer.

Falsification of Financial Statements

There are as many ways to falsify financial statements as there are to interpret them.

Generally, a business gets into trouble because it can't sell enough of its products or services to people who are ready, willing, and able to pay for them. This, in turn, renders the company unable to pay its creditors. This is referred to as a cash-flow problem. A firm can stave off disaster for a while by borrowing. As long as it can make interest payments out of current income and continue to sell its paper, that is, get more loans, it can keep going.

Selling merchandise to dubious credit risks or "booking" fictitious sales can make a failing company look prosperous. Likewise, a company can improve its apparent image by making the collection process look more effective than it is. For example, a firm could carry uncollectable debts as accounts receivable, or treat receivables as cash. Factoring of invoices is a common way to obtain a short-term loan. Sometimes the factor collects on the account; alternatively the factor simply holds the invoice while the merchant collects on the account and sends the proceeds to the factor. It is not unknown for a merchant to factor the same invoice twice. If the firm is able to make the expected payments, it has fraudulently received an unsecured loan.

Many asset accounts lend themselves to wild overstatement. Intangibles such as trademarks and copyrights, goodwill, and franchises have no generally agreed upon value, and the figures set down on a balance sheet are seldom susceptible to checking. In addition, it is also possible to play inflationary games with fixed assets such as land and buildings, production equipment, and merchandise, raw materials or work-in-progress inventory.

The Challenge of Automation

Although traditional bookkeeping methods possessed a great deal of built-in protection from fraud, they also led to a great deal of paper shuffling and large, marginally productive staffs of white-collar workers.

In the mid-1960's, many accounting operations became automated as harried businessmen endeavored to reduce paperwork costs. Many clerical jobs were eliminated. The work of many bookkeepers and clerks was taken over by computers. The computer programs sometimes followed the form of the manual system, but lacked substance because nobody was left to check for approvals and supporting documents. This checking process, which was formerly performed manually, was not always built explicitly into the computer's program.

This is one type of fraud; it is frequently reported as computer-based crime affecting input documents.

CHARTS OF ACCOUNTS

Debit Accounts	Credit Accounts
Assets	Liabilities
Cash	Accounts Payable
Accounts Receivable	Notes Payable
Notes Receivable	Sales Tax Payable
Land and Buildings	Excise Tax Payable
Machinery and Equipment	Sales Commission Payable
Furniture and Fixtures	Outbound Freight Payable
Prepaid Insurance	Income Tax Payable
Prepaid Taxes	Social Security Tax Payable
	Unemployment Insurance Tax Payable
Expense	Equity
Interest Expense	Owner's Equity
Salary Expense	
Sales Expense	*Reserves*
Discounts Given	Reserve for Depreciation
Shipping Expense	Reserve for Bad Debts
Insurance	
Depreciation	*Imprest Accounts*
Bad Debts	Petty Cash
Rentals	Payroll
Supplies Expense	
Corporate Income Tax	Income
Employees' Income Tax	Sales
Social Security Tax	Trade Discounts
Unemployment Insurance Tax	Interest Income
Property Taxes	Miscellaneous Income
Excise Tax	
Customs Duties	
Scrap, Trim, Salvage	

Chapter 4

CONTROLLING
WHITE-COLLAR CRIME

There are really only two principles behind all the things we do to prevent white-collar crime. The first is that of <u>personal accountability</u>. <u>It states that</u> <u>every sensitive transaction must be positively identified with at least one</u> <u>named individual</u>. An audit trail is then the sequence of personalized transactions concerning the acquisition or disposition of some company asset.

The use of passwords, checksums, and codes are techniques that ensure the personalization of transactions. These procedures are designed so that transactions can be carried out quickly and easily by authorized, and hence named, persons; but only with great difficulty, if at all, by unauthorized persons.

The second principle is that of forced collusion. It requires that two authorized persons participate in at least the most sensitive transactions. It rests on the premise that it is harder to subvert two people than one. This principle is reflected in the requirement for double signatures on checks, use of two keys in safety deposit boxes, never-alone-zones such as currency packaging rooms, double sign-off on security-relevant changes to computer programs, and two witnesses to the destruction of redeemed bonds.

Both these principles lead to making it more difficult, and expensive, to commit crimes (i.e., sharing the loot with more confederates, or paying more in bribes to get passwords, etc.). The rationale is that good security will make it so uneconomical for criminals to attack a company's assets that they will go elsewhere or desist altogether.

Incidentally, this is the difference between commercial crime and national security. Measures that deter thieves by making it uneconomical to steal may not deter adversaries who act from motives of patriotism or ideological conviction.

The essence of control in any large company today is control of the data-processing (DP) department. At the heart of the matter is the uncomfortable fact that DP personnel tend to identify more with their function than with the business of the company they work for. For example, in a bank, most employees regard themselves as bankers while the DP staffers tend to regard themselves as computer people who happen to work in a bank.

For this reason, it is essential that the relationship between the DP department and the users of its services be formalized and that responsibilities be fixed for the security of data at the time it is delivered to the DP department for processing; for the security of reports at the time they are returned to the user; and for specification of the processing operations to be performed, including liability for loss, compromise or error.

Today, many of the assets of the company may reside exclusively in machine-readable media: customer lists, invoices, marketing plans, money itself. It is within the computer that changes of policy are actualized. Through the computer must flow the documents that determine the profit position of the firm. If top management loses control of the data-processing department, it loses control of the enterprise.

The history of computer abuse is replete with incidents where tapes containing employee names and addresses were surreptitiously supplied to union business agents for use in organizing drives, or where lists of shareholders were supplied to persons preparing a tender offer as part of an attempt to take over control of the corporation.

If some subordinate operating arm of a company is placed in a position where it can exercise undue control over the data-processing department, the resulting advantage it would be able to realize over other divisions could distort its relative position to the detriment of overall corporate planning.

SEPARATION OF DUTIES

A key factor in maintaining control over data-processing is to make sure that no one person, or clique, possesses detailed knowledge of the entire operation. There should be both spatial and functional separation of duties.

Incoming and outgoing mail rooms should be separated so clerks can't intercept remittances and mail them home.

The functions of programming and machine operation should be separated so a programmer can't insert codes that would cause the computer to print extra checks and then pick them up when he runs the program.

A tape librarian should keep custody of software and data so a third-shift machine operator can't make an unauthorized copy of a valuable mailing list without leaving evidence of having signed the tape out of the library.

Involving two or more persons in every sensitive action may not insure that no unauthorized actions will occur, but it almost guarantees that someday the truth will come out.

PREVENTION OF FRAUD

There are at least four things that should be done routinely to help in prevention or detection of fraud:

1. Maintain systems and programs effectively. No item of data-processing equipment should be left in service with an uncorrected mechanical or electrical defect, especially when such a defect might affect a protective mechanism. Nor should a computer program having known logical errors be left in use. Such programs can give erroneous and unexpected results that may aid the depredations of an embezzler or unlawful user.
2. Prevent and detect accidental errors. There is no way to tell whether an erroneous or unexpected result arises from accidental error or from deliberate falsification. Such falsification may be undertaken either to facilitate a defalcation, or to erase traces of one. Furthermore, a so-called "error" can, in some cases, facilitate a defalcation by creating a distraction, or by forcing the bypassing or exposure of a protective mechanism.
3. Prevent fraudulent manipulation of data or misuse of classified information. This is the heart of the matter and appropriate control mechanisms will be presented in the next chapter.
4. Prevent accidental destruction of records; ensure continuous operation. The only way to avoid accidental destruction of records is to store back-up copies in a secure off-site location, otherwise operators may thoughtlessly spoil all the copies in abortive attempts to correct a systems malfunction or "bug." If back-up tapes are not immediately accessible, machine-room personnel will be forced to follow proper procedures and use simulated data while the error is being located and corrected.

SYSTEMS CRASHES

The systems crash is the most common event that causes interruption of computer operations. It occurs when the computer's operating system encounters a dilemma which it cannot resolve; consequently the system gives up and quits. Many crashes are caused because of design deficiencies in their control programs which render them incapable of coping with processing events not forseen by the designers.

However, systems crashes can be a sign that some users are doing unanticipated things to the system. Usually these things turn out to be honest mistakes. But sometimes aberrant user behavior can be an indication that someone is probing the security mechanisms of the computer system, preparing to make an unauthorized penetration of another user's address space or data files.

Few penetrators are able to crack a system on the first try—unless they have previously practiced on a similar system. Therefore, a rash of unexplained systems crashes often means a would-be penetrator is at work learning how to compromise the system.

Sometimes users may find it self-advantageous to force a crash. In at least one computer system, all current accounting charges are wiped out when the system crashes; so a programmer can save money by causing a crash.

I knew of one programmer who was working on a simulation program that was extremely expensive to run. He would work for several hours using up many hundred dollars worth of computer time. He would then give the command:

OUTPUT filename to OUTPUT

It turned out that OUTPUT was the name of a part of the computer's operating system as well as the name the programmer had given to one of his files. This instruction caused the computer to become confused and overwrite its own operating system, which is the sequence of instructions that control the computer's operation.

Operating systems are designed so that the computer automatically checks instructions whenever they are called into its program register. In the case being described, when it began to call up instructions from the part of its operating system that was overwritten, it found itself unable to continue operations because every instruction it called up turned out to be unacceptable. The system crashed. In doing so, it wiped out all the current accounting records including the very large bill my friend had just incurred.

A deliberate systems crash can also be a device for harassing other users or for spying on them.

When a system crashes, it automatically dumps the current contents of its central memory to help systems programmers diagnose the reason for the crash. By studying the dump, an astute programmer can discern what each user was doing at the time of the crash and thereby gain insight into possibly sensitive data or programs. In another case, a programmer was interested in forcing crashes to harass other users. He found he could do so by issuing the systems command:

ATTACH*

Asterisk (*) is a so-called "wild card" and stands for "everything."

The consequence of issuing this command was that all the computer's peripheral devices: card readers, printers, disk files and the like, were attached to his program. There weren't any devices left for any other users. Every time another user asked to use a peripheral device, his request was put onto a queue and the computer stopped further work on that user's program. Soon, everybody was waiting in line and nothing was getting done; the computer sensed this impasse and brought itself to a stop. The programmer had successfully caused a crash. Under these conditions, a user who had just typed a lengthy program at his keyboard would lose it and have to start all over again. And programmers hate to type!

The malicious user made sure his victim was in just such a vulnerable position when he caused the system to crash.

CONTINGENCY PLANNING

To cope with a longer-term service interruption it is necessary to have a contingency plan. It may be based upon transferring operations to an alternative site, making use of someone else's site on a temporary basis, or purchasing data-processing services from a computer service bureau.

A contingency plan must address every aspect of data-processing operations: hardware (*i.e.* computers and peripherals) telecommunications devices; data conversion/entry devices; software (*i.e.* operating systems, utility programs); data bases and applications programs; data; forms; procedures; working space; electric power and air conditioning; and assignment of personnel.

A contingency plan has at least six phases: definition, setting forth functional procedures, design, implementation, testing, and maintenance or updating to accommodate changing conditions—everything from purchase of a new computer to change of personnel, titles or telephone numbers.

Software and data are crucial to any recovery plan. You can buy new hardware, but you can only replace data at prohibitive cost. Data files that are periodically updated should be kept for at least three generations. Only the most recent ones should be kept in the machine room, and at least one generation should be stored in an off-site vault. If data is updated continually, copies of the file, or dumps, should be taken at regular intervals and a continuous record kept of changes.

The acid test of a contingency plan is to declare an emergency to see if you can continue operations using only resources and procedures set forth in the plan.

The key to effective contingency planning is to have a nucleus of loyal and competent employees, all of whom know what to do in an emergency and have practiced their responses until they are confident they can handle it.

Exit Procedures

Contingency planning must address everyday emergencies as well as catastrophies. There should be standard exit procedures from all abnormally terminated programs. Usually, these procedures are an integral part of the program. Upon encountering a so-called fatal error, the program directs the computer to print out diagnostic information, restores the data being processed to some specified prior state, and leaves the user's view of the machine in a designated state.

Although it is the responsibility of the computer technologists to make use of these clues to find and correct the error, procedures must be formalized regarding the handling of diagnostic data such as dumps, which could expose sensitive information; the subsequent use of questionable programs; and who can certify that a defect has, in fact, been corrected.

In contingency planning, steps must be taken to protect customer data, records and reports. Naturally, the loss of data, whether it be your own or a customer's, is a loss in itself. However, in the context of fraud investigation, these losses can also represent cover-up mechanisms available to an embezzler.

COMPLETENESS, ACCURACY, AUTHORIZATION

All control mechanisms exist to guarantee completeness, accuracy, and authorization. If any one of these qualities is missing, an accounting system cannot be said to be under control.

Completeness of processing means that all tests and indicated actions have been carried out on all data items of all records submitted for processing. It can be ensured by serially numbering all records, checking to see that all data fields in input and output records are filled—even with phrases such as not "applicable," and by arranging for a feedback response to indicate when a processing program has run to completion.

Accuracy of processing means that all results correspond to standards.

These standards are the expected values of results over the entire range of possible inputs. This requirement implies that a program must have been subjected to exhaustive pre-implementation testing and appropriate checks built into the released version.

Authorization for processing must be evidenced in some positive way such as by signing or initialing a request form or by the use of a key, card, or password whose distribution has been controlled and whose authenticity has been verified manually or automatically.

MANAGEMENT TRAILS

A management trail consists of the documents attesting to the initiation, approval, and implementation of an executive action or policy statement. Its objective is to fix the responsibility for action or inaction upon the advisors, decision makers and supervisors who participated in it.

This fixing of responsibility has the two-fold benefit of deterring irresponsible management behavior by the sure knowledge that blame will come to rest on its perpetrators, and of showing upper echelons of management where remedial training and education can most effectively be applied.

An audit trail is a type of management trail that provides a form of *ex post facto* protection from fraud. It should be possible, in respect of any monetary transaction above some nominal floor value, to locate documentary or machine-readable evidence as to who authorized it, and how and when it was carried out.

DOCUMENTATION

Adequate documentation is necessary, first, because during its preparation, errors and contradictions may be disclosed in the logic of the systems, programs, and procedures.

Documentation is necessary to ensure the proper operation and maintenance of hardware and software; after all, one cannot go by the book if one does not have a book.

Documentation is essential in the training of new staff and any business is sure to experience some turnover. In fact, turnover is so high in some DP departments that the managers of these departments call them revolving doors.

Only where adequate documentation exists is it possible to make an operational audit and thus determine if rules exist and whether things are being done according to them.

Finally, only documentation can spell out completely the conditions of work and standard operating procedures, thus putting employees adequately on notice and laying the groundwork for subsequent termination or other disciplinary action in the event rules are violated or procedures disregarded.

List of Documents

In a typical data-processing department, documentation would include:

Organizational chart
Job descriptions
Departmental terms of reference
Employee rules of work and conditions of employment
Standard procedures for:
  systems analysis studies
  program design and development
  machine operation
  hardware and software maintenance
Employee names, addresses, phone numbers, regular and collateral duties
Authorized visitors list
Schedule of standard service and material charges
Contingency plans
Library holdings list
Building facility plans
Hardware interconnection diagram
Telecommunications diagrams; cable maps; cable reference cards
Systems password and access-control lists
Hardware documentation:
  General description
  Theory of operation
  Operations manual
  Reference and troubleshooting manual
  Maintenance and modification log
  Performance (benchmark) data
Software documentation:
  General description and objectives
  System flow charts
  Program interfaces
  Program documentation:
    General description and objectives
    Hierarchical input-processing-output diagram
  Logic flow chart or pseudo-code logical description

Sample command/response sequence
Main program source code in structural format with explanatory sequence
Module interfaces
Module documentation:
    Statement of objectives
    Inputs and outputs
    Detailed logic flow chart
    Sample command/response sequence
    Logical state diagrams
    Source code listing
Operators' manual
Programming reference manual
Chronological file of change letters
Program test data (test decks)
Program run book
Sample input coding forms or terminal dialog/sample printout
Data-base documentation:
    Data-base dictionary
    Data-base administrator's terms of reference
    Data-base schema
    Subschema; data-base password and access-control lists
    Data-description-language reference manual
    Data-manipulation-language reference manual
    Operating procedures
    Recovery procedures
    Telecommunications protocol
    Sample input/output
    Sample dump of files showing structure
Master copies of all forms used

Chapter 5

HOW TO ACHIEVE CONTROL

Presented in this chapter are 28 control techniques recommended by the Canadian Institute of Chartered Accountants and the American Institute of Certified Public Accountants. These techniques can be used to implement the guidelines given in the previous chapter. In most cases, several ways to realize each control technique will be given.

AUDIT CONTROL TECHNIQUES

1. Design forms properly.
2. Write procedure manuals.
3. Implement proper training and supervision.
4. Preprint standing data.
5. Division of duties.
6. Establish a control group.
7. Use self-checking digits.
8. Take advantage of computer editing.
9. Use manual editing also.
10. Make simultaneous entries of data.
11. Verify your key-punching.
12. Make use of control totals.

13. Make sure hardware controls are working.
14. Keep transaction logs.
15. Use "ANSWER BACK" communications.
16. Keep up preventative maintenance.
17. Control the computer's environment.
18. Establish data conversion standards.
19. Put external labels on files.
20. Make use of software controls.
21. Set up a media ("TAPE") library.
22. Control computer programming.
23. Take advantage of arithmetic and overflow tests.
24. Restrict access to sensitive areas and items.
25. Rotate operators.
26. Keep console logs.
27. Keep error logs.
28. Help users anticipate results.

1. Design Forms Properly

Data should be recorded on specially designed documents. These documents should be coded and filed for convenient retrieval. The design of a form should be such that it inhibits the omission of data and inadvertent use of the wrong form.

Some forms will be used for direct entry of data. These forms should incorporate safeguards to prevent loss of data and inaccuracies due to transmission errors. It is a good idea to use fixed-length fields and boxed characters even though these features may not be strictly necessary as they are in the case of batch entry of data (*i.e.* keypunching).

In direct-entry systems, it is important that terminals be identified by number and the operators be identified by password. Terminals and operators should be restricted as to their range of permissible activities.

A form should be designed with ease of completion and data conversion in mind. It is a good idea to preprint common codes and amounts so as to minimize incorrect interpretation.

A direct-entry system should be able to function when the host computer is inoperative. Some mechanism, such as serial numbering or time stamping of forms, should exist to ensure that data entered when the computer is down are subsequently processed by the system.

Five specific considerations in forms design are use of (a) redundancy checks, (b) rationalized numbers, (c) dating, (d) approval and authentication, and (e) cancellation.

(a) *Redundancy checks.* When data is critical, ask for it in at least two ways. For example, ask for AGE and for DATE-OF-BIRTH (DOB); check one against the other by mathematically determining the difference between AGE and DOB using the current date.

(b) *Rationalized numbers.* Identifying numbers should, when possible, be used to encode personal data. For example, the Canadian taxpayer number, which is used to check for persons working under two or more Social Insurance (Security) Numbers, consists of the first five characters of the last name concatenated with the sum of the taxpayer's Julian day of birth (001–365/6) plus the modulo-9 sum of the last two digits of the year of birth (1925 = 7) plus 500 if the taxpayer is female. (The modulo-9 sum means the remainder after the sum has been divided by 9; it can also be found by adding the digits: $2 + 5 = 7$.)

(c) *Dating of forms.* A time limit or expiry date prevents fraudulent entry on "stale" forms.

(d) *Approval and authentication.* The original form should contain space for a signature or initials to show that the transaction was properly authorized before being entered into the system.

(e) *Cancellation.* Provisions should be made for invalidating a form once the transaction has been terminated. It can be done by perforating or stamping, but the technique should be uniformly applied and clearly recognizable by all operators.

2. Procedure Manuals

Documentation should cover input preparation, data conversion, activities of the control group, systems programming, computer operation, and user procedures. Procedure manuals should be clearly written, complete, and up-to-date. They should be distributed to all personnel who require them. Operators, and especially supervisors, should be familiar with their contents. Manuals in the workplace should exhibit evidence of use. Changes should be distributed, entered in the manuals, and put to use without delay.

Procedure manuals should deal explicitly with administrative safeguards, cancellation, and confirmation.

Administrative safeguards include requirements for shared or simultaneous authorization of sensitive activities. It can be implemented by double sign-off, never-alone zones, and two-key systems.

Cancellation is especially important in the case of paid invoices and checks.

Confirmation of instructions received by telephone should entail calling back the caller's supervisor.

3. Proper Training and Supervision

There are five important precepts in the training and supervision of input preparation, data conversion, data transmission, activities of the control group, systems programming, computer operations, and user procedures. They are as follows: (1) A regularly scheduled operator training program should exist. (2) Evidence of supervisory review, such as initials, should exist on utilization logs, output reports, control group logs, and programs. (3) Supervisors should be adequately trained and advised when new procedures have been taught to personnel under their control. (4) Training and supervision standards should not be permitted to lapse during peak periods. (5) A one-over-five span of control is considered the maximum consistent with good management practice.

4. Preprinting or Precoding

Standing elements of data should be preprinted on forms or precoded on machine-readable input such as punched cards. These techniques should be used whenever possible and all systems should be reviewed to discover opportunities to best use them. Prenumbered serialized forms should be checked when received from the printer to ensure that the stock is correctly serialized, that the number sequence is compatible with that currently in use, and that numbers on the forms agree with those on the stubs. It is important that numbered sequences used at remote locations be compatible with those used at the data center and at other remote locations.

The principles of serial prenumbering should apply to forms for data input, punched cards, and optical-character-recognition documents.

Forms for data input should include preprinted serialized numbers.

Punched cards should be prepunched with serializing numbers and other identifying data elements.

Optical-character-recognition (OCR) documents should, if possible, be designed as turnaround documents with the maximum amount of data pre-entered before the form is given to an operator for completion.

5. Division of Duties

The principle of division of duties dictates that the implementation of a sensitive procedure should not be carried out by the same people who initiated it. The input of transactions should be segregated from their authorization. The custody of assets should be separated from the act of accounting for them. Computer programmers should not be permitted to operate computers and, conversely, operators should not be permitted to write programs. The control group should not participate in the activities they are expected to control. Access to the unused stock of critical forms should be restricted to persons whose duties involve the duly authorized input of transactions.

6. Control Group

The control group should be involved in input, processing, and output. The day-to-day activities of the control group should only be bypassed with prior approval—and then only if alternative arrangements have been made to see that adequate control procedures are carried out.

Input. The control group should be responsible for receiving input and verifying its authorization.

Processing. The control group should reconcile processing. This can be accomplished by periodically running test decks, by manually processing random samples of work, and by sending out queries to users for audit conformation.

Output. The control group should be responsible for distributing output to intended recipients and for ensuring that all errors have been corrected.

Members of the control group should be experienced persons, screened for reliability and loyalty to the company. The leader of the control group should not report to the senior executive of any department whose activities the control group is charged with scrutinizing.

7. Self-Checking Digits

Self-checking digits should be used on key codes to detect inadvertent or intentional errors.

There are many kinds of self-checking digits. These include (a) hash totals, (b) check sums, (c) simple summation, (d) the Luhn check digit, and (e) the International mixed modulo system.

(a) *Hash totals* are the sums of unrelated numbers present in a record such as SSN + DOB + WEIGHT + *ETC;* they protect against alteration.

(b) *Check sums* are the sums of the binary equivalents of all computer words in a block of text taken modulo some larger number, usually the largest that can be held in the computer's registers. This technique also protects against alteration.

(c) *Simple summation* of the digits of a key code gives 100 percent protection against single-digit substitution. Note that slideovers can be regarded as a special case of single-digit substitution. It does not protect against transposition.

For example, consider the number 1 2 3 4 5 6 7 8. The sum of digits is: $1+2+3+4+5+6+7+8=36$.

The remainder taken modulo 10 is 6. (Taking a number modulo some base, in this case the base equals 10, involves dividing the number, *i.e.*, 36, by the base and retaining only the remainder, *i.e.*, 6.) This is the self-checking digit. It is appended to the number making it 1 2 3 4 5 6 7 8 6.

The self-checking digit should be recomputed automatically whenever the key code has been transcribed manually.

(d) *Luhn check digit* assigns weights to adjacent digits according to the series 1 2 1 2 1 2.... . The products of the weights and the digits are reduced modulo 9 and their sum is reduced modulo 10. The remainder is subtracted from 10. The Luhn self-checking digit gives 100 percent protection against single-digit substitution and transposition of adjacent digits. It does not protect against transposition of digits 1 and 3, 2 and 4, etc. A form of the Luhn digit is used as the last number of the Canadian Social Insurance Number. Example:

Data to be checked	Multiplier		Modulo-9 Product
1	1	=	1
2	2	=	4
3	1	=	3
4	2	=	8
5	1	=	5
6	2	=	3
7	1	=	7
8	2	=	7
			38

Modulo 10 remainder = 8

$10-8=2$: this is the check digit. The key code would be written: 1 2 3 4 5 6 7 8 2.

(e) *International mixed-modulo* (11/10) system checks digits give 98 percent protection against single-digit substitution; 90 percent protection against random multiple digit substitution; 98 percent protection against transposition of adjacent digits; and an average of 94 percent protection against transposition of non-adjacent digits. It has been proposed by a working group of the International Standards Organization. Example: mixed 11/10 modulo system.

Data to be checked	Multiplier		Modulo-11 Product
1	1	=	1
2	2	=	4
3	4	=	1
4	8	=	10
5	5	=	3
6	10	=	5
7	9	=	8
8	7	=	1
9	3	=	5
1	6	=	6

44 (SUM)

MODULO-10 SUM = 4

number with check-digit = 1 2 3 4 5 6 7 8 9 1 4

Note the multipliers are increasing powers of two reduced modulo 11. For example $2^5 = 32$ and $32-22 = 10$, which is the sixth multiplier.

In contrast, the International "pure" modulo 11/2 system gives 100 percent protection against single-digit substitution, 100 percent protection against transpositions of all kinds, and 90-percent protection against multiple-digit substitution. The tests that produced these results were made on ten thousand randomly selected 8-digit numbers.

The disadvantage of the "pure" system is that the check digits may range in magnitude from 0 to 10. This means that either two digit positions must be provided to accommodate the check digit, or that the 10, when it occurs, must be encoded as an X.

8. Computer Editing

The capabilities of the computer should be exploited whenever possible to ensure that input and output are error free. The computer can be programmed to edit for

(a) *Reasonableness checks.* Example: "Age must be less than 150."
(b) *Limit (range) checks.* Example: "No monthly paycheck can be written for more than $7,333."
(c) *Consistency checks.* Example: On hospital records: "if service-OBSTETRICS; then sex must be FEMALE."
(d) *Year-to-date checks.* Example: year-to-date-hours-worked X

mean-hourly-rate = year-to-date-payroll-expense; check this against the sum of year-to-date detail totals.

(e)   *Serial-sequence checks*. Check to see that 2 follows 1, that 109 follows 108, etc.

(f)   *Read-after-write checks*. Check to see that the computer is not producing spurious output.

(g)   *Count of transactions, records or lines*. Used to ensure that processing has been carried out to completion.

(h)   *Completeness checks*. Are all the blanks filled in?

(i)   *Field format checks*. Verify the length of fields; whether negative numbers are allowed and whether alphabetic or special characters are allowed.

9. Manual Editing

Visual review can be used to catch glaring errors and should be applied to all transactions rejected by the computer to ensure that they are properly corrected or cancelled. It is also advisable to scan printed output for reasonableness. It is important to determine the reasons for anomalous conditions such as negative balances.

The reconciliation of documents often involves manual intervention. Cancelled checks should be reconciled with stubs; receipts should be reconciled with deposit slips; invoices should be checked against receiving reports and purchase orders; sales slips should be checked against receipts and orders; and payroll vouchers should be checked against employee time cards.

10. Simultaneous Entries of Data

Critical data like receipts should be entered in such a way that two or more documents are automatically made available for subsequent checking.

This principle should be applied to (a) documents, (b) batch input, (c) direct on-line entry, (d) computer operator console logs, and (e) computer terminals.

(a) *Documents*. The use of multipart forms is exemplified by a system in which a sales receipt is prepared in quadruplicate. The canary copy becomes the customer's proof of purchase. The salmon copy is the authority for the stockroom to release goods. The white and blue copies remain locked in the machine. The white copy is reconciled with the cash register tape; and the blue copy is sent to the internal auditor.

(b) *Batch Input*. When data is key punched, a punched card becomes the data entry vehicle while the key-punching form is retained to verify authorization. The key-punch may simultaneously make a machine-sensible copy on punched paper tape for additional and mechanized checking.

(c) *Direct on-line entry* devices can be backed up by simultaneously recording data on a tape cassette. This can become important when data is "lost" because of computer malfunction.

(d) *Computer operator console logs* are useful for checking operator procedures. Some computers also internally record a day-file that the operator is not able to change or erase, except by employing extraordinary (hence, highly noticeable) measures. Breaks in the continuity of the log should not be permitted.

(e) *Computer terminals*. It is a good idea to create a duplicate printout at the computer terminals, using carbon or NCR copy. This ensures that an intact chronological record of activity remains even if the users tear off pieces of the original output. A video screen display can be backed up by a remote printing terminal.

11. Verification

Key verification of punched-card input is valuable to ensure that errors do not find their way into computer processing. This involves having a second operator type the data using a machine called a verifier. The verifier notches a punched card if the verifier operator's work coincides with that of the original keypunch operator.

Supervisors should be alert to see that verifier operators do not improperly use the "skip" key to omit parts of the punched card, thereby inflating their apparent output by failing to perform their intended task.

The provision for an echo display on the video screen gives some protection against errors. Supervisors should make sure that direct-entry operators do not immediately strike the return key after entering a record, thereby sending data to the computer.

12. Control Totals

Batches of checks or other documents are often accompanied by adding machine tapes showing their totals. These totals should be reconciled with input totals produced by the computer.

Batch or intermediate totals can be produced during the processing of long lists of transactions. The sum of the batch totals should be checked against the grand sum of detailed transactions.

Use of batch totals can provide convenient fall-back positions from which to isolate and rectify processing errors. These are known as check-point/restart procedures.

13. Hardware Controls

Computers have built-in or hardware controls that can reduce the occurrence of errors. It is important that a computer not be used when these control mechanisms are inoperative. Programmers should not be permitted to bypass these controls with program statements except with prior approval. Hardware controls include: (a) parity checks, (b) cyclic redundancy checks, (c) fail-safe operation, (d) bounds registers, (e) hardware monitors, and (f) hardware usage meters.

(a) *Parity checks* are used to detect bit errors on tape or in memory.

Character	Binary code	Lateral redundancy check (LRC)
A	0110101	0
B	0110110	0
C	0110111	1
D	0111000	1
E	0111001	0

	0110101	0 Vertical redundancy Check (VRC)

Parity bits are chosen so the modulo-2 sum of rows and columns equals zero. The following paradigm summarizes the rules of modulo-2 addition, also known as "XOR":

$$0 + 0 = 0$$
$$0 + 1 = 1$$
$$1 + 0 = 1$$
$$1 + 1 = 0$$

(b) *Cyclic redundancy checks* (CRC) are used to detect bit errors on disks.
Assume the message is 1010010001 (10 bits)
Given that the generator is 101011 (6 bits)

Annex five (5) zeros to the message; reverse the order of the bits; and repeatedly XOR the generator and message until a difference sequence is left that is shorter than the generator.

```
          110101      100010010100000
GENERATOR             110101     MESSAGE WITH APPENDED ZEROS
                      101110
                      110101
                       110111
                       110101
                        100100
                        110101
                         100010
                         110101
                          101110
                          110101
                           110110
                           110101
          DIFFERENCE =      00011
```

The check bits are obtained by reversing the bits of the difference and appending them to the message:

$$11000 \qquad 1010010001$$
$$\text{check bits} \qquad \text{message bits}$$

Upon reception, this procedure is repeated. At this time, however, the difference must be zero. If it is not, then an error has been introduced in transmission or within the computer system.

The actual CRC used on magnetic disk memories is 7 bits long. The generator is 57 bits long. It has ones in the following bit positions: 56, 55, 49, 45, 39, 38, 37, 36, 31, 22, 19, 17, 16, 15, 14, 12, 11, 9, 5, 1, and 0.

The CRC appears in the home address header of every disk track and in the header of every record. It is capable of detecting errors even if they occur as bursts of up to 22 spurious bits.

(c) *Fail-safe operation.* If a protective mechanism fails, the computer system should become inoperable.

(d) *Bounds registers.* Exists to enforce isolation of users from each other and from the system. They store the addresses of the upper and lower limits of each user's allocated space in main memory.

(e) *Hardware monitors.* These are built-in mini- or microcomputers that record pertinent statistics regarding a computer's operation, like the number of calls to the disk. These statistics are used principally by systems programmers to optimize the processing function, but can also provide clues to computer misuse.

(f) *Usage meters.* These are clocks, usually digital, that tell how many hours a computer has been used. Their output may disclose unauthorized use of computer resources.

14. Transaction Logs

These are control logs for data transmission devices. The duplicate terminal log also serves as a transmission log. It can be supported by a bound register (book) in which the operator signs on and off, as indeed can the computer operator's console log. Transaction logs exist to protect against the sending of spurious messages or the alleged non-receipt of legitimate messages. It is important that the operator's password not appear on transaction logs; this can be achieved by suppressing the computer echo or by automatically overstriking it with M's, W's, etc.

15. Answer Back Communications

Answer-back procedures should be used for on-line transmissions. They help ensure that the terminal on the other end is the one which you intend to communicate with. Answer-back is implemented automatically by printed circuit cards or silicon chips built into computer terminals. When two machines establish communications, one sends a character that means "Who are you?" The other responds automatically with its "Here is" code. The assigned number of the second terminal is then displayed on the sender's screen. Encrypted designations can be used when sensitive traffic is being sent.

16. Preventative Maintenance

Computers should receive regularly scheduled maintenance consistent with manufacturers' recommendations. Particular attention should be paid to seeing that no computer is permitted to remain in service with uncorrected defects in its hardware controls.

The ratio of computer up-time to down-time should be similar to that experienced in centers using similar equipment.

17. Environment Controls

Large computer main frames should be located in computer rooms where temperature, relative humidity, and atmospheric purity can be kept within manufacturers' recommended specifications. Smaller computing equipment should, if possible, be aggregated within similar environmentally controlled enclosures. Precautions should be taken to ensure early detection and suppression of fire in computer rooms. Computer files and related records should be stored in fireproof areas. Environmental conditions should be monitored by chart recorders to enable determination of whether erratic behavior of equipment is due to environmental conditions or human mistake. Computing equipment should not be left in service if proper environment cannot be maintained.

18. Conversion Standards

Master-file data should be kept in an agreed upon format and computer code. Control should be exercised before, during, and after master-file conversion. Errors introduced in master-file compilation should be corrected and the data immediately reentered.

19. External Labels

Magnetic tapes, cassettes, disk packs, floppy and mini-disks should bear external labels as well as internal machine-sensible identification in headers and trailers. External labels can prevent inadvertent mismounting of computer files containing sensitive data.

20. Software Controls

Software controls available in operating systems and teleprocessing monitors should be implemented locally, and operating procedures should not permit them to be bypassed. A password system should exist to authenticate the identity of users to the system, to control the access of users to sensitive files and volumes, and to limit the range of activities permitted to users and terminals, The computer should keep a record of its activity in an internal day file or series of periodic systems status reports to aid in reconstructing audit trails.

Other protective features implemented in software should include (a) password protection, (b) program comparison utilities, (c) address comparison checks, (d) software monitors, and (e) provision for marking output.

(a) *Passwords* should not be printed out. Computer echo should be suppressed or the password should be masked. Provision should be made for easily changing passwords. It is a good idea to assign passwords to users to prevent them from choosing meaningful passwords.

(b) *Program comparison utilities* should exist in order to make line-for-line checks between the object code of a program (*i.e.* the load module) and a copy of the object code stored under secure conditions.

(c) *Address comparison checks* should be made on transactions involving storage of data. The objective of this rule is to enforce read-only restrictions.

(d) *Software monitors* can be used as a substitute for hardware monitors where the system does not support hardware monitors.

(e) *Provisions for marking output* should exist so that sensitive output can be appropriately marked for special handling.

21. Media Library

A media library should exist along with a system of request slips, usage logs, and file listings in which magnetic tapes, disk files, and documentation can be stored under safe, secure, and environmentally controlled conditions. Storage of files should be neat and orderly. Operators and programmers should be allowed access to library files only after following the formal request procedure. There should be a media librarian on duty unless the library is securely locked.

22. Control Over Programming

Control over programming should be exercised by demanding that external documentation follow a specified format and that the program be documented internally by comment statements liberally sprinkled throughout the source code. Rules of structural programming should be enforced by specifying use of a high-level block-structure language that does not admit abuse of the GOTO statement. Use of tested and approved routines and program modules should be encouraged. Programming logic should be readable from the top of the page downwards, and its import should be apparent even to non-technical managers. A chief programmer should bear ultimate responsibility for accomplishment of a programming task. He/she should have the services of a back-up programmer and a project librarian to ensure compatibility of the names of constants, parameters, and variables.

23. Arithmetic and Overflow Tests

Arithmetic and overflow/underflow tests should be programmed and per-formed in hardware or software to avoid processing errors. These tests include: (a) crossfooting, (b) performing operations twice, (c) inverting operations, (d) casting out nines, (e) nines complement subtraction, (f) overflow tests, (g) underflow tests, (h) formula checks, and (i) proof costs.

(a) *Crossfooting* means that the sum of row totals is checked against the sum of the column totals.

(b) *Perform operations twice* and compare the results.

(c) *Inverting operations* or interchange factors:

$$A + B = C \qquad\qquad B + A = C$$
$$A - B = C \qquad\qquad B + C = A$$
$$A \times B = C \qquad\qquad B \times A = C$$
$$A/B = C \qquad\qquad A \times 1/B = C$$

(d) *Casting out nines* checks addition and multiplication.

$$(A+B) \bmod 9 = (A\ [\bmod\ 9] + B\ [\bmod\ 9])\ \bmod\ 9$$
$$(A \times B) \bmod 9 = (A\ [\bmod\ 9] \times B\ [\bmod\ 9])\ \bmod\ 9$$

Example: $37 + 49 = 86$ $1 + 4 = 5$
                $17 \times 33 = 561$ $8 \times 6 = 3$

(e) *Nines complement subtraction.* Some computers do all subtraction this way.

    A−B = (9's complement B + 1) + A (dropping leftmost 1)

Example:

895	999	895
−747	−747	253
148	252	1148
	+1	−1000
	253	148

(f) *Overflow checks.* If a number is moved to a register that is too short for it, the higher order digits will be lost. Programming the computer to do double-precision arithmetic (*i.e.* to use two registers) will circumvent most overflow problems. Use of so-called "floating" point technique addresses the register overflow problem by preserving the highest order digits and order of magnitude of the result while sacrificing precision altogether.

(g) *Underflow checks.* Since a computer performs subtraction by two's complement addition, an attempt to subtract a number from a smaller one may yield an extremely large result, if provisions are not made for accommodating it in the form of a negative number. Underflow can also result in loss of lower order digits, if the computer is not programmed to handle the precision of the data.

(h) *Formula checks.* For example, in an inventory system, the basic formula must be maintained in balance:

Amount available (AA) = Balance-on-hand (BOH) + On-order (OO)

	AA = BOH + OO		
Placing an order (O)	+O		+O
Receiving a shipment (S)		+S	−S
Making an issue (I)	−I	−I	

(i) *Proof costs.* A proof cost (K) is a random integer by which one detail factor in an extension is multiplied. Use of this technique can help defeat attempts to introduce spurious processing steps. For instance, when extending:

$$P \text{ (price)} = C \text{ (cost)} \times Q \text{ (quantity)}$$
$$K \sum P = \sum (KC \times Q)$$

This means that the constant multiplied by the sum of all prices should equal the sum of the detail costs multiplied by the constant and the quantities.

24. Restricted Access

The computer, its remote terminals, computer programs, and critical forms should be regarded as sensitive assets. A formal system of badges and passwords should be used to restrict access to them. This system should not be bypassed except to admit service technicians, including telephone service-men, who should be properly identified and escorted while on the premises. Restriction of access can be implemented by automatic terminal identification, use of operator passwords, and limitation of activities.

Automatic terminal identification can be implemented by the "here is" circuit board, or chip.

Use of operator passwords such as project numbers, programmer codes, and unlisted telephone numbers all help in implementing restricted computer access.

Limitation of activities permitted at some terminals and/or by some operators can be implemented in software.

25. Rotation of Operators

On sensitive runs, operators should be rotated or joint operation should be required to reduce the opportunities for dishonest employees to introduce fictitious transactions or perform unauthorized processing steps by making all operators unsure when they will be running a sensitive job or with whom they will be working.

26. Console Logs

Console logs should show operator actions taken during computer HALTS. They should be reviewed regularly by knowledgeable supervisors. The console log should be supported by operator sign-on registers (bound volumes), machine utilization logs, internally maintained logs or "day files," computer usage meters, and monitors (hardware or software) that keep a count of processing cycles.

27. Error Logs

A well-defined system should exist to correct errors. Rejected data returned for correction should be entered on an error log. Entries should be followed up by the control group to clear them for re-entry. Control totals should be established on re-entered items.

Exception reports should be made regarding error conditions. Items should be investigated to verify data for correction and re-entry, and also to assess responsibility. Trends in errors should be studied to determine whether they are due to hardware malfunction, software deficiencies, procedural shortcomings, inadequate personnel training, or a fraud attack. Appropriate and prompt remedial action should be taken when one of these conditions is recognized.

28. User Anticipation

User departments should be able to expect return of output according to a prearranged schedule. A formal system should exist so that users can identify their output. Such a system can be implemented by stubs retained by the user and use of transmittal forms or letters. An example is the remittance advice that accompanies a payment, or a duplicate deposit slip sent to the bank with money.

RECENT DEVELOPMENTS

The foregoing protective measures represent the conventional wisdom of designing secure automated accounting systems. However, their codification dates back to 1974 and there have been substantial improvements in the state of the art since then.

New developments, only a few of which had widespread implementation at the time of writing, take the following directions:

1. Design of secure computer operating systems.
2. Control of access to systems and surveillance of user behavior.
3. Protection of exterior data communications.
4. Verification of authority to execute remote transactions.
5. Automatic authentication of user access privileges.
6. Control over unauthorized extension of privilege by legitimate systems users.

Design of Secure Computer Operating Systems

The ultimate Achilles heel of any computer is the existence of latent defects in its operating system. If a skillful and malevolent technician can discover such a defect he/she could potentially override any other security mechanism. These defects are often referred to as "trapdoors." Some are the result of faulty logic on that part of the system designers. Others result from the errors or omissions of programmers who made subsequent modifications to the system. Still, others were deliberately created to help technicians fix the computer in case of electrical circuit malfunctions or serious programming errors.

The first attempt to design a secure operating system resulted in the Multics system, designed at MIT in 1967. It relied on so-called rings of protection. These rings were actually operating states. There were eight of them. The computer's operating system could recognize the state of any executing program. The programs executed in the more highly privileged states could make use of commands and resources denied to programs executed in less privileged states. The effect was that the programs of highly trusted users would be allowed to operate in highly privileged states where they could read data of less trusted users whose programs executed in less privileged states. But the programs of less trusted users could not read the data of more highly trusted users. The programs implementing the underlying control mechanisms of the computer were accorded the most highly privileged state of all. Over the years, flaws have been discovered and corrected in the logic of Multics. But the operating system is huge and no one can say for sure that hidden flaws do not remain. Multics is now available commercially for some main-frame computers produced by Honeywell.

In 1974, or thereabouts, some computer scientists decided that they would start anew and write a secure operating system for a modern medium-sized computer. They picked on the military version of the then-popular PDP–11/45 computer made by Digital Equipment Corp. Their design strategy was to seek out all the data and functions relevant to the securty of the computer in order to segregate them into a so-called security kernel, or reference monitor. The system was designed so that any time an executing program started to take a security-relevant action it would have to check with the reference monitor to make sure that the program was privileged to take the action, and the intended action was correct. The result was the KSOS (Kernalized Secure Operating System). Presently, the U.S. military is using it experimentally. It has a few problems. It is painfully slow; it supports only 4 to 6 concurrent users instead of the two dozen or so that could be supported, if it were not for all the checking. Moreover, there is no way to prove that the designers were able to correctly identify every security-relevant action that deserved to be checked, or that they could anticipate the proper sequence of steps of which such action should consist.

Control of Access to Systems

The biggest supplier of computers to the business world is IBM. Their operating systems have never been noted for security. For one thing, their systems are often huge with thousands of files and hundreds of users. In 1978, a number of software products began to appear that could be added onto the more popular IBM operating systems. These products provided for validating the authorization of users (USERID), and in some cases the terminals they were using, and the authority these users were allowed to have over programs and data files. These products also provided a continuous record of improper attempts to enter the system or to exert improper authority over programs and data files. They allowed for access privileges to be conveniently and securely granted, modified or withdrawn, and they provided for real-time warning messages and surveillance of the system by a security officer. They do not, however, protect against any trapdoors in the operating system, and they are as vulnerable as any other program to a successful penetration of the operating system. Under the heading "Security" in its summary of specifications, one supplier warrants that their product does not contribute to any exposures which are not already present in the operating system. These security add-on packages go by names like SECURE, ACF-2, RACF (an IBM product) and, more recently, TOP SECRET.

Protection of Exterior Data Communications

It has long been known that anybody who takes the time, trouble and risk to wiretap a data communications link can compromise any remotely accessed computer system. Until recently, few users outside of the Defense Department or the State Department took any counter-measures. SWIFT (Society for World-Wide Interbank Funds Transfer) which uses the Swiss GRETACODER to encrypt its wire funds transfer messages was the principal exception.

In 1976, the U.S. National Bureau of Standards promulgated DES (data encryption standard) based upon a design submitted by IBM. It was intended to be used for all sensitive, but unclassified, U.S. government wire and radio communications. Devices conforming to the DES are available to private American and friendly foreign buyers from several suppliers. It is now possible to secure both ends of a data communications link by plug-in devices retailing for about $4,000 each. There are other hardware implementations of DES that allow a user to encrypt files before storing them on magnetic tape or disks.

Presently, despite the availability of encryption devices, and the fact that only encryption can offer meaningful protection from wiretapping, there are only a few users. A perfume manufacturer with offices in Manhattan uses encryption on the line to its laboratory in New Jersey. The American Bank Note Company has an encrypted line between its New York headquarters and its printing plant in Dallas. And one large New York bank has encrypted the lines linking its branch offices in Manhattan.

Verification of Authority

With the advent of the ATM (automatic teller machine) banks found themselves confronting a major security risk. It was not sufficient to rely for customer identification simply on the numbers recorded on his debit card. Cards can be lost, stolen or counterfeited using numbers obtained from sources like discarded statements. It has become standard practice to require customers to authenticate ATM transactions by giving another number, the PIN (personal identification number). To avoid customer disavowal of ATM transactions by alleging that a bank employee compromised his PIN, many banks now let customers select their own PIN's which are then transformed by a one-way encryption device so that no bank employee ever sees their clear-text form. Some ATM's are equipped for total or partial encryption of transaction data sent to the bank. With the imminent coming of POS (point-of-sale) funds transfer, banks are planning to take similar measures to confirm the identity of the merchant by use of an enrypted CIN (customer identification number). Merchants, in turn, may be expected to take similar measures to personally identify each of their clerks.

However, no electronic mechanism presently has the potential to commit a party to a legal transaction to the same extent as does his written signature. A major unsolved problem is the search for a digital signature.

One contender is the public key cipher. This is a new mathematical formulation in which one key is used to encrypt a message, while a second unrelated key is used to decrypt it. In one implementation of the digital signature mode a person would make public his decryption key and keep his encryption key private. The fact that the recipient was able to successfully decrypt the signature might provide a way to legally bind the sender on the premise that he alone would have been able to encrypt it. Two versions of the public key cipher have been announced: the Hellman-Diffie knapsack cipher developed at Stanford University and the RSA (Rivest, Shamir, Adleman) cipher developed at MIT.

Authentication of User Access Privileges

A lot of people are uncomfortable about entrusting the authentication of access credentials to the possession of a password or cipher key even when these tokens are provided with additional safeguards such as countersigns, one-way encryption, masks, or one-time-use provisions. There has been a great deal of interest in biometric identification systems. Researchers have studied all sorts of human characteristics for use as identifiers: lip-prints, blood vessels of the retina, electro-encephalograms, skull geometry, height, weight, etc. The leading contenders are (a) palm geometry, (b) single fingerprint recognition, (c) dynamic signature analysis, and (d) voice recognition. At the time of writing, any of the first three could be obtained commercially. With any of them, however, there is a small probability of improperly admitting an unauthorized person, or of improperly excluding an authorized person. Unfortunately, any "fine tuning" of the system to ameliorate the former effect tends to exacerbate the latter.

Unauthorized Extension of Privilege

In 1982, at least 4,000 mainframe computer users in North America were using some kind of DBMS (data-base management system) that had some security features. A DBMS is a large program that acts as an intermediary between the users' programs and the computer's operating system when it comes to storing information in files or retrieving information from files. It is, of course, as vulnerable to unauthorized penetration of the operating system as is any other program. However, there is substantial reason to believe that data-base machines, special computers dedicated to the task of storing and retrieving information, may be better able to withstand technically-based penetration attempts than any general-purpose computer—whatever its operating system.

A DBMS protects information by first giving each user a view of the data base that incorporates only such information as that user is privileged to see. Secondly, it forces the user to give a proper password before opening certain sensitive files to him even if he is allowed to know of their existence. Finally, it may demand the user give a second (or third or more) password before he will be allowed to do certain things to a file, like change data. As an example, in respect to a personnel file, at one level of trust, an employee might not be allowed into the collection of files at all. At a slightly higher level, he might be allowed in, but not permitted to know that an area of the personnel file contained employee salary data. And among those employees permitted knowledge of the existence of the salary area, only those possessing a password would be enabled to read it. Still another password would be required before an employee would be allowed to make changes to it.

In some DBMS these protocols are enforced by storing the data in encrypted form and making the password the key needed to decrypt it. Many DBMS keep a record of the date and exact time each file is opened, what was done to it, from which terminal the user addressed it, and who he said he was.

Chapter 6

EXAMINING SYSTEMS FLOW CHARTS

Many security-relevant features of the design of an accounting system can be depicted graphically. A particularly informative representation is the flow chart. There are two kinds of flow charts. The systems flow chart shows the flow of documents around a computer. The summary flow chart shows the flow of information within a computer. Either kind can reveal whether or not sensitive information is crosschecked by data arriving over two or more independent routes. This is one of the hallmarks of secure systems design.

The systems flow chart is popular with external auditors. The reason is that the external auditor can make-up flow charts for the principal accounting systems of a client on his first engagement, and on subsequent engagements need only to refer to these charts to determine where the critical controls (checkpoints) exist and how the system has changed during the past year. Systems flow charts make it easier for the external auditor to acquaint new staff with the systems configuration of a client. They also provide the auditor with a standard against which to compare past and present performance.

From the security director's point of view, if there is the slightest hint of theft connected with a system, be it payroll, accounts receivable, inventory or whatever, he can refer to systems flow charts to find out who was involved in the transactions in question. He can also ascertain which documents figure in it, and thus begin to look for forged entries or other evidence of cover-up. Auditors use flow charts to reveal.weaknesses in accounting systems. In a theft investigation, if the source of loss has not already been determined, the security director can review flow charts with the internal auditor on the premise that loss is most likely to occur where controls are the weakest.

Flow charts may also contain volume summaries which indicate the monthly load of documents processed at various work stations. Auditors use this information to determine what size samples to examine in order to establish whether procedures are being properly carried out. To the security director looking at every document for evidence of dishonesty, the volume summary will disclose the magnitude of the task confronting him.

We will discuss the properties of systems flow charts, describe their configuration, tell how an auditor goes about deriving information from one, and conclude with an example showing how a cash receipts system can be described by one.

Systems flow charts facilitate the analysis of audit control and detect weaknesses or spots areas in which improvements could be introduced. They directly help to determine:

1. Whether the powers of authorization and approval have been delegated to specified individuals, and whether control mechanisms exist to see that authorizations and approvals are properly executed.
2. Whether each record is checked by another record created independently. (An example of this principle can be seen in a payroll system in which labor costs for the labor distribution journal are determined from job time tickets, and payroll costs are determined from employee time cards. These costs should be equal, but they are independently determined so that the paths over which the supporting documents travel do not come in contact. Thus, there is no opportunity for collusion which could force costs to come out the same.)
3. Where documents leave the system, thus indicating where it may become necessary to go outside to interview recipients.

They indirectly help to determine:

1. Whether the recording of assets and transactions has been separated from physical custody or access to assets. If it has been done there will be two different paths on the chart; one for custody and one for accounting for custody. The procedures in these paths will involve different players.
2. Whether procedures exist to verify the existence of assets shown on records. For example, in a cash-receipts system, the sum of

transactions recorded on cash receipts in the cash box must equal the amount of cash.

3. Whether proper physical control of assets exists including dual custody of valuable negotiable assets. For example, in some establishments, accounts payable must issue a voucher before cash disbursements can write a check. In this way, two different departments become involved in any payments.

FLOW CHART SYMBOLS

The symbols in Figure 6.1 are used on systems flow charts depicting manual accounting operations. The subject on the chart is the flow of documents. A document is depicted by a rectangle. A black triangle in the lower right hand corner of the rectangle signifies that the document is prepared at this point. A square tab indicates that the document is initialed (letter I in square) or signed (letter S in square).

Permanent files are shown as pyramids. The letters, A, N, or D within the pyramid tell how the documents are filed (*i.e.* Alphabetically, Numerically, or by Date). A lozenge depicts a temporary file. A blackened square signifies that a document is destroyed in the step depicted. A square with a diagonal stripe signifies an operation in which two documents are joined together.

Figure 6.1. Flow chart symbols (manual)

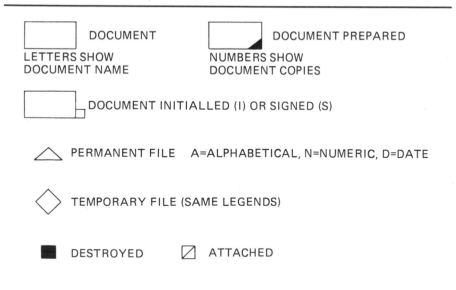

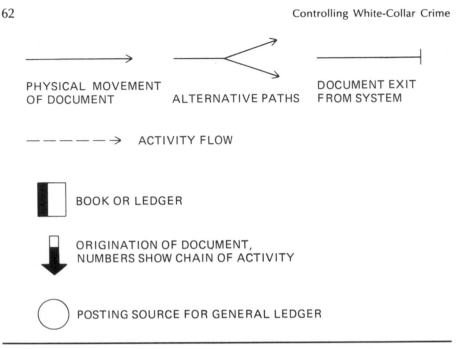

Figure 6.1. (continued)

Solid lines represent the flow of documents; broken lines indicate the flow of human activity. A large square, the left hand third of which is blackened, denotes a book or ledger. A heavy arrowhead signifies the entry of a document into the system. A circle indicates whether the step depicted is a source of information subsequently to be posted in the general ledger.

Systems flow charts and volume summaries are prepared from information derived from interviews with officials and employees.

VOLUME SUMMARIES

A volume summary is the monthly number of key transactions and the number of key accounts.

It is prepared by tabulating the following accounts and transactions:

Accounting system	*Monthly volumes of*	*Total number of*
Sales, Receivables and Receipts	Sales Orders	Active Customers
	Sales Invoices	Inactive Customers
	Shipments	Customers by
	Units Shipped	Category
	Back Orders	Salesmen

Accounting system	*Monthly volumes of*	*Total number of*
	Credit Notes	Order Clerks
	Checks Received	Billing Clerks
	Accounts-Receivable Postings	Accounts-Receivable Clerks
	Cash Sales Slips	
Purchases, Payables and Payments	Purchase Requisitions	Purchasing Department Employees
	Purchase Orders	
	Purchase Invoices	
	Receiving Slips	
	Suppliers Debits	
	Vouchers	
	Checks Issued	
Payroll	Daily Work Tickets	Office Employees (monthly, semi-monthly)
	Payroll Checks	
	Piecework Tickets	
	Time Cards	Plant Employees (weekly) (range and peaks for year)
		Employees by Category or Location
		Payroll Department Employees
Inventory	Production Orders	Production by Product Line
	Units Produced by Type	Manufactured Parts; Subassemblies
	Production Change Notices	Inventory Accounts by Category
	Scrap Reports	Cost Ledger Accounts
	Perpetual Inventory Postings	Cost Department Employees
	Cost Ledger Postings	

MAKING FLOW CHARTS

1. The first step in making a flow chart is to divide an accounting system into subdivisions whose images will fit on charting paper. This can be done by getting an overview of the system from the comptroller. In this chapter, the subdivision that will be used as an example is a cash receipts system.

2. A rough chart is then prepared on the basis of on-site interviews conducted with employees. It is a good idea to first ask the supervisor what is supposed to happen; then interview employees to find out what really happens.
3. An outline chart may be prepared to facilitate rapid comprehension of the system. The outline chart shows the accounting information that is transferred among players, but it does not specify media or mechanisms.
4. The final chart should be drawn after the rough chart has been confirmed by performing a *flow audit* based upon it. A flow audit is performed by actually tracing a half dozen, or so, assorted transactions through the system.

Before preparing the final chart, it is important that the rough chart cover all possible types of transactions.

1. Do any transactions described or implied in the description of the business fail to appear on the chart? If so, you missed something.
2. Can reference to all transactions shown on the chart be found in books, ledgers, or files? If not, somebody could be carrying on a business outside of the duly authorized activities of the firm.
3. Does the chart cover processing during slack periods, peak periods, vacations, illnesses, or coffee or lunch breaks?
4. What might be the consequences of substituting one employee for another in a given job slot?

CHART PREPARATION

A flow chart shows the receipt or preparation, flow, processing and disposition of documents, books and other records. It also notes the debits and credits appropriate to ledger postings.

Flow charts are both horizontal and vertical in nature. Document flow is shown by horizontal movement between vertical columns representing employees or departments. Vertical movement represents the progression of a document from its origination to permanent storage or destruction.

A flow chart starts in the upper left-hand corner of a rectangular field and progresses toward the lower right-hand corner. All documents should eventually exit from the system, wind up in permanent storage, or be destroyed.

Charting paper measures 14 × 18 inches; it is divided into six or more vertical columns. So-called computer print-out paper works very well in this application.

Good practice in making flow charts dictates that:

- Lines should not cross each other.
- Lines should not backtrack.
- Irrelevant detail should be omitted.

THE CASH-RECEIPTS SYSTEM

A business is most vulnerable at the cash box. A turn-of-the-century improvement was the introduction of the cash register. Money, cash receipts and the "float" that the cashier uses to make change, was kept in a locked cash drawer, and the key was kept by a supervisor. The drawer opened in response to entering the dollar value of a sale on the machine's keyboard. A "no-sale" key could open the drawer to make change or reverse a prior transaction. Sales amounts and no-sale openings were recorded, timed and dated on a two-part endless tape. One part was kept locked in the machine and portions of the other part were torn off and given to customers as receipts. Periodically, supervisors collected cash, in excess of float, from the drawers and balanced it against totals maintained on the internal tape. Refunds and other no-sale openings had to be noted on the tape manually and explained to the supervisor.

Over the years, dishonest clerks discovered many ways to cheat the system. There were "no-rings" when clerks simply handed over merchandise and pocketed the payment. There were "underrings" when clerks rang up less than sales price and stole the difference. Clerks exploited "buy-back" situations where customers exchanged one item for a more costly one after the sale was rung up. They let the original transaction stand and kept the difference.

There were "till dips" when clerks rang "no-sale" and skimmed the cash drawer when no one was looking. There were "false refunds" when customers failed to take their receipts and clerks retrieved them and used them to substantiate illegal refunds the clerks made to themselves. Dishonest clerks were able to explain shortages by alleging that they made honest mistakes or were victimized by "short-change" artists. Sometimes, the short-change artist was the clerk himself who rang up the correct price, but collected more from the customer and kept it. At times when dishonest clerks were too closely supervised to dip into the till, they would "overring" or record more than the amount of sales, deliberately creating fictitious shortages so the pattern would remain the same even though they had no opportunity to steal. There were collusive schemes in which sales clerks, stock boys, customers and even supervisors conspired to cheat.

As a result, most stores handling "big ticket" items—like lumber yards, hardware stores, jewelry stores, and camera shops—have adopted more secure systems for handling cash receipts.

FLOW CHART CASH RECEIPTS

Figure 6.2 illustrates the appearance of the systems flow chart of a manual accounting operation for handling cash receipts. The same operation is shown in abbreviated format in the drawing at the bottom. The actors involved in this operation are, from left to right, order clerks, warehouse stock chasers, cashier, inventory records clerks, and accounts receivable clerks.

Referring to the topmost drawing, money enters the system in the form

Figure 6.2. Flow chart

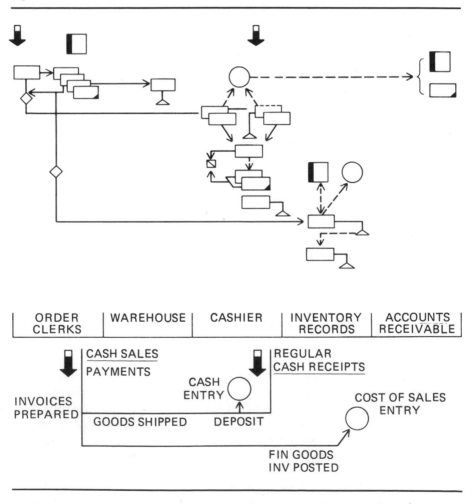

| ORDER | WAREHOUSE | CASHIER | INVENTORY | ACCOUNTS |
| CLERKS | | | RECORDS | RECEIVABLE |

of a cash sale over the counter. Four copies are made of the receipt. Two are given to the customer. One of these is presented at the warehouse enabling the customer to collect what he has purchased; it is filed there permanently. The other one leaves the system as the customer's evidence of having paid. The third copy is put into the cash box with the money. The fourth copy remains locked in the machine in which the receipts are prepared. The journal shown at this point is the retail price list.

The cash box goes to the cashier. Regular payments from customers accompanied by letters advising of payment (remittance advice) also go to the cashier. The cashier makes appropriate entries in the cash book and permanently files the remittance advices. The cashier makes up duplicate bank deposit slips for money. One copy is returned from the bank and permanently filed by the cashier.

The fourth copy of the customer's receipt goes to the inventory records. It is used to support a reduction in the perpetual inventory of finished goods, as well as an entry to the cost-of-goods-sold account in the general ledger. The receipts are filed permanently among the inventory records. Periodically, the receipts are summarized and these summary records are also filed.

Entries in the cash book are used to support debit entries in the accounts receivable ledger as well as reductions in balance-due entries which are periodically mailed to regular customers.

Take note of the controls at work here, or absent, in some instances. If the order clerk pockets cash receipts, he must still make out a receipt so the customer can get his purchase out of the warehouse. Thus, there will exist a receipt copy on file at the warehouse not supported by an entry in the cash book. It is not clear what the cashier does with his copy of the receipt. But, if the cashier's receipts are retained and can be checked against those in the warehouse, the fact that the order clerk had short-circuited receipts would thereby be disclosed.

Warehouse receipts can be reconciled against entries made to inventory records and their supporting receipt copies, thus ensuring that merchandise leave only pursuant to purchase by a customer, and that warehouse personnel are not diverting it for their own use.

Probably the worst problem here is that there is no provision for a systematic audit of procedures. In particular, the cashier counts the cash receipts, makes bank deposits and retains custody of the duplicate bank deposit receipts. The cashier also retains custody of customer remittance advices, and the accounts receivable department is simply taking the cashier's unsubstantiated word that someone has or has not paid the said amount. In fact, in one company using this system, the cashier and the accounts receivable clerk were one and the same person—and that person, literally, had a license to steal.

MODIFIED CASH-RECEIPTS SYSTEM

A modification of the cash-receipts system is shown in Figure 6.3. The first row shows that money passes from customer to sales clerk to cashier to the bank. The cashier makes an entry in the cash-book and fills out duplicate deposit slips, one of which is filed with internal audit. This provides a check on the cashier and the bank messenger. The sales clerk rings up the sale on the cash register and the cash-register tape goes to internal audit; here it is reconciled with the bank deposit slip. The existence of the internal audit function institutionalizes the principle of a regular follow-up.

The four-part receipt is used as before. The customer gets two copies. One he keeps as evidence of sale in case he wants to reverse the transaction or

Figure 6.3. Cash receipts

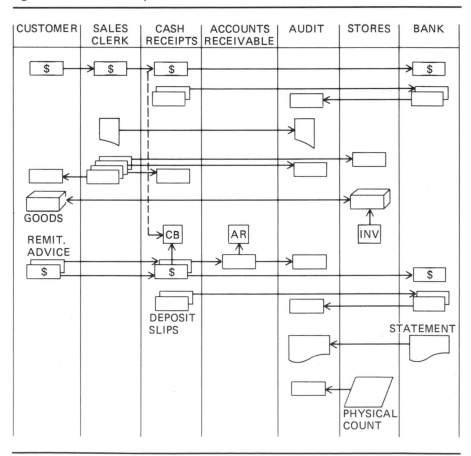

exchange or return the merchandise. No refunds or exchanges will be made without presentation of this receipt. He takes the other copy to the warehouse in order to get his merchandise. This receipt stays in the warehouse to support the recorded decrease in inventory. The third copy of the receipt goes to the cashier along with the money. This copy will remain there as evidence that the cashier did, in fact, receive the money. The last receipt copy goes to internal audit; audit now has two automatically prepared documents attesting to the fact that the sales clerk received the money, one of which (the receipt copy) passed through the cashier's hands while the other (cash register tape) did not.

When customers pay bills by mail, they send along a letter advising what their remittance covers. These letters go to the cashier. He enters the amount of money in the cash book and makes out duplicate deposit slips as he does in the case of cash sales. The cashier stamps the date on the remittance advice, it is then sent to accounts receivable to support a debit, and ultimately is filed in internal audit.

Internal audit reconciles duplicate bank deposit slips with periodic bank statements to check on the cashier, bank messenger, and bank teller.

At random intervals, the internal auditor makes a physical count of inventory. The three-way reconciliation of item count, reductions in stated finished goods inventory, and receipts from the fourth copy provide a check on the honesty of the storekeepers.

EVALUATION OF FLOW CHART

Flow charts may be used in the following way to evaluate the strength of a system of controls:

1. Trace, from cradle to grave, four or five transactions along each path of the charted system. Compare related books, ledgers and permanent files. In particular:
    a. Verify the arithmetic in each transaction.
    b. Check for agreement between matched sets of documents such as purchase requisitions, purchase orders, vendor invoices, and receiving reports.
    c. Make sure that files contain only those types of transactions noted on flow charts.
    d. Check files for serial continuity.
2. For each step, ask yourself what would happen if the step were omitted or performed incorrectly.
3. Determine how such errors or omissions would be detected. In general, two independent paths to each destination must exist. Pay

particular attention to diagonally-slashed squares (attachment); these are your principal check points or threat gates. Find out what the consequences of destroying documents are; should this ever be done; if so, when?

4. Determine for the system as a whole whether it is possible for large errors to occur.

5. Determine whether small errors could occur in sufficient numbers to amount to a significant total.

6. Identify the key controls in the system and try to think up procedures to verify compliance.

Once a flow chart has been made, you can concentrate your subsequent investigations on the differences between the flow chart and what you actually observe.

Look to see if:

- Differences are consistent with updated procedure manuals, or do they signify a trend to circumvent controls?
- Altered procedures stem from prior recommendations you've made, or do they stem from some other attempt to tighten controls? If so, what precipitated these moves? Is there evidence that the problem persists?
- Altered procedures represent short-cuts that tend to weaken controls? If so, why was this course pursued and who instigated it?

Chapter 7

INTRODUCTION TO COMPUTER CHARTS

It is more difficult to investigate theft in a computer system than in a manual system because computer systems are more complicated and their actions are less visible. Indeed, auditors used to talk about auditing around the computer as opposed to auditing through the computer. The former approach treated the computer as a black box and asserted that if you could verify what went in and what came out, you could assume that all was well. An increasing number of computer-based thefts have proved this assumption to be false.

Of course, every security man knows that the six letter word ASSUME can make an ASS out of U and ME. Today, most auditors at least attempt to audit through the computer. They have varying degrees of success in doing so.

The general approach to understanding a complex system is one of progressive decomposition. There are at least five levels of understanding.

LEVELS OF DETAIL

Figure 7.1 summarizes the steps in the progressive decomposition of business information systems by graphical aids. One objective of this decomposition is to facilitate understanding of complex systems. Another is to concentrate on progressively smaller parts of the system so that increasingly precise levels of detail can be documented.

PROGRESSIVE DECOMPOSITION
OF SYSTEMS

BLOCK DIAGRAM
SYSTEMS FLOW CHART
(AROUND THE COMPUTER)
SUMMARY FLOW CHART
HIPO DIAGRAM
(THROUGH THE COMPUTER)
RUN DIAGRAM
PROCEDURES   LOGIC FLOW CHART
MANUAL   DECISION TABLE
NASSI DIAGRAM
PSEUDO-CODE

SOURCE CODE (HLL)
ASSEMBLER
OBJECT CODE

Figure 7.1. Levels of decomposition

The first level is the block diagram. Each block may represent the part played by a department of the company.

The systems flow chart shows the flow of paperwork around the computer, usually from one person or office to another. The summary flow chart shows the flow of information through the computer using symbols to represent the principal files involved by the media on which they are held. An equivalent but more narrative presentation is found in the hierarchical-input-output-processing diagram.

The run diagram provides positive identification of the files used in the system.

The logic flow chart explains, in detail, the steps taken in processing an item of information in the computer. It corresponds to a procedures manual in the manual environment. The decision table and Nassi-Shneiderman diagram are equivalent to the logic flow chart; so is pseudo-code, a curt English language description of the processing logic. A pseudo-code description follows the general syntax of computer language but at a higher level of abstraction (*i.e.* less detail). Computer code is written from the logic flow chart or its equivalent, usually in a high-level language (HLL) like Cobol, PL/1, Fortran, Basic, or Pascal. Code for smaller computers may be written in RPG or Assembler. The final step of translating high-level computer code into numerical (an unreadable) object code is performed within the computer by a special program called a compiler.

The block diagram treats the system under consideration in the context of the company's overall operations. As an example, we show the sales system of a merchandising house. The system exists to move merchandise to the customer, keep track of the customer's indebtedness to the company, and ultimately receive the cash that discharges the customer's obligation.

BLOCK DIAGRAM

The block diagram of a merchandising house is shown in Figure 7.2. In the center of the diagram is the inventory department confirming that the merchandise available for sale is, literally, a merchandising house's stock-in-trade. At the top are the functions that replenish inventory: purchasing, receiving and accounts payable. At the bottom are the functions that turn inventory into income: order (sales), shipping, and accounts receivable.

The second level of understanding is the sytems flow chart which depicts the total environment surrounding the system and was described in great detail in Chapter 6.

The third level is the summary flow chart. At this level, the system under consideration is decomposed into functional data-processing activities.

Figure 7.2. Block diagram

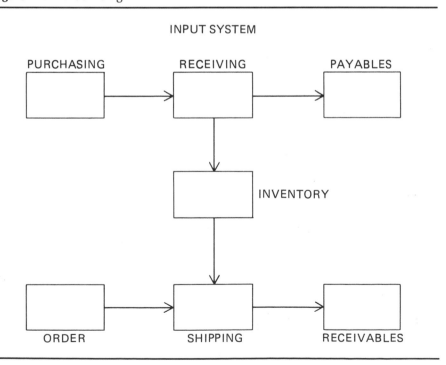

We can decompose the sales system into entry of customer orders, fulfilling the customer order, adjusting our inventory to reflect the fulfillment of customer orders, keeping track of the customer's indebtedness to the company, recording the receipt of cash to discharge these obligations, and determining how much money the company has made or lost on the transactions. We will do this in Chapters 12, 13 and 14. Summary flow charts make use of stylized symbols to indicate the media on which input and output data are recorded and where the various data-processing steps take place. Observe that each block contained in the block diagram is developed into a summary flow chart.

SUMMARY FLOW SYMBOLS

Summary flow charts and run diagrams make use of symbols (see Figure 7.3) that tend to depict computer hardware and information media in symbolic fashion. A file in which information is stored on punched cards is symbolized by an outline drawing of one of these cards (top, left). A magnetic tape file is symbolized by its circular form with a line at the bottom showing a little of the tape unreeled; sometimes this feature is missing. A file held on magnetic disk is symbolized by a perspective drawing of a disk pack. Files were also held on magnetic drums. This kind of hardware is not widely used anymore, but both kinds of files were represented by the same symbol. Sometimes the view of the right-hand end of the disk pack is completed by drawing another 180-degree arc. The important distinction is the one between sequential files (typified by magnetic tape) and direct-access files (either disk or drum). In the former case, records must be read in and out in order and you may have to unreel 2,400 feet of tape to get the one record you want. A record on a disk or a drum can be recalled directly.

Transmittal tape is symbolized by an abstract drawing of a piece of adding-machine or cash-register tape and that's just what it stands for. Punched paper tape isn't used very much any more, but may be encountered in older installations. It is roughly an inch wide and has a small sprocket hole and a row of up to eight larger perforations across it every 1/8 inch or so.

Any kind of computer operation is symbolized by a rectangle.

The symbol for a printout is an abstract representation of a torn piece of fan-fold computer paper. It stands for permanent (or so-called hard) humanly readable output.

The symbol for an on-line keyboard is an abstraction of a typewriter keyboard. The symbol for a video display unit is apparently somebody's idea of what a cathode-ray (tv picture) tube looks like. In any event, it stands for temporary (soft) humanly readable output.

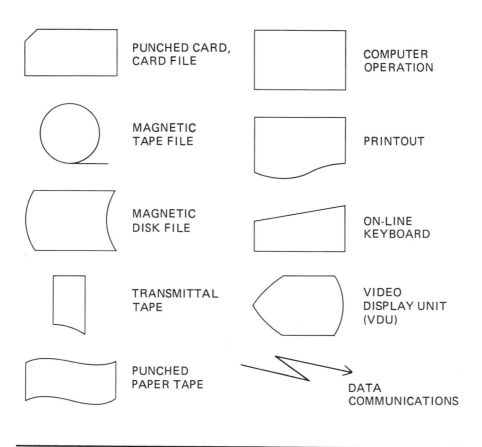

Figure 7.3. Flow chart symbols (computer)

The lightning bolt symbolizes data communications which can be accomplished by wire line, radio, microwave, satellite, fiber optics or whatever.

For each subsystem, a summary flow chart shows:

1. Processing steps and their relationships.
2. Main systems inputs (transactions, files).
3. Principal processing functions.
4. Main system outputs.
5. Source of any general-ledger entries.

The operations described should include those concerned with:

1. Procedures for maintaining and balancing control information.
2. Conversion to machine readable format.
3. Procedures for following up and correcting errors rejected by the computer (suspense files).

The summary flow chart shown in Figure 7.4 uses these symbols to depict the information inputs and outputs. It represents the computer's central processing unit as a small rectangle.

As shown on the flow chart, a payroll job record is fed in the form of a deck of punched cards. The payroll master file is on magnetic tape, and the payroll rate table resides on magnetic disk. Error messages are printed by a high-speed line printer, and the updated master payroll file is written out on another magnetic tape, as is the gross pay file which is the desired product of this operation.

Figure 7.4. Summary flow chart

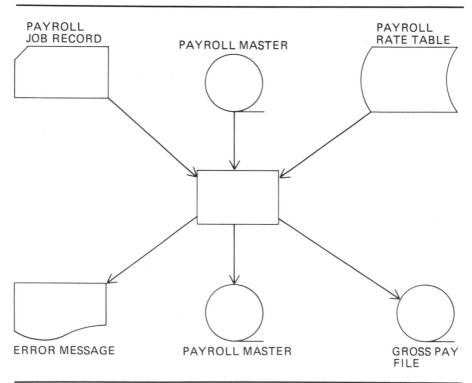

Recently, there has been some dissatisfaction with the conventional summary flow chart. Consequently, in some engagements, you may run into the HIPO diagram: HIPO stands for Hierarchy: Input, Processing, Output. For each step formerly shown by a summary flow chart there will be a HIPO diagram.

While the summary flow chart specifies the media of inputs and outputs, the HIPO diagram doesn't concentrate so much on media; it is more compact and permits an expanded description of the work performed by the computer program. Instead of just showing a box indicating that there is computer processing involved, HIPO lets us know that the computer performs three principal tasks: it accumulates the hours worked, finds the correct pay rate for each job classification, and calculates gross pay.

Figure 7.5 is the HIPO diagram of a payroll system. It consists of three boxes. In the first box are found the inputs: the payroll job record (*i.e.* time cards), the payroll master file, and the payroll rate table.

The second box contains the major processing steps: first, add up the hours worked by each employee; secondly, find the correct rate of pay for that employee's job classification; and third, calculate his/her gross pay.

The third box contains the outputs: the (updated) payroll master file, a gross pay file, and error messages, if any.

The fourth level of understanding is represented by the run diagram. The run diagram specifies which data files and computer programs are

Figure 7.5. HIPO diagram

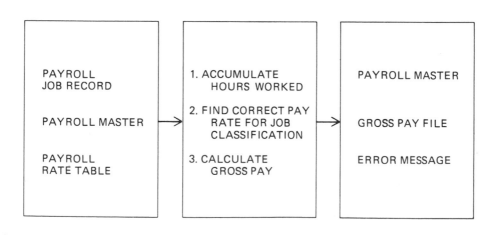

actually used in carrying out the operations indicated in summary flow charts. In case of suspicion that theft is being perpetrated, the security director can refer to a run diagram to determine on which magnetic file or disk pack reside the electronic images of the transactions in question. Then he can have these records printed for examination.

A run diagram is a chronological record in graphic form of the computer processing operations described within a rectangle on a summary flow chart. In other words, the summary flow chart processing step tells *what* is done (*i.e.* edit input, check credit, check inventory available, etc.); while the run diagram tells how it is done and with what.

The computer processes described may include:

1. Updating of master files.
2. Summarization of data into a condensed form.
3. Arithmetic calculations such as the pricing and extension of sales invoice data.
4. Sorting and merging.
5. Extraction of data from one or more data files based upon predetermined criteria.
6. Printing of reports.

The processing blocks shown on a summary flow chart may each include several programs, whereas each processing block on a run diagram refers to a specific program, which can be identified right on the diagram. The input and ouput files are denoted on summary flow charts in a general way, like "cash receipts transactions," whereas the inputs on a run diagram denote specific files such as "labor distribution XYZ–01–06." In these ways, the run diagram expands upon the summary flow chart.

The run diagram (Figure 7.6) shows a level of detail intermediate between that of the summary flow chart and the logic flow chart. It is a level of detail appropriate for the tape (media) librarian who must release files for processing and for the computer operator when setting up the job to run. The computer operator also has a complementary run book that tells him on which spindles to mount which disk packs; on which drives to mount which tapes; what console switches to throw; when to feed which decks of punched cards into the card reader; how long the job should take to run, and what to do with the input media; intermediate products; and output media.

For anyone interested, this program is one for cost accounting. It apportions labor cost, materials cost, and some overhead costs such as city tax among products manufactured during a certain period, and thereby assigns a cost figure to each item. The purpose here, however, is to show the level of detail in the run diagram. Scratch tapes are tapes used for intermediate calculations; they are kept in the machine room and automatically erased and

COST-OF-GOODS RUN DIAGRAM

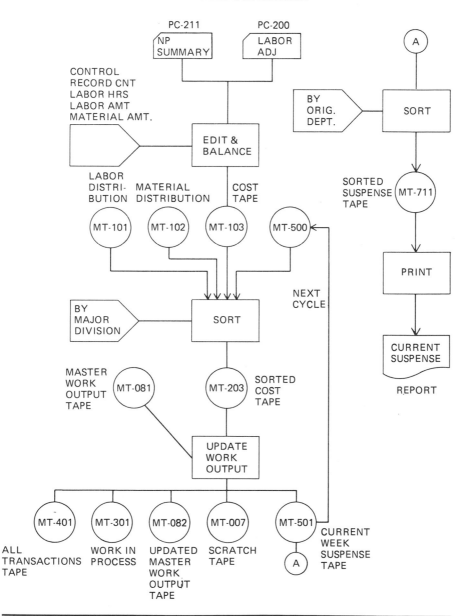

Figure 7.6. Run diagram

overwritten as required. Suspense files contain items about which final determinations have not been made because of errors, lack of authorization, absence of supporting documents or data. It is the duty of the control group to follow up these items and dispel the uncertainty surrounding them before the next processing period.

REPRESENTING PROGRAM LOGIC

The fifth level tries to show what goes on within the rectangles that have been used to indicate computerized data-processing steps. The traditional way to do this entailed the use of logic flow charts. These charts used stylized symbols to depict computer operations like "read," "write," and "compare." Arithmetic operations like "add" and "subtract" were still shown in rectangles but these rectangles could now be filled with mathematical equations or text that described what was actually being done. There are, however, other ways to describe detailed data-processing steps besides the logic flow chart. We will describe two of them. One is the decision table, the other is the Nassi-Shneiderman diagram. When an investigation reaches this level it is best to seek guidance from a skilled and reliable data-processing professional to assist in determining whether unauthorized alterations have been made in data-processing steps.

Logic Symbols

The symbols shown in Figure 7.7 are used principally on logic flow charts. The big arrowhead, top left, is used to draw the reader's attention to steps where comments are relevant, especially regarding modifications made to a program subsequent to its first being implemented. The hexagon denotes a predefined operation, usually a program subroutine or function. The "baloney-like" symbol is the terminal symbol; it denotes either the beginning or the end of a program. The keystone is used by some authors to mean an input (e.g. "read") or output operation. To other authors, it denotes a clerical operation. The lozenge always signifies a decision or logical choice. The triangle denotes off-line storage (e.g.: a file cabinet). The parallelogram is used by some authors to indicate a clerical operation, and by others to denote an input or output operation. The small arrowhead signifies that the draftsman has run out of room and that the chart is to be continued on the next page. The small circle is used to join two points in a logic flow chart when it would be messy to draw a line connecting them; it is often used in looping (repetition) operations. The diamond, or large circle, is used by some authors to designate a sorting or collating operation. Most authors just use properly labelled rectangles, however.

SYMBOLS FOR LOGIC FLOW CHARTS

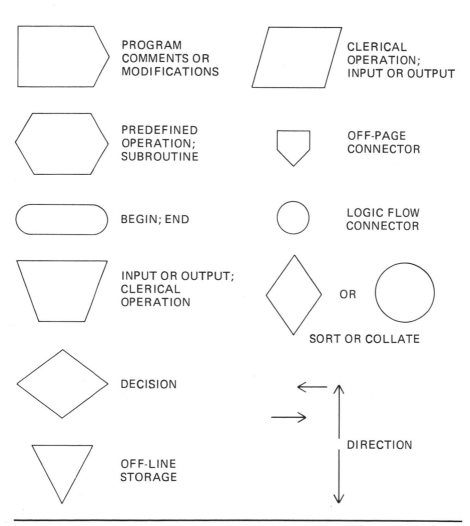

PROGRAM
COMMENTS OR
MODIFICATIONS

CLERICAL
OPERATION;
INPUT OR OUTPUT

PREDEFINED
OPERATION;
SUBROUTINE

OFF-PAGE
CONNECTOR

BEGIN; END

LOGIC FLOW
CONNECTOR

INPUT OR OUTPUT;
CLERICAL
OPERATION

OR

SORT OR COLLATE

DECISION

DIRECTION

OFF-LINE
STORAGE

Figure 7.7.   Logic symbols

Logic Diagram

Figure 7.8 is a conventional logic flow chart. It shows one small step in the processing of a new insurance policy by an insurance company. The logic connector symbol (numeral 1 in a small circle) shows that the computer returns to this point after processing each record of a new insurance policy

LOGIC FLOW CHART

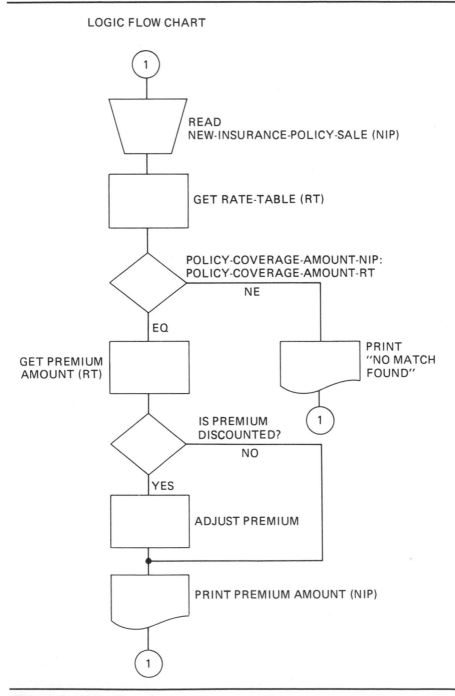

Figure 7.8. Logic flow chart

sale. The keystone indicates that the computer reads the record of a new-insurance-policy-sale. One would have to consult the run diagram to find out whether this record came from a deck of punched cards, a magnetic tape, or a disk file. The rectangular box tells us that the computer calls up a prestored rate table. Since no call to a disk unit is shown, we presume that the rate table resides within the computer's main memory.

The lozenge-shaped decision symbol indicates that the computer searches its rate table to determine whether the policy coverage amount (face value) in the record of the new-insurance-policy-sale matches one of the policy-coverage-amounts listed in the rate table. If no such match is found, an error or an exception has occurred and a message to that effect is printed on the high-speed printer. An error or exception such as this must be investigated after the run by a member of the control group. If a match is found during the running of the program, the flow of program logic proceeds to the next rectangular block which shows that the computer consults its prestored rate table to get the premium amount appropriate to the policy coverage amount of the new insurance policy.

The next decision lozenge instructs the computer to determine whether or not the record of sale indicates that the policy is to be discounted. One reason a policy might be discounted would be because the customer has installed certain approved safety or security measures to reduce his suscepti-bility to loss. If the premium is to be discounted, the flow of processing logic enters the third rectangular processing block. The computer thereupon calls up some mathematical formula (subroutine) or consults another prestored table to find the appropriate discount amount and adjusts the premium accordingly. Then it prints the correct premium amount on its high-speed printer. The connector symbol with the numeral 1 indicates that the computer now loops back to the beginning of this program segment and reads the next record describing a new insurance policy sale.

If, back at the second decision lozenge, the computer had found that the premium of the new insurance policy was not to be discounted, it would have printed the premium amount initially found in the prestored rate table and forthwith looped back to read the next record.

Some people have never been comfortable with logic flow charts, and as an alternative the use of decision tables has been suggested. They make a combinative "explosion" of logical possibilities to make sure that each possibility is explored. That is to say, if there are two dichotomous (YES or NO) choices in series, there are four logically possible outcomes. If there are three choices, then there are eight logical outcomes. Some of these outcomes may be impossible within the context of the process, but others might occur so infrequently as to be overlooked, thereby giving rise to a potential "bug" or latent software error. Forcing consideration of these unlikely and potentially troublesome cases is the principal virtue of the decision table.

DECISION TABLE

IF	AND	AND	THEN	AND
CONDITION	CONDITION	CONDITION	ACTION	NEXT ACTION
NEW INSURANCE POLICY SALE	POLICY COVERAGE AMT FOUND	PREMIUM DISCOUNTED	ADJUST PREMIUM	PRINT PREMIUM AMT
NEW INSURANCE POLICY SALE	POLICY COVERAGE AMT FOUND	PREMIUM NOT DISCOUNTED	PRINT PREMIUM AMT	
NEW INSURANCE POLICY SALE	POLICY COVERAGE AMT NOT FOUND		PRINT "NO MATCH FOUND"	
NO NEW INSUR-ANCE POLICY SALE			GOTO END-OF FILE ROUTINE	

Figure 7.9. Decision table

DECISION TABLE

The decision table shown in Figure 7.9 is then an alternative way to depict the logic inherent in the program step of processing new insurance policy sales.

The columns to the left of the double vertical line are conditions. The vertical line at the left-hand margin is read "IF." The two vertical lines following are read "AND." The double vertical line is read "THEN."

The columns to the right of the double vertical line are actions. The first vertical line is read "AND." The vertical line on the extreme right is read "NEXT." It stands for "go to the next row" if unsuccessful or "process the next record" if successful.

The first row signifies that "IF" (1) there has been a new insurance policy sale "AND" (2) the policy coverage amount has been found listed in the computer's prestored rate table "AND" (3) the premium is to be discounted, "THEN" the actions to be taken would be to adjust the premium downwards "AND" proceed to print the premium amount; then get the next record of sale.

If any of the three conditions are found to be false, the second row is entered: "IF" (1) there has been a new insurance policy sale "AND" (2) the policy coverage amount is found in the rate table "AND" (3) the premium is not to be discounted "THEN" only one action is taken before getting the next record, namely, print the premium amount found in the prestored rate table.

If any of the conditions specified in the second row is untrue, the third row is entered: "IF" (1) there has been a new insurance policy sale "AND" (2) the policy coverage amount is not found in the rate table, "THEN" the computer prints an error message "NO MATCH FOUND" and after doing so gets the next record.

The decision table is designed to test all possible conditions, and in doing so exposes a logical error in the logic flow chart. If condition 1 is false, that is, if there has not been a new insurance policy sale, we must enter the fourth row; "THEN" the action to be taken is to go to the end-of-the-file routine. In other words, the job is finished and it is time to either shut down the computer in an orderly fashion or else (and more likely) start processing the next job.

NASSI DIAGRAM

For various reasons, neither decision tables nor logic flow charts have pleased all systems analysts. When there are a lot of conditions that must be fulfilled simultaneously, there are a lot of rows in the decision table. For example, if there are five dichotomous (*i.e.* YES/NO) choices, there must be 32 rows. That is a lot of information to have to assimilate at a glance.

Logic flow charts can become very complex, also. In fact, with looping back and everything else a logic flow chart does, it soon begins to resemble a bowl of spaghetti, at which point it becomes nearly impossible to visualize what's going on in the process.

The Nassi-Shneiderman diagram forces systems designers to break their creations into readily understandable segments each containing not more than, say, three decision elements. Figure 7.10 is a Nassi diagram that portrays the processing of a new insurance policy sale. Every command is written in a box. The command at the top of the page sets up the looping condition:

DO FOR EACH NEW INSURANCE POLICY SALE

It runs the full width of the page and communicates with a similar box at the bottom of the page by a channel at the extreme left. This box at the bottom contains the single word: RETURN. Its effect is to mark the termination of the loop and with it the end of the program segment.

The next command exists within the loop and is therefore framed within the fence formed by the left-hand channel and the DO and RETURN rectangles. The second command is:

SEARCH 'RATE' TABLE FOR POLICY COVERAGE AMOUNT

Now comes the first decision element. It splits the rest of the diagram into two parts; the one on the left is entered if the outcome is YES; the one on the right is entered if the outcome is NO. The portions of the decision box above the YES and NO regions are split by diagonal lines coverging to form an arrowhead pointing to the line separating the YES and NO regions. Each region is labelled YES or NO in the triangular area directly above it. The substance of the decision is written within the arrowhead. In our example it is: MATCH FOUND?

The NO region drops down immediately to the RETURN box and contains the command:

PRINT "NO MATCH FOUND"

In the YES region we encounter the command:

EXTRACT PREMIUM AMOUNT

This is followed by a second decision element. The decision element's arrowhead contains the legend:

IS PREMIUM DISCOUNTED?

NASSI-SHNEIDERMAN DIAGRAM

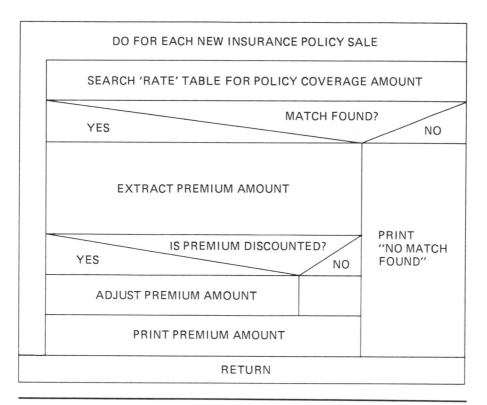

Figure 7.10. Nassi diagram

The YES region following it contains the command:

ADJUST PREMIUM AMOUNT

The next command, that is, PRINT PREMIUM AMOUNT, extends over the entire width of the decision box indicating that whether or not the premium amount is discounted, the computer is still to print it. The empty box following the NO region of the decision element brings us directly to the print command.

The fact that the designer is forced to split the diagram everytime a decision element is encountered tends to restrict the number of choices that can be represented on a page. Moreover, there is no provision for off-page continuation. Thus, the designer must explicate his logic in small bites. This makes it easier to comprehend the import of each program segment. Coupled with the HIPO diagram to specify inputs and outputs, the Nassi diagram encourages systems designers to document their work in readily understandable page-sized elements.

Chapter 8

CONTROLS IN ACTION: PAYROLL SYSTEM

So far, we have discussed several techniques for validating data and procedures to protect integrity. In this chapter, we are going to examine several applications of these techniques and procedures in the context of a payroll system.

This is an actual case, but I've simplified and abbreviated it so as to make the security-relevant aspects stand out. The company is medium-sized, employing about 200 people.

Initially, the company processed payroll in the batch mode making heavy use of punched cards. After that, it went to on-line processing using computer terminals and a modern data-base management system (called a DBMS in data-processing jargon).

We will first look at the administrative environment with the aid of a systems flow chart. Next, we will examine the batch processing system using a static summary chart to identify the important files and a summary flow chart to illustrate the various processing steps. We will then see how the processing is done in the on-line mode and then look in detail at the data dictionary of each of the five principal files used.

PAYROLL SYSTEM

Figure 8.1 is a modified systems flow chart depicting the administrative environment of the payroll system. The decision to hire or fire an employee is made by plant management. When such a decision involves creation of a new job or a reduction in force, the action taken must conform to the company budget, and requires approval of the (financial) comptroller; this step is not shown on the diagram. Whether the job is old or new, plant management must show evidence of having advertised the job to avoid the appearance of nepotism. (Such advertising is placed by the advertising department with approval of the personnel department to see that it does not contravene any applicable human rights code; this step is also not shown). Drops from, or additions to the payroll are made by the personnel department and implemented by the payroll department.

In a similar way, changes in pay or status (*e.g.* from hourly to salaried) are authorized by plant management, made by personnel, and implemented by payroll. Changes in an employee's dependent status (marriage, birth, divorce, etc.) are entered by the personnel department upon presentation of supporting documentation and implemented by payroll.

Job time tickets (authorizing the expenditure of labor on a job) are issued by plant management. They are delivered to timekeeping. Timekeeping keeps track of the actual expenditure of labor against these job time tickets and reports any variances they discover. The amended job time tickets are sent to the labor distribution department where the labor cost is charged against specific goods manufactured. The labor expense account must be reconciled with the payroll document in the general ledger.

Meanwhile, timekeeping delivers time cards (or the information contained on them) to payroll. The payroll is processed and the pay statement is sent to the accounts-payable department. Here, a voucher or request for payment is made up. An entry is made in the general ledger payroll account and the voucher is sent to the cash-disbursements department. On the strength of the approved voucher, a check is deposited in the imprest payroll account. Duplicate deposit slips are returned to internal audit. Pay checks are issued to employees by the payroll department. Uncollected checks are sent to internal audit for release, individually, upon proper identification. Cancelled checks returned by the bank and the periodic bank statements are sent to internal audit for reconciliation.

Figure 8.2 is a summary chart that shows the files of the old batch payroll system. In the center is a rectangle labelled CPU (central processing unit). This is the part of the computer in which comparisons are made and arithmetic operations carried out.

Coming into the CPU we find the old master payroll file (represented as magnetic tape), sorted hourly pay transactions (represented as a magnetic

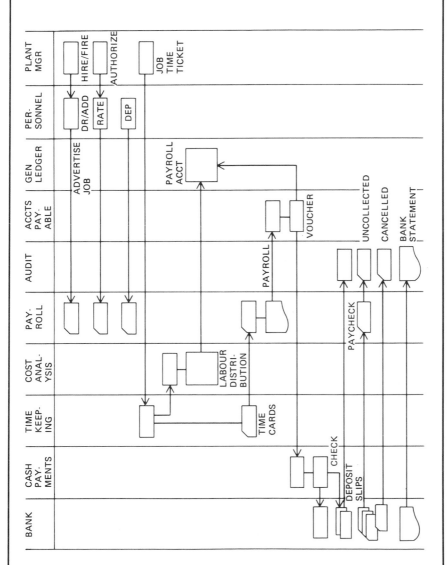

Figure 8.1. Payroll system

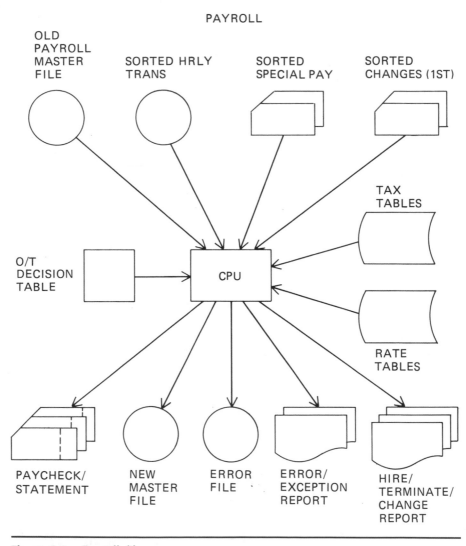

PAYROLL

OLD
PAYROLL
MASTER   SORTED HRLY   SORTED   SORTED
FILE   TRANS   SPECIAL PAY   CHANGES (1ST)

TAX
TABLES

O/T
DECISION   CPU
TABLE

RATE
TABLES

PAYCHECK/   NEW   ERROR   ERROR/   HIRE/
STATEMENT   MASTER   FILE   EXCEPTION   TERMINATE/
                 FILE   REPORT   CHANGE
                                                            REPORT

Figure 8.2. Payroll files

tape), sorted special pay transactions (represented as punched cards) and sorted changes to the personnel file (represented as punched cards).

The federal tax table and wage rate tables are represented as files stored on magnetic disk. The table used to make decisions regarding the payment of overtime pay is shown as residing in extended "core" storage.

Coming out of the CPU we find pay checks with stubs, an updated ("new") master payroll file, an error file, represented as a magnetic tape, an error and exception report printed in duplicate, and a hire/terminate/change report on personnel, printed in triplicate.

BATCH PAYROLL

Figure 8.3 shows the way payroll processing is handled. The file of punched cards indicating changes in pay status, special pay, and hours worked are first sorted in employee number order and validated by computer to create three magnetic tape files: changes to pay status, special pay, and regular pay.

First, the change file is run against the old copy of the payroll master file to record name or department changes; changes in salaried, hourly, or pay grade status; termination or hiring. In this procedure a new file, the updated master payroll file, is created. This file is run against the special pay file and the New Master I is created. This sets current pay to zero and adds in positive or negative pay adjustments and bonuses.

The New Master I file is run against the hours worked (pay) file. Appropriate data is called in from disk to ascertain the correct federal tax rate and the pay rate appropriate to this employee's current pay grade. The logic to be used in deciding whether or not to pay overtime resides in "core" (that is, immediate access storage). This creates a magnetic tape file called New Master File II and the Errors and Exceptions file. The New Master II file is run against the error file to fix errors or to kick erroneous records out for manual processing. Then the corrected master file is run through the computer one more time; paychecks are printed, reports used to apply labor costs to various company operations and to reconcile cancelled pay checks are printed, and the current totals are added to the cumulative year-to-date files. The final tape produced will be the starting file (old payroll master file) for the next payroll preparation cycle.

ON-LINE PAYROLL

The new on-line payroll system is illstrated in Figure 8.4. The personnel file resides in a disk storage unit of the central computer. Changes to it are entered directly from an on-line terminal in the personnel department. The federal tax table also resides on disk. Each year the new tax rates are entered from an on-line terminal in the wage/salary/benefits administration department. Weekly entries to the disk-resident special pay file are made from another terminal in this department. Likewise, the hours-worked file resides on disk. Entries on it are made from an on-line terminal located in the timekeeper's department.

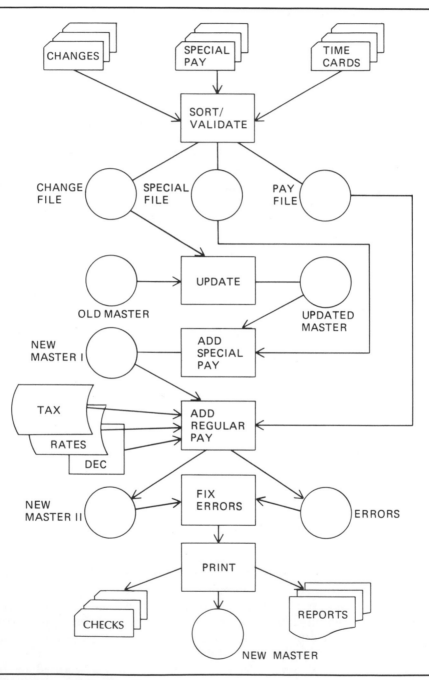

Figure 8.3. Batch Payroll

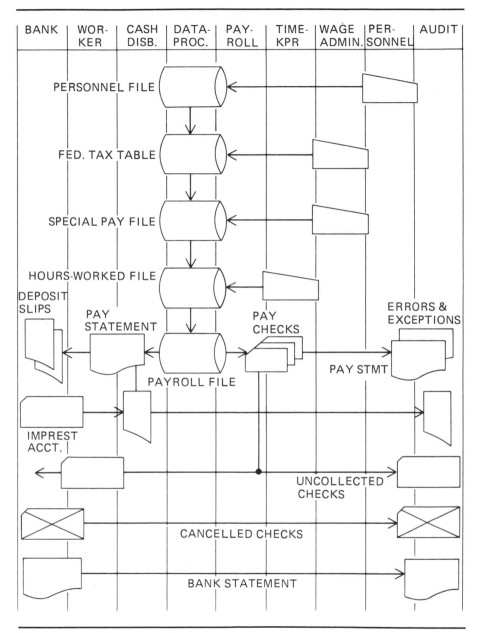

Figure 8.4. On-line payroll

The four files are processed in the computer's central processing unit to produce the payroll file, also on disk, and a subsidiary errors-and-exceptions file. The pay checks with stubs attached are printed under secure conditions by a remote printer within the payroll department. Copies of the pay statement are printed and delivered to the cash-disbursement department and the internal auditor. Copies of portions of the pay statement are given to the various manufacturing and service departments to help them to assess labor costs as part of the overall cost of goods manufactured.

The cash-disbursement department uses the pay statement as its authority to draw a single check on the company's general account and to deposit that check in the special imprest account for payroll. In some companies, this account is maintained at a bank or bank branch separate from the one that handles the company's general account. The deposit slip is made out in duplicate. One copy remains at the bank; the second is returned to cash disbursements as evidence that the payroll check has indeed been deposited, then routed to internal audit where it is reconciled against the pay statement.

The internal auditor checks the errors-and-omissions report to see that all erroneous or exceptional occurrences have been resolved satisfactorily. The auditor may sometimes require a print of the payroll file or of one or more of the subsidiary files to carry out this investigation. The actual resolution of these contradictions is a a duty of a data control group within the payroll department.

The payroll department delivers pay checks to workers. Uncollected checks are delivered to the internal auditor. Here, the payee must identify himself and sign for his check when he gets around to collecting it.

Cancelled checks are returned from the bank and delivered to internal audit along with the periodic bank statement. Cancelled checks, uncollected checks and deposit slips are reconciled against the bank statement and the pay statement.

We will now look at the principal files used in the payroll system and see how it has been possible to build validation checks into the system for every item.

The payroll is made up from input files:

1. Federal tax table
2. Personnel file
3. Statement of special pay
4. Report of hours worked

The information, both current and year-to-date, is processed by computer and stored on the payroll file, which is not normally printed. Every week, a pay statement is printed as well as the paychecks for employees.

The four input files are updated at computer terminals remote from the main computer room. The tax table is updated yearly; the other files are updated weekly. The operators work at display terminals (cathode-ray tubes) and a paper copy of their work is printed on a typewriter terminal slaved to the screen. The copy is printed on a continuous roll of paper and is reviewed by the operator's supervisor.

The tax table and the special pay file are updated in the wage administration department. The personnel file is updated in the personnel department. The hours-worked file is updated in the timekeeper's department. The computer's operating system ensures that the programs to update these files can be run only from designated terminals, as identified by their "here-is" chip. Before updating is done, the documents the operators will copy are approved. They bear two signatures: one of the officer who created it (or in the case of the tax table the one who received it); and of the officer who reviewed it.

Each document bears a time and date; the DBMS checks the date and time that the operator enters before starting to process a file. The file won't be opened unless the date and time entered correspond to the current date and time. Likewise, the operator must enter his or her personal password and the file will not be opened unless the password entered corresponds to the one stored in the program. When entering data regarding a particular employee, the operator must give the employee's number as it appears on the input document, otherwise the DBMS will not accept the data. A lot of tricks can be used to compose checkable employee numbers like some mathematical combination of his/her date of birth and the numerical representation of his name; alternatively some range like 130–1000 can be chosen.

If data is unacceptable, the DBMS sends a warning message to the operator and the operator is given a chance to fix it. If it is not fixed, that employee's record is made part of the errors-and-exceptions report. This is printed on the continuous paper roll of the typewriter-like terminal (the console log). The operator's supervisor and perhaps the security officer can then decide if the operator needs more training or transfer to a less sensitive position. Since the time, date, and place of updating and the operator's ID are preprogrammed into the DBMS, the supervisor can even make it a point to look over the operator's shoulder if this seems desirable.

A lot of security principles are working for us here.

1. Responsibilities are divided. The person who has custody of payroll funds cannot authorize their disbursement.
2. Duties are separated. Different parts of each task are performed by different people in different departments.
3. Every transaction is automatically validated.
4. Provisions are made for direct supervision of sensitive tasks.
5. Every participant in every transaction is positively identified.
6. An audit trail is created and reviewed in the normal course of business.

Now, we'll look at each field (data item) of each input transaction and see how some of the principles stated in Chapter 5 have been implemented.

FEDERAL TAX TABLE

The federal tax table is dated. If the table is stale or not yet operative, the table cannot be used. Every number in the table is automatically added to every other number at the time it is first entered into the DBMS. The total is stored in the table as a checksum. Every time the table is opened, the total is automatically recomputed and compared with the checksum. If the two figures are not equal, the table cannot be used, on the premise that an unauthorized change may have been made. If the table cannot be used, a warning message is printed for the security director.

TAX FILE

This payroll system was programmed in DPL (Data Processing Language), a product of National Information Systems, Cupertino, CA, which runs on DEC (Digital Equipment Corp.) computers.

Figure 8.5. Tax table

```
          LIST DSD TAXDESC

                SYMBOLIC FIXED
          10 INCOME,N,10,2
          20 TAX,N,3,2 OCCURS 7


          *OPEN TAX

          8 RECORDS

          *SELECT
             6000.00 .00 .00 .00 .00 .00 .00 .00
             8000.00 .16 .18 .16 .14 .13 .11 .09
            12000.00 .18 .16 .14 .12 .11 .18 .09
            15000.00 .22 .20 .18 .16 .15 .14 .13
            20000.00 .24 .22 .20 .19 .18 .17 .16
            35000.00 .28 .26 .24 .23 .22 .21 .20
            60000.00 .32 .30 .29 .28 .27 .26 .25
           200000.00 .36 .34 .32 .30 .29 .28 .27

          8 MASTER RECORDS READ
          8 SELECTED RECORDS
```

The data dictionary is prepared as a by-product of programming. Figure 8.5 shows the DSD (data set description) of the federal tax table. The name of the file is TAXDESC. It is symbolic (as opposed to binary) and its records have a fixed length. The table has two types of data. The field called INCOME is numeric. It has 10 places, two of which exist to the right of the decimal point. It is the lower limit of each tax bracket.

The field called TAX is also numeric. It has three places. Both numeric places exist to the right of the decimal point. There are seven occurrences for each tax bracket. Each occurrence corresponds to a dependency category, i.e., 0, 1, 2, 3, 4, 5, 6 or more.

The checksum is verified by automatically running a validation program against this table when it is first opened. To enhance security, the checksum is stored as an entry in this program.

The "dump" of the table displays dummy data that was used to test the program during the development cycle. The file containing data is called TAX to distinguish it from the description of the file above.

SPECIAL PAY STATEMENT

The special pay statement contains the fields NEGATIVE-PAY-ADJUSTMENT, POSITIVE-PAY-ADJUSTMENT and BONUS (Suggestion Award).

These fields normally contain zeros. If an employee had an entry last week, it is automatically echoed to the operator for review before being reset to zero.

The NEGATIVE-PAY-ADJUSTMENT cannot exceed a negative amount previously determined by management nor can it be positive because this would be a way to steal from the company.

The operator cannot enter a POSITIVE-PAY-ADJUSTMENT if a NEGATIVE-PAY-ADJUSTMENT has previously been entered. A POSITIVE-PAY-ADJUSTMENT cannot exceed a predetermined amount and cannot be negative because this would be a way to cover up a fraud.

The BONUS cannot be negative either, nor can it exceed a predetermined amount.

Figure 8.6 shows the format of the special-pay file description. Its name is PAYADJDESC (pay-adjustment description). It contains four fields, one, EMPLOYEENO is integer. The other three are numeric. The lines which begin with an exclamation point are comments used to document the file description. Note that the field called PADJ is described as containing the positive (upward) pay adjustment. The effect of the validation clause is that the value of this field must be greater than zero (it cannot be negative) and must not exceed one week's pay at the highest rate in effect ($15) based on 40

```
*LIST DSD PADJDESC

      SYMBOLIC  FIXED
  10 EMPLOYEENO,I,3 VALID IF VALUE GE 130 AND LE 300
  11 ! EMPLOYEENO--CONTAINS EMPLOYEE'S NO--IT MUST BE SMALLER THAN 300
  12 ! AND GREATER THAN 130.
  20 PADJ,N,8,2 VALID IF VALUE GE 0. AND LE 600.
  21 ! PADJ--CONTAINS THE POSITIVE PAY ADJUSTMENT--MUST BE GE TO ZERO
  22 ! ANCAN NOT EXCEED ONE WEEK'S PAY USING 40 HOURS WORKED.
  30 NADJ,N,8,2 VALID IF VALUE LE 0. AND GE -92.
  31 ! NADJ--NEGATIVE PAY ADJUSTMENT--MUST BE NEGATIVE AND MUST NOT
  32 ! BRING WORKER'S WEEKLY PAY TO ZERO.
  40 SUGAWD N,7,2 VALID IF VALUE EQ 0. OR VALUE GE 1. AND LE 6000.
  41 ! SUGAWD--CONTAINS SUGGESTION AWARD--IT CAN BE ZERO ,BUT NOT LESS
  42 ! THAN $1.00--AND MUST BE LESS THAN $6000.00.


*OPEN PAYADJ

4 RECORDS

*SELECT
130     10.00      .00      .00
131       .00   -40.00      .00
133       .00      .00  5500.00
145     20.00      .00      .00

4 MASTER RECORDS READ
4 SELECTED RECORDS
```

Figure 8.6.   Special-pay file

hours worked, (*i.e.* that rate belongs to a salaried employee). The fields called NADJ (negative or downward adjustment) and SUGAWD (suggestion award) are documented in a similar manner. The file containing special-pay data is called PAYADJ.

HOURLY PAY FILE

Figure 8.7 shows the hourly pay file description called HOURSDESC. It consists of two fields. The first is called EMPLOYEENO. It is a three digit integer. The validation clause prohibits the computer from accepting an employee number unless it is in the valid range, (*i.e.* equal to or greater than 130 and less than 1000).

The HOURSWORKED field is numeric. It allows for three digits to the left of the decimal point and two digits to the right of it. The validation clause

```
*LIST DSD HOURSDESC

     SYMBOLIC  FIXED
 10 EMPLOYEENO,I,3 VALID IF VALUE >= 130 and < 1000
 20 HOURSWORKED,N,6,2 VALID IF VALUE >= 0.00 and < 168.00


*OPEN HOURS

4 RECORDS

*SELECT
130   45.00
131   40.00
133   40.00
145   55.00

4 MASTER RECORDS READ
4 SELECTED RECORDS
```

Figure 8.7. Hourly-pay file

will not permit entry of negative numbers or values greater than 168 hours (this could be set to 80 or even some lower value, if desired). The file that contains time data is called HOURS.

PERSONNEL FILE

The personnel file contains several fields. They are NAME, SOCIAL-SECURITY-NUMBER (SSN), NUMBER-OF-DEPENDENTS (DEP), DEPARTMENT (DEPT.), RATE, TYPE-OF-EMPLOYEE (TYPE), DATE-OF-BIRTH (DOB), DATE-HIRED, DATE-TERMINATED, and CAUSE.

Three kinds of transactions are permitted: hire, change, or terminate. All entries are made from a statement compiled by the personnel department.

If the operator elects to enter a "hire" transaction, only the fields NAME, SSN, DEP, DEPT, RATE, TYPE, DOB, and DATE-HIRED can receive data.

The NAME field is 20 characters long. It must be alphabetic (we won't put R2D2 on the payroll). It must contain at least one space (between first and last names).

The SSN field is alphanumeric with hyphens between the third and fourth, and the fifth and sixth digits. It has 10 digits. The 10th digit is a checking digit. It is computed when the employee first presents his social-security card at the personnel office. The checking digit is computed in the following way: add the first, third, fifth, seventh and ninth digits to form subtotal #1. Make a four-digit number out of the second, fourth, sixth and eighth digits; add it to itself; add the digits of the resulting number to form subtotal #2. Add subtotal #1 to subtotal #2 and subtract from the next highest multiple of 10. This is the checking digit, the 10th digit of the SSN field. It it automatically calculated when the SSN is entered into the database. If it is not equal to the number in the 10th digit position, the DBMS will not accept the employee's record on the premise that the SSN has inadvertently, or intentionally been altered by substituting an incorrect digit or by transposing two adjacent digits.

The DEP field must be a whole number between zero and the largest number allowed in the tax table. It cannot be negative.

The DEPT field is alphanumeric and must correspond to a valid company department designation. A list of them has previously been stored in the DBMS.

The RATE field is numeric (numeric fields are also called real or decimal). Its value must be between a minimum and maximum as determined by management. Of course, it cannot be negative.

The TYPE field is alphabetic. It must be either "S" for salaried, or "H" for hourly.

The DOB field in this DBMS is a special "date" field. If company rules state that no person younger than 16 or older than 65 may be hired, then the DOB must be earlier than the current date minus 16 years and later than the current date minus 65 years. In this pay system DATE-HIRED cannot be later than the current date minus 14 days — the company withholds two weeks pay against which offsets can be made to liquidate damages done by departing employees; therefore, the employee's name will not appear on the payroll until he/she has worked for two weeks. DATE-HIRED cannot be earlier than the date the company started business.

If the operator elects to enter a "change" transaction, only the NAME, DEP, DEPT, RATE and TYPE fields can receive new data.

If the operator elects to enter a "termination" transaction, only the DATE-TERMINATED and CAUSE fields can receive data. In this pay system DATE-TERMINATED cannot be later than the current date plus 14 days so a terminated worker can get the two weeks pay withheld, less any authorized offset (NEGATIVE-PAY-ADJUSTMENT) but no more. In this company, management has decreed that only the entries "VOLUNTARY," TRANSFERRED," or "TERMINATED" shall appear in the CAUSE field.

The description of the personnel file PERSNLDESC is shown in Figure 8.8. It contains 11 fields. These have already been described. Each field has a validation clause that prevents improper data from being entered. Each field is followed by one or more comment statements that explicate the contents of the field and describe the effect of the validation clause.

```
*LIST DSD PERSNLDESC

        SYMBOLIC  FIXED
    10 EMPLOYEENO, I,3 VALID IF VALUE GE 130 AND LE 300
    20 ! EMPLOYEENO--CONTAINS THE EMPLOYEE #, AND IT MUST BE
    30 ! SMALLER THAN 300 AND GREATER THAN 130
    40 NAME,A,20 VALID IF HAS " "
    50 ! NAME--CONTAINS THE NAME--IT IS VALID IF IT HAS A BLANK.
    60 SIN,C,11 VALID IF VALUE HAS "-" and "-"
    70 ! SIN--CONTAINS THE SOCIAL INS. NUMBER--IT IS VALID IF IT
    80 !    CONTAINS TO HIPHENS.
    90 DEPD,I,2 VALID IF VALUE GE O AND LE 6
   100 ! DEPD--CONTAINS THE NUMBER OF DEPENDENTS--IT CAN NOT BE
   110 !      NEGATIVE OR GREATER THAN 6
   120 DEPT,I,3 VALID IF VALUE = 100 OR 200 OR 300 OR 400 OR 500
   130 ! DEPT--CONTAINS THE DEPARTMENT #--IT CAN ONLY BE 100,200
   140 !       300,400 OR 500.
   150 RATE,N,7,2 VALID UNLESS VALUE GT 15.00 OR LT 2.50
   160 ! RATE--CONTAINS HOURLY RATE OF PAY--IT HAS TO BE BETWEEN
   170 !      $15.00 AND $2.50 INCLUSIVE.
   180 ETYPE,A,1 VALID IF VALUE = "H" OR "S"
   190 ! ETYPE--TELLS UIF THE EMPLOYEE IS SALARIED OR HOURLY
   200 DBORN,D VALID UNLESS VALUE+65 LE @DATE AND VALUE+16 GE @DATE
   210 ! DBORN--CONTAINS THE DATE OF BIRTH--EMPLOYEE CANNOT BE OLDER
   220 !       THAN 65 OR LESS THAN 16.
   230 DHIRED,D VALID UNLESS VALUE#14 GT@DATE AND @CAL"800101"
   240 ! DHIRED--CONTAINS THE DATE OF EMPOYMENT--CANNOT BE EARLIER
   250 !        THAN THE DATE THE COMPANY WAS STARTED NOR LATER
   260 !        THAN 14 DAYS PRIOR TO THE CURRENT DATE.
   270 DTERM,D VALID UNLESS VALUE LT @DATE-14
   280 ! DTERM--CONTAINS THE DATE THE EMPLOYEE STOPPED WORKING--
   290 TCAUSE,A,11 VALID IF VALUE = "TRANSFERED" OR "VOLUNTARY"
OR "TERMINATED"
   300 ! TCAUSE--TELLS WHY THE EMPLOYEE LEFT THE COMPANY--


*OPEN PERSNL

4 RECORDS

*SELECT
130 TOME B               478-666-365   1 100    5.00 S 12/25/45 07/01/80 ***

131 SLONE RENE           478-922-511   4 500    9.00 S 11/08/47 03/01/80 ***

133 SMITH J              450-911-896   6 400    7.00 H 02/02/49 05/02/81 ***

145 SMITH FRANCIS        456-662-816   4 400    9.45 H 08/02/45 07/01/81 ***


4 MASTER RECORDS READ
4 SELECTED RECORDS
```

Figure 8.8. Personnel file

Note that three new field types appear in this file description. The field called NAME is alphabetic. It can be 20 characters long and it must contain a space between the first and last names of the employee.

The field called SSN is a character field. It can contain any kind of character. It is 11 characters long and must contain two hyphens. A special validation program is run against this data file to recompute and thus validate the checking digit of this number.

The field called DBORN is a special date field. It contains the employee's date of birth.

The data file corresponding to this file description is called PERSNL. It contains only four records of dummy data used in program development.

PAYROLL FILE

The payroll file contains the fields: CHECK-NUMBER (CKNO), REGU-LAR-PAY (REG), OVERTIME (OVT), POSITIVE-PAY-ADJUSTMENT, NEGATIVE-PAY-ADJUSTMENT, BONUS, GROSS, FEDERAL-TAX (FED), FEDERAL-INSURANCE-CONTRIBUTION-ACT (FICA), NET, YEAR-TO-DATE (YTD) -GROSS, YTD-FED, YTD-FICA, and YTD-NET.

The CKNO is an integer made up by mathematically combining the employee number with the date and time the payroll was processed. This procedure affords a certain amount of protection against forgery and gives every check printed in every pay period a unique number to help in reconciling bank statments and following audit trails.

POSITIVE-PAY-ADJUSTMENT, NEGATIVE-PAY-ADJUST-MENT and BONUS fields are transferred directly from the special-pay file to the payroll file without further checking. This is the first step in processing payroll. At this time, it is essential that all current amount fields, as distinguished from cumulative or year-to-date totals, be reset to zero so no employee will get unearned pay carried over from the last pay period. It is also essential that steps be taken to ensure that terminated employees, who must be carried to the end of the current quarter for tax purposes, do not improperly receive pay.

Next, the hours-worked file is run against the payroll file; the federal tax table and the personnel file are both opened for reference. The fields DEP, RATE, TYPE, and DATE-TERMINATED are taken from the personnel file. OVT is set equal to zero if TYPE is equal to "S" or if HOURS-WORKED is less than or equal to 40. Otherwise, OVT is equal to 1.5 (for time-and-a-half) × RATE × HOURS-WORKED ÷ 40) with no negative values allowed; REG is equal to the lesser of RATE × 40 or RATE ×

HOURS-WORKED if TYPE is "H" and HOURS less than 40. REG is equal to RATE times 40 if TYPE is "S."

The value of GROSS is then the sum of REG plus OVT plus POSITIVE-PAY-ADJUSTMENT minus NEGATIVE-PAY-ADJUSTMENT plus BONUS. Gross pay will be set to zero if DATE-TERMINATED is more than 14 days prior to current date, otherwise values of zero or less will be printed for investigation. Values over a stipulated maximum result in the records of the employee in question in the personnel, special-pay, hours-worked, and payroll files being printed on the errors-and-exceptions file for investigation. Another job for the security director.

The value of FED is found by first multiplying GROSS by 52 (this is the employees' purported annual gross earnings called YEARN), then entering the federal tax table with this value and the value of DEP to get the appropriate tax rate, and then multiplying GROSS by that decimal value from the tax table. The control is that FED cannot be zero or less or greater than a predetermined maximum.

A common payroll fraud consists of shaving a little bit off several employees' FED entries and adding it to that of the thief, or one or more of his confederates. This way, the ripoff is realized in the form of an unlawfully augmented income-tax refund. This is called a "salami" fraud.

The value of FICA is obtained by multiplying GROSS by a rate set by the federal government until the YTD-FICA total exceeds an amount, also set by the federal government. The control is that FICA cannot be negative or greater than a stipulated maximum. In no case should YTD-FICA exceed the legal maximum.

The value of NET is then GROSS minus the sum of FICA and FED. It should not be negative or more than a previously stored maximum. Zero values must be printed for reconciliation with attendance and vacation records.

Year-to-date fields may be used by thieves as repositories for small amounts of money shifted from diverse debit accounts on a weekly basis, then stealing them at the end of the year or quarter. The YTD fields can also be used to cover up thefts by falsely augmenting credit accounts so that overall accounting totals appear, contrary to fact, to be in balance.

You may wonder how the YTD fields could be in error when we take such pains to ensure that all the inputs are valid. One answer is that clever and strategically situated technicians in the data-processing department have frequently been able to override the controls and/or insert transactions outside of the normal data-processing cycle or suppress transactions made during the normal data-processing cycle.

The YTD-NET, YTD-GROSS and YTD-FED fields should never be negative; they should be equal to zero only at the start of the year, and they

```
*LIST DSD PAYROLDESC

     SYMBOLIC  FIXED
 10 EMPLOYEENO,I,3
 20 !  EMPLOYEENO--CONTAINS EMPLOYEE NUMBER.
 30 CKNO,I,5
 40 !  CKNO--IS A CONTROL  ==EMPLOYEENO*CURRENT HOURS+CURRENT MINUTES
 50 OVT,N,8,2
 60 !  OVT--CONTAINS OVERTIME--
 70 REG, N,7,2
 80 !  REG--CONTAINS REGULAR PAY--
 90 PADJ ,N,8,2
100 !  PADJ--POSITIVE PAY ADJUSTMENT--
110 NADJ ,N,8,2
120 !  NADJ--NEGATIVE PAY ADJUSTEMENT--
130 SUGAWD, N,8,2
140 !  SUGAWD--SUGGESTION AWARD--
150 FED ,N,8,2
160 !  FED--FEDERAL TAX--
170 CTY, N,6,2
180 !  CTY--CITY TAX--
190 FICA,N,7,2
200 !  FICA--FEDERAL INSURANCE CONTRIBUTION ACT--
210 GSEARN,N,10,2
220 !  GSEARN--GROSS EARNINGS--
230 TOTFED,N,9,2
240 !  TOTFED--TOTAL FEDERAL TAX--
250 TOTCITY,N,8,2
260 !  TOTCTY--TOTAL CITY TAX--
270 TOFICA,N,9,2
280 !  TOFICA--TOTAL FED. INSURANCE CONTRIBUTION ACT--
290 NETPAY,N,8,2
300 !  NETPAY--NET PAY--


*OPEN PAYROL

4 RECORDS

*SELECT
130  2103     .00 200.00  10.00      .00      .00 37.80    2.10    13.6
    210.00    37.80    2.10    13.65 156.45
131  2119     .00 360.00     .00  -40.00      .00 48.00    3.20    20.8
    320.00    48.00    3.20    20.80 248.00
133  2151     .00 280.00     .00      .00 5500.00 520.20  57.80   375.7
   5780.00   520.20   57.80   375.70 4826.30
145 2343   212.63 378.00  20.00      .00      .00 91.59    6.11    39.6
    610.63    91.59    6.11    39.69 473.24

4 MASTER RECORDS READ
4 SELECTED RECORDS
```

Figure 8.9. Payroll file

should never exceed a stipulated maximum. In addition, the difference between the appropriate YTD total and the product of current NET, GROSS, or FED multiplied by the current week number must fall within pre-stored limits. These controls will not stop all payroll fraud but they will reduce losses.

Figure 8.9 is the description of the payroll file. It is called PAYROL-DESC. It contains 15 fields. There are no validation clauses. This file cannot be altered manually. It is updated automatically within the computer by running the four files previously described against it. The comment statements here merely spell out the meaning of the names given to each field. Validation is accomplished by the sets of instructions in the program used to update it. The name of the corresponding data file is PAYROL.

Payroll Statement

In this system, a payroll statement is printed from the payroll. It is dated and it gives, for each employee, his/her NAME, DEPT, EMP-NO, CKNO, NET and GROSS. For each department, subtotals are printed and sent to the managers concerned to check against their labor costs. Grand totals are printed for comparison against budget forecasts. Internal auditors use the payroll statement to reconcile the CKNO's and NET amounts of paychecks returned from the bank. The DBMS prints the payroll statement with title and company letterhead and automatically marks it as COMPANY CONFIDENTIAL.

Paychecks and Stubs

The paychecks are printed with stubs that carry all the entries on the payroll file, but experience has shown that a security director cannot rely on employees checking their own stubs even though these employees have been given all the information needed to do so. Some employees do check, however, and some thieves have been caught as a result of this.

The checks are printed on serially numbered and inventoried water-marked stock to guard against forgery or against removing one or more checks, printing one or more of them two or more times, or printing fictitious checks. Exactly the number of checks on the payroll statement are printed. The checks are protected by printing the amount in figures and words flush right and filling the space on the left with asterisks to prevent forgers from changing the amount. Signature plates are stored under secure conditions and used under the control of two senior employees.

Even though this has been a very much simplified treatment of the subject of payroll processing it still contains a lot of detail that probably made for dry reading. However, this case incorporates, explicitly or implicitly, all of the controls set forth in the last chapter. Today most companies have a computer as well as modern data-base software (it is a lot cheaper than even one major white-collar theft). With it you can make a start toward controlling white-collar crime starting with the payroll department, one of the most attractive targets.

These controls do not need to be expensive and they will probably save as much in avoidance and correction of non-malicious errors as they do in forestalling theft. After all, the objective of security is to reduce loss from any source; crime is just one of them.

The main point is that unless the controls are designed in, as part and parcel of, a data-processing system, they can become very expensive to install later on, and they won't work very well either.

Systems analysts should be conscious of threats to security, and some internal auditors do become involved in the system design process despite the "independence" shibboleth. However, the payroll system (and other data-processing systems like receivables, payables, and inventory) is too attractive a target for protection to be left to chance. This is one reason why the security director should arm himself with a knowledge of internal control procedures, and become directly involved in the systems design process or the management review of it.

Chapter 9

VERIFICATION OF PROCESSING

Chapter 7 described some of the methods used to indicate what is supposed to be happening inside the computer. None of these methods are satisfactory. In fact, there is no direct way to prove whether a computer program is correct or not. Nevertheless, some auditors have developed approaches that help isolate potential troublespots. The security director should become familiar with them.

Parts of this chapter presume that the reader has an acquaintance with the art of computer programming. We do not believe this is unreasonable because many recent graduates of safety and security technology programs have taken at least one course in computer programming. Therefore, it is likely that you have, or someday will have, someone on your staff who can track down IF and GOTO statements so you don't have to become personally involved in the details of auditing computer programs. Alternatively, if a serious case of computer-based white-collar crime presents itself, you may want to call upon a reliable employee of the data-processing department or hire an outside consultant. In either case, it is wise, from a management point of view, to understand their general approaches.

This chapter deals with methods of verifying processing. These methods can be used in either manual or computer environments. Even in a manual environment, the sheer volume of data sometimes dictates that the computer be used for verification.

Three techniques that will be introduced are: the use of questionnaires to investigate programming practices, standards, and processing procedures; the auditing of computer programs and documentation; and the use of the computer as an audit tool.

QUESTIONNAIRES

The environment in which computer programs are prepared can be assessed by questionnaires. Questionnaires can be structured as a checklist, a series of yes/no answers, or opinion or choice questions.

Questionnaires should be constructed according to the following guidelines:

1. Explain the purpose of the study to the respondents.
2. Give detailed instructions for answering questions.
3. Impose a time limit to respond to the questionnaire.
4. Ask positive and precise questions. Instead of asking "Do workers regularly consult procedure manuals?" ask "Do procedure manuals in the workplace exhibit evidence of regular use?"
5. Plan for computer tabulation (*e.g.*, by programs such as the Statistical Package for the Social Sciences or SPSS).
6. Leave enough space for comments.
7. Phrase questions clearly.
8. Avoid eliciting predictable responses. Don't ask "Are receipts regularly deposited in the bank?" It is predictable that the response will be "Yes." Instead, ask "How often are receipts deposited in the bank?"
9. Elicit specific comments. Instead of asking "Are regular physical inventories taken?" ask "When did you last take a physical inventory?" and "What discrepancies did you discover?"
10. Explain questions.
11. Identify respondents. Anonymous tips are okay for discovering that an investigation is necessary, but once it is underway we should look for evidence and accountability.

Typical questions include:

1. Are there procedures for a periodic review of obsolete, surplus or slow-moving inventory items? The lack of movement renders these items vulnerable to undiscovered theft.
2. Can book inventory be reconciled with physical inventory? When was this last done? With what results?

3. Are credits for returns and allowances approved by an employee with no access to cash receipts or other funds? Identify the employee. Also identify those with access to cash receipts.
4. Is every shipment promptly and accurately billed? What is the average time between shipping and invoicing? Is there any history of customer complaints about inaccurate billing?
5. Are invoices supported by evidence of shipment? Are the documents filed together? How are they reconciled?
6. Are customer payments recorded, promptly deposited and properly credited? How often are deposits made? Are duplicate deposit slips made? Is there any history of customer complaints about double billing?
7. Are past due accounts receivable identified as to amount and days past due?
8. Can payments be supported by requisitions, purchase orders, receiving documents, and invoices? Are the documents filed together? How are they reconciled?

AUDITING THROUGH OR AROUND THE COMPUTER

Auditing around the computer assumes that the computer is a black box; therefore an audit consists of determining whether the output generated by the computer can be traced back to valid input. This approach accepts computer processing as gospel.

Auditing through the computer investigates control procedures over computer operations and programs, and the correctness of internal programs. In this approach, the auditor views the computer with healthy skepticism.

Only by auditing through the computer can sophisticated computer-assisted embezzlement be discovered.

The process of auditing computer programs consists of the following steps:

1. Review programming and documentation standards.
2. Select a particular program such as payroll, inventory, order-entry, etc.
3. Get a copy of the source code listing; the object code listing, or load module, is, except to technologists, unreadable. Make sure the code you choose can be compiled into that which is being used.
4. Get a copy of the program documentation.
5. Find out what input and output files are being used. Compare Cobol SELECT clauses to the FILE SECTION of the DATA DIVISION so as to ascertain what data is being processed; check

the effects of REDEFINES clauses on the data being processed. REDEFINE is an instruction that gives another name to a data file or field.

6. Compare the dump of two or three pages of each file with the file structure and record layouts. These should be shown in the program documentation.

7. Make sure an OPEN and CLOSE command exists for each file. If a file is left open, it can be improperly entered into by a spurious program sequence.

8. Locate all IF statements and obtain an explanation of the logic behind them. The IF statement is the hallmark of a decision or branch. These statements contain the logic of the program.

9. Locate all GOTO statements and find out what they do. Modern structured programming techniques try to eliminate these statements altogether. A GOTO statement transfers control elsewhere in the program. Where it goes is determined by a statement name in COBOL or a statement number in FORTRAN or BASIC. If a GOTO statement transfers control to a step further along in the program, its use may be acceptable in some situations. If it transfers control back to a previous step, its presence should be taken as evidence of poor programming practice.

   Use of the GOTO statement may be encountered in common computer frauds such as the salami technique, or the logic bomb.

- The *salami technique* consists of shaving off insignificant sums from many balances, and then crediting them to the account of the thief or one of his confederates. A statement is introduced in the routine that processes all accounts; it could look like this:

```
PROCESS–ACCOUNTS
IF CREDIT–BALANCE IS GREATER THAN 50. THEN
    CREDIT–BALANCE = CREDIT–BALANCE–1.44
GOTO FRAUD
FRAUD. CROOKS–ACCOUNT = CROOKS–ACCOUNT + 1.44
GOTO PROCESS–ACCOUNTS
```

- The *logic bomb* embeds statements in a program that have a deleterious effect, but they are actuated only if a certain condition is sensed. For example, a perpetrator might use the logic bomb to threaten an employer; hence if the crook got fired then the files would be wiped. A spurious statement such as the one below could be inserted in the routine that processes all payroll accounts:

```
IF EMPLOYEE–NAME EQUAL TO "IMA CROOK"
    THEN TRIGGER = TRIGGER + 1
```

At the end of the program, this statement will be inserted:

IF TRIGGER LESS THAN 1 THEN GOTO WIPE=FILES

10.   Check for external influences admitted by ACCEPT, CALL, ENTER, FILL, RETURN and ZAP statements and find out what they do. ACCEPT means data can be entered from a keyboard. CALL and ENTER statements transfer program control to subroutines whose purpose you have to discover by reading elsewhere in the documentation. RETURN transfers program control back to the main flow of program logic. FILL inserts zeros, blanks or other specified characters into data fields. ZAP is a powerful statement that can alter program instructions; its use in routine business data-processing is not recommended.

11.   Use automated program study aids such as flow charts, cross-reference listings and test-data generators.

THE COMPUTER AS AN AUDIT TOOL

We have seen that audits rely heavily on taking random samples of transactions and carrying out mathematical operations on them. If a large number of transactions are involved, the investigator will need a computer. This means he also needs computer programs for it. There are four ways to satisfy this requirement.

1.   The auditor can write the programs himself. This is usually not a reasonable approach. Auditors often lack programming skill and, even if he can program, programming takes a lot of time.

2.   The auditor can have the company's data-processing department write the programs. This, however, is an unsatisfactory alternative. If there are white-collar criminals in the data-processing department, it would be like hiring a fox to guard the henhouse. Moreover, it costs a great deal of money to write good programs; even if there was money available, most data-processing departments are too overloaded with their own work to take on major projects from other departments.

3.   The auditor can buy or lease special audit software programs from software suppliers. Usually, this turns out to be cheaper than writing in-house programs because a software supplier is usually efficient and can spread his program development costs over many customers. Thus, he can sell you software cheaper than you could write it and still make a profit. Even if you buy or lease this software the problem of running the test still remains. The auditor is faced

with the same dilemma: "Can he trust the data-processing department?" He could bring in his own operators, but the data-processing department may not have any running time available. The auditor is then faced with finding a reliable outside service bureau; there, he must also consider the risk of exposing sensitive company data to outsiders.

4. A comparatively recent development is the audit computer. This is a specially configured minicomputer designed so that the auditor can run it himself. A security director could run one as well. The minicomputer comes with special audit software. It can be customized to translate data from the code used by the company's data-processing department to one readable by the minicomputer. Developers of the audit computer claim the process of code translation itself can help catch irregularities.

Some of the functions audit programs perform on computers are:

- Search for, and retrieve specified items from data files.
- Select statistical samples of data.
- Perform calculations.
- Prepare subtotals.
- Compare, sort and merge data files.
- Copy data from one file to another.
- Let auditors insert their own program. However, it is necessary to make sure that the auditor is not a crook.
- Summarize records by totals and subtotals.
- Print-out audit results in any format desired.

SPECIFIC USES OF THE COMPUTER

Here are several things the computer can do for the auditor:

1. List all employees who worked more than a predetermined number of hours. This tells who is piling up overtime. Exempt employees should not be receiving overtime payments.
2. Prepare footings and subtotals of any master file.
3. List all accounts over 90 days old. These accounts are likely to default.
4. Calculate rebates due for a group of loans. Rebates arise because lenders will offer reductions in interest (points) to obtain the business of frequent borrowers having good credit ratings. By the same token, borrowers with poor credit ratings may have to pay points.

5. Prepare trial balances for a group of loans to see how much they are making from interest and other charges.

6. Calculate cost-to-retail ratio of selected items to estimate the expected profit margin.

7. Select stratified random samples of inventory.

8. Find differences between *Lifo* and *Fifo* pricing. Lifo pricing means that we take as the cost of an item sold, the latest price we have paid for a similar item. It is a way to cope with the effects of inflation. Fifo pricing means that we take as the cost of an item sold, the price we actually paid for it.

9. Compare last year's inventory balances with current balances. List for review: new items, discontinued items, accounts changing 20 percent or more, and slow moving items. This tells which items are selling and which are being left on the shelf.

10. Calculate ratios: capital to liabilities; current assets to current liabilities; working capital to current liabilities; sales to inventory; cost-of-goods-sold to average inventory; sales to receivables; and net to invested capital.
    - Capital to liabilities tells how much of the business we own as opposed to how much is owed to creditors.
    - Current assets to current liabilities tells whether we are operating in a favorable business climate from day-to-day.
    - Working capital to current liabilities tells whether or not we are capable of paying our bills.
    - Sales to inventory tells whether or not our stock is selling satisfactorily, and if we are meeting demand.
    - Cost-of-goods-sold to average inventory is another measure of inventory movement.
    - Sales to receivables tells how much of our business is being done on credit.
    - Net to invested capital is the percentage return on our investment.

11. Check prices against price list to find out whether unauthorized discounts or markups are being made.

12. Verify extensions and summarizations.

13. Select random samples for statistical analysis.

14. Stratify data elements by age (*e.g.* checking accounts inactive for 9 months), type, status, and amount. In a bank, inactive accounts are vulnerable to theft.

15. Sample on a systematic basis.

16. Perform a "lower of cost or market" analysis; this compares stated costs of goods with what they are actually worth.

17. List outstanding checks.

18. Age accounts receivable; list those over 90 days for review because the customers might default.
19. List customer accounts exceeding credit limits. This can be a source of fraud or subsequent default.
20. List suppliers' invoices exceeding a set limit. Someone can be overstocking, possibly with theft in mind; suppliers could be improperly billing; or a purchasing agent could be paying off to a "sweetheart" supplier.
21. List numbered source documents missing from files; these events can mean someone is covering up.
22. Select accounts for confirmation. Flag past due accounts for positive confirmation, that is, sending a query letter to the customer.

In their approach to white-collar crime, there is a big difference between the auditor and the security director: the auditor is usually on a fishing expedition; the security director is on a hunting trip.

An internal audit on a part of the business may be done in response to a suggestion of dishonesty; more commonly it is carried out just because that department's number came up. Company departments or branches should be selected for audit on a random basis to prevent thieves from covering up; or honest, but sloppy employees from projecting an atypical image of competence. Usually, when the security director becomes involved, there is suspicion of unexplained loss, or there is reason to suspect one or more members of some loosely defined group.

A crook has to have a motive, the opportunity and the means. Traditionally, a white-collar employee is motivated to become a crook because of an unsharable financial problem: catastrophic medical bills, gambling losses, disastrous investments, expensive divorce settlements or other adverse legal judgments, alcohol or drug addiction. Another motive is disgruntlement: a missed raise or promotion, transfer to unpleasant duties, reprimand, personality conflict with supervisors or coworkers. Then there is pure and unvarnished greed. Some employees may have ideological motives dating back to the confrontational tactics of the 1960's. A few just want to prove to themselves how clever they are, and how much they can get away with.

The need for a white-collar crook to have opportunity suggests that checking up on people who have and make use of after hours access, opt for pay in lieu of vacation, eschew help and insist on working alone, eat lunch at their desks and go home regularly with bulging briefcases for no apparent reason.

The need for a culprit to have the means to commit white-collar crime suggests focusing more attention on people who have custody over assets or authority to authorize their disposal. However, today the prevalence of computer systems means that the security director has to cast his net wider than before. Persons with access to computer terminals or who are able to submit jobs for computer processing or make changes to programs have the capability to "forge" authorization by improperly obtaining the passwords of authorized persons.

This suggests looking critically at persons who seem to be overqualified for the jobs they hold, ask questions about the details of transactions that are outside their ambit of responsibility, are found in sensitive areas or in possession of sensitive documents or manuals without proper authorization, have "friends" in sensitive positions, or have histories of frequent changes in employment.

If an internal audit suggests that weaknesses exist in controls and that the company is suffering unexplained losses, it is then incumbent upon the security director to fix responsibility.

The most vulnerable areas are those company operations that have recently undergone financial losses; here is where the "looting" syndrome appears to infect some employees: "I'll get mine before they close the place up."

Alternatively, there is a high level of vulnerability in parts of the company that are in the process of expanding rapidly. Here, controls have not yet become institutionalized; managers may be new to their jobs and uncertain as to how and when to exert authority; and employees at this time don't really know each other. The theft syndrome here may be summed up in the philosophy: "Get yours while the getting is good."

A knowledge of how accounting systems work, what controls are or should be in place, and what tests internal auditors use to evaluate systems is essential at the beginning of an investigation. The personalization of guilt, however, calls for application of the people skills the security director has built up over the years.

INTERVIEWING SOURCES

There is at least one gossip in every office who will go on at length about the problems, work habits and foibles of co-workers if given the opportunity. There are un-persons: elevator operators, messengers, caretakers, and maintenance men who observe a great deal more about the comings and goings of employees than is generally realized. Exit interviews can be productive—a common sneak thief may be only too happy to finger a bigwig who is ripping off the company for far more than he/she ever stole. Approaching a smart-aleck, or alienated person with a question like: "How do you think a person would go about stealing receipts, getting an unearned payroll check, or getting valuable merchandise out of the stock room?" will open the floodgates of a theft scenario to which it may be relatively easy to affix names and faces.

ANALYZING RECORDS

There is a surprising amount of useful information buried in personnel and payroll files. In these records you can find out who has exhausted his medical benefits, required pay and expense advances, borrowed heavily from the credit union, keeps changing his address and the beneficiary of his life insurance. Which employees were hired recently, had a prior history of job jumping, stepped down from a more responsible position elsewhere, received noncommital references from past employers? Which employees arrive early, leave late, don't go out for lunch, pass up vacations, come in on holidays and weekends?

FOLLOWING THE AUDIT TRAIL

Does a particular employee seem to somehow be involved in a number of loss-causing transactions? Do his apparently random errors and mistakes seem to occur at or about the time unexplained losses are sustained? Can losses be correlated with the presence of specific persons?

As the circle of suspicion becomes narrower, the security director may wish to consider surveillance, polygraph screening where permitted, and ultimately interrogation of suspects and search of the suspect's workspace, car, home and person. These investigative techniques are well covered elsewhere and are beyond the scope of this book.

The security director's knowledge of business practices and controls, and his ability to work productively with internal audit and systems analysis, can narrow the circle of suspicion until the problem of stopping loss from white-collar crime becomes manageable with his unique and well-honed traditional skills.

Chapter 10

GO/NO-GO TESTING FOR FRAUD

By now, it must be apparent that the chances of being able to prove programming correct by direct examination is discouraging, to say the least. For a long time security officers, law-enforcement officers, and auditors have wanted a simple go/no-go test. They would like to have a program which could be run against a questioned program, one that would say *okay* or *here is trouble*. There are three possible programs to implement. None of the programs does all that is desired, but each can be helpful in special circumstances.

The first is the *code-comparison program*. It compares production programs, line-for-line, with other copies that have been stored under secure conditions. It is the actual load modules which are compared. These are also known as object programs and exist in the form of numerical sequences of machine-readable code. In order to instruct the computer a program must follow this form. The program is written by the programmer; the so-called source program is automatically converted to an object in a process called compilation. This process uses a systems program called a compiler. Compilers exist for computer languages such as COBOL and FORTRAN. By making comparisons with the load modules, we are able to exclude the possibility of someone subverting an applications program by tampering with the compiler.

The disadvantages of using a code-comparison program are two-fold.

First, to be effective, it should be run each time the object program is loaded into the computer. Code-comparison programs are slow to run and, consequently, their use may incur an unacceptable amount of overtime. More significant is the fact that every time a change is made to the object program, a corresponding change must be made to the program used for comparison with it. The making of the change, which must be made to the source program, and the recompilation of the exemplar, must be accomplished under secure conditions. This also takes a lot of time and may constitute an unacceptable interruption of the routine work of the data-processing department.

A second kind of go/no-go test may be accomplished by using an integrated test facility (ITF). An ITF consists, in the first instance, of a computer controlled directly by the audit department or by the security department. This computer must be capable of emulating any computer used in the company to process sensitive jobs. Emulation is a software-based procedure that causes one computer to look, operationally, exactly like another. Traditionally, emulators were used when a company bought a newer, larger and faster computer but did not want to go to the trouble and expense of rewriting all of the company's application programs.

It is then established that a copy of every sensitive applications program used by the company must be deposited with the ITF. Moreover, every time a new program is written or an old one revised, a copy must be sent to the ITF. In a sense, the ITF is a shadow data-processing department even though it need not be capable of large-scale production operations.

With the ITF infrastructure in place, the audit or security department embarks on a continuing program of taking and processing random samples of sensitive production jobs at irregular intervals, and compares the results with the results produced by the regular data-processing departments. Moreover, the ITF may be directly connected to the data-processing departments over high-speed data communications lines to enable samples of work to be taken without human intervention, indeed without regular employees even becoming aware that their work is under surveillance. The ITF procedure may expose the most sensitive information of the corporation; therefore, it is essential that employees working in the ITF be cleared to the highest level and that communications circuits used be secure, using encryption, if necessary. These requirements may substantiate an argument for putting the ITF under operational control of the security department.

The third approach to go/no-go testing is the exact opposite of the integrated test facility. In the ITF, samples of real data were processed through a computer system known to be as correct as possible, and the results were compared with those obtained in regular operations. Presumably, any discrepancy could then be attributed to unauthorized changes having taken place in the operational system.

The third approach uses test decks. A test deck is a simulated job comprised of data specifically contrived to exercise the operational system in all its allowable modes of operation. The results of having run the test deck when the system was new are stored under secure conditions; the test deck is also. Any discrepancy between a recent run against the test deck and the original run when the system was new, can be taken as evidence that unauthorized changes have been made in the operational system.

Just as in the case of the code comparison program where the standard of comparison must be continually updated to reflect authorized changes, so also must the configuration of the ITF be continually updated as well as the expected results of running the test deck.

Years ago, the most common form of input to a computer was a deck of punched cards, hence the name test deck. Today's test decks may be magnetic tapes, disk packs, floppy or mini disks, decks of prepunched card/badges, or sheaves of documents coded for optical-character-recognition (OCR), magnetic-ink-character-recognition (MICR), or universal packaging code (UPC) scanning.

OBJECTIVES

Test decks are used to:

1. Evaluate a system of accounting controls. Do controls exist that will properly reject spurious or erroneous data?
2. Test the worst-case limits of applicability. How will the system behave when confronted with zero or negative values, or with extremely high values?
3. Discover erroneous logic embedded in the programs. Every case is distinct, but totals should rise when incremented, and fall when decremented. If they do not do so in every instance, it is a symptom that logical errors exist.
4. Determine the effectiveness of system controls. Will controls continue to function when faced with a high error rate?
5. Evaluate the viability of the user/computer interfaces. Can the integrity of the system survive user errors?
6. Find weaknesses in accounting controls that could lead to fraud. The way to do this is to insert potentially fraudulent transactions and observe how the system reacts to them.
7. Improve system quality and the effectiveness of controls. Find out what conditions cause unpredicted behavior, and insert program steps to counter them.

HOW TO CREATE A TEST DECK

To create a test deck it is necessary to:

1. Define the objectives and scope of the test. Are particular problems to be diagnosed or is it to be a general evaluative exercise?
2. Study the documentation of the system including: file structure, record layout, run diagrams, and logic flow charts. The file structure is the kind of files involved and how they interface with each other. The record layout contains the size and configuration of the fields making up each record.
3. Interview the programmers and systems analysts responsible for the design, implementation or maintenance of the software system. This will let you know the intended purpose of the system.
4. Interview users and operators. This will disclose how a system actually works.
5. Determine what data records are to be tested.
6. Define what error conditions are to be tested.
7. Develop, create or design the test transactions.

The test transactions can be obtained by using:

1. Actual data from current transactions.
2. Data created to simulate anticipated error conditions.
3. Reference records which may have been the records that were used to originally test the system when it was designed. This deck can disclose the presence of unauthorized programming changes. But, the original results must be available.
4. Outdated master file records.
5. Special conditions implied by situation or not allowed for in the system.
6. Data generated by test-data generator software packages.

Generally, option two, in which data is created and errors are anticipated, is the preferred test. It is necessary to test for both erroneous results and processing errors that occur because of inaccurate or unreliable data, and those resulting from logic loopholes as well as common operator errors such as mounting the wrong tape.

Most test decks investigate system response to common data errors such as:

1. An attempt to divide by zero.

2. Use of zero instead of letter O.
3. Use of 1 instead of letter I or small L. It is also possible to confuse *six* and the letter G, *two* and the letter Z, letters V and U, and numerals *one* and *seven*.
4. Other alpha vs. numeric substitution.
5. Failure to observe the algebraic sign of a number.

Likewise, it is necessary to test for design oversights or the outcome of created conditions such as register overflow or underflow, or the triggering of special conventions peculiar to the programming language used; machine processing conditions peculiar to the hardware in use (*e.g.* how it handles an attempt to divide by *zero*); and conditions that may be produced in the on-line or communications portion of the system (*e.g.* missing bits, noise, pulses, burst errors, that is, a number of bits lost in sequence or a string of spurious bits introduced).

In testing the logic of a system it is well to write out the program logic as a *decision table* and see if every possible combination of circumstances either cannot physically occur or is handled by either a logic branch or an error routine. All possibilities should be represented by test transactions including use of special characters (*e.g.* /, #, *, ?) in the card code. The effects of multiple punches in a card column should be considered.

The preparer of a test deck should be aware that error conditions can arise on a record as well as a field basis. For example, the whole record can be shifted over one character space so that the last character of one field becomes the first character of the next. This is called *slideover*.

You can get ideas on preparing test data by:

1. Reviewing the type of test data used by the systems analysts that developed the system. Try to think of what they may have missed.
2. Preparing a checklist of conditions you want to test while you review the systems documentation and interview staff.
3. Review the flow charts examining all the points of logic (look for the diamond symbol) or use of tables. These show up at the branches. A table reference is often made by changing the subscript of a program variable.
4. Review the principal mathematical formulas such as extensions or interest computations.
5. Look up reference literature or existing test decks for applications similar to yours: payroll, accounts payable and receivable, notes payable, inventory, order processing and invoicing.
6. Use a commercial test-deck package.

HOW TO USE A TEST DECK

After the test deck has been created, the following steps need to be taken:

1. Precalculate or anticipate the results of each transaction. When using designers' data, work out the results yourself and check on their work.
2. Convert transactions to appropriate machine-readable form.
3. Secure copies of the programs or files to be tested. You want the one actually used in production, not one that may have been fabricated to deceive auditors. There are two ways to do this:
   - Intercept the program immediately following a production run.
   - Get a copy of the program and run it against old data for which results are known and have been verified.
4. Determine at which point, and when the test deck should be fed.
5. Prepare detailed procedures for the test runs.
6. Run the test; be there yourself if at all possible. Make sure it is not possible to insinuate spurious data or commands from remote terminals.
7. Compare results against known or anticipated results.
8. If the test fails, repeat the steps to make sure you didn't make a mistake.
9. Analyze, draw conclusions, make recommendations.

It is important to keep careful records of a test as you may discover evidence of fraud. Be sure you have:

1. Clearly stated the objectives of each test.
2. Kept a file of working forms and schedules.
3. Previously made flow charts of procedures you have followed.
4. Kept a good record of the master file transactions to be used by type, volume and categories especially if you are using stratified random sampling.
5. Maintain custody over input data, program copies, and results to preserve the chain of evidence.

WHAT TO LOOK FOR

These are some of the improprieties that can be uncovered by use of test decks:

1. Duplicate payments, this often requires bypassing serial checks.

2. Fictitious employees ("horses" on the payroll). One federal agency had Donald Duck on its payroll.
3. Fictitious vendors.
4. Ability to pay more than allowable maximum.
5. Payments to former employees.
6. Payments to former creditors.
7. Employees working under two social security numbers.
8. Overtime payments to exempt employees, that is, management or office staff ineligible for overtime pay.
9. Credit extended or goods shipped to customers who have exceeded credit limits.
10. New employees added without authorization.
11. New vendors added without authorization.
12. Credit customers added without credit check.
13. Shipments authorized on insufficient, zero, or negative inventory; or from reserved stock, that is, stock earmarked for specific authorized use.
14. Checks issued with blank amount, or issued with some absurd amount like a million dollars.
15. Checks issued with payee blank.
16. Payroll checks issued to employees who did not work.
17. Unauthorized overtime payments.
18. Discounts allowed beyond maximum limit.
19. Checks treated as though they were cash.

These are some of the common error conditions that should be tested for:

1. Incomplete record or data.
2. Alpha instead of numeric or vice versa.
3. Signed instead of unsigned numerical values, or vice versa.
4. Invalid codes, dates, or times.
5. Missing input.
6. Duplicate records.
7. Same code for different entities, or overuse of a non-specific or catch-all code.
8. Digit transposition.
9. Digit substitution.
10. Field slide-over into neighboring field.
11. Data beyond valid range.
12. Master file out of sequence.
13. Input records out of sequence.
14. Inconsistent data.

15. Transaction against non-existent master file item.
16. Truncation error (field too short).
17. Use of non-existent entry in reference table, especially cases due to zero or out-of-range subscripts.
18. Erroneous batch total.
19. Wrong record count.
20. Last transaction not processed, or processed twice.
21. Missing document number.
22. Re-entry of previously processed data.
23. Duplicate items or transactions.
24. Zero division.
25. Overflow or underflow.
26. Missing codes.
27. Edit-routine conditions violated.
28. Wrong file loaded.
29. Out-of-sequence job stream.
30. Wrong JCL (job control language) instruction.

Chapter 11

CONFIRMATION OF AUDITS

This chapter will discuss the four kinds of audit confirmation, and will then explain how to carry out an audit confirmation in terms of preparation, performance and followup. When dealing with large data bases it is necessary to apply the principles of random sampling. Four kinds of sampling will be covered including sampling both for materiality and number.

There are four kinds of audit confirmation:

1. *Positive* - The confirmation form contains the status and amount of the confirmation object (*e.g.* accounts receivable or some other file that is being scrutinized). This confirmation report is mailed to the respondent (*e.g.* customer) who is asked to report directly to the auditor as to its accuracy (*e.g.* balance owed). Positive confirmation calls for a reply in every case. This technique is used when the potential for loss is high.
2. *Negative* - Same as above except that the respondent need only reply if the confirmation report is incorrect. This technique is used when the potential for loss is low.
3. *Physical* - The auditor views the confirmation object to determine its existence. An example of a physical confirmation is an inventory audit where the physical count of items is compared with inventory records.

4. *Third Party* - The auditor relies on an official third source to confirm the existence of the confirmation object. (*e.g.* Vendor names may be run against a Dun and Bradstreet file to confirm that they belong to real companies.)

PREPARATION

There are 11 steps in getting ready for an audit confirmation:

1. Set the date.
2. Decide on size: *all* accounts; 10 to 33–1/3%; a number set by a regulatory agency; small sample.
3. No advance notice to the people in charge of the accounts to be verified.
4. Rent a separate post office box for replies.
5. Prior notice and consent from respondents (usually when account is opened). People sometimes tend to be touchy about what might be regarded as an invasion of privacy. Today, it is not sufficient merely to get legal consent by putting some fine print above the line for the customer's signature or on the account application. The account representative should take the time, and trouble, to explain audit confirmation when the customer opens the account.
6. Decide on scope in terms of types of accounts.
7. Selection of accounts: random, stratified, zero balance, large balance, past-due, employee or officer, dormant.
    (a) Random selection entails estimating the prevailing conditions of an entire file based on the study of a small sample selected by chance.
    (b) Stratified selection enables the auditor to select random samples from recognizable subgroups from the entire file. One might choose to select samples from groups of high-balance accounts, dormant accounts, etc.
    (c) Zero balance accounts or accounts that appear to have no balance. They are suspect because a devious programmer may have "zapped" zeros into the print-out file to obscure some suspicious condition such as a large positive or negative balance used for fraudulent purposes.
    (d) A large credit balance in accounts receivable could be the repository for "salami" sliced off legitimate credit balances by a dishonest programmer. A large debit balance can mean that a customer is over his head in debt and likely to default or that someone has fraudulently bypassed a credit check.

    (e)   Employee or officer accounts can be repositories for money taken from customer accounts.

    (f)   Dormant accounts (credit balances) have often been stolen by dishonest employees or officers.

8. Positive form for low-volume accounts, loans or collateral; here, the loss potential is high.
9. Negative form for high-volume accounts. These tend to be scrutinized more closely by the customer so loss potential is lower.
10. Order sufficient supplies like paper, envelopes and punch cards.
11. Plan the work: PERT. This acronym stands for Project Evaluation and Review Technique; it is a scientific way to schedule a major undertaking, in this case, the audit.

PERFORMANCE

There are ten important steps in performing an audit confirmation:

1. Seize control of the records subject to confirmation.
2. Investigate suspense accounts and cash items that may have temporarily been used to fill a shortage in the accounts being checked. If an employee has been improperly dipping into the petty cash or cash receipts box, he could slip in IOU's to cover the shortage before the auditors examine the box. Alternatively, he could dip into the petty cash to cover a shortage in cash receipts, then, after the cash receipts have been checked out, dip into the cash receipts to cover the shortage of petty cash.
3. Keep copies of the confirmation reports sent. This is in case a dishonest employee intercepts incriminating replies, and without a copy the auditor would probably never miss them.
4. Release records only after they have been proved, balanced, and the verification forms mailed.
5. Make a telephone check of addresses to make sure that they are not phoney.
6. Date forms and inform customers of the fact. Audit confirmation is a "snapshot" and time move on.
7. Personally investigate cases where the record shows the customer has asked to receive no audit confirmation requests. This is often done in investment accounts when the investor doesn't want the spouse to learn the extent of holdings. Sometimes a flag is placed on these accounts. Embezzlers often put such a flag on accounts they have been stealing from.

8. Personally mail all forms in order to prevent interception and short-circuiting.
9. Investigate cases where audit confirmation forms are returned because of incorrect addresses.
10. Mail with self-addressed envelopes. Use big type and big check boxes; many investors suffer from presbyopia.

FOLLOW UP

There are six follow-up activities:

1. Promptly review replies. Replies that are incorrectly completed or those that report exceptions should receive a response. Auditors should send letters of apology if exceptions are due to mistakes made in preparing the forms. Customers deserve a letter of explanation if exceptions arise due to items crossing in transit.
2. Verify all signatures against signature cards if time permits, otherwise do this on a sample basis.
3. Unsigned, or incorrectly signed replies should be returned to the customer with a polite letter requesting correction.
4. After two weeks (two months foreign; send foreign requests airmail) send another request. A copy of the first stamped "SECOND REQUEST" will do. If a third request must be made, send it by registered mail. Request a receipt in special cases.
5. Strive for a 100% response; sometimes phoning local customers will help. Usually the response varies from 33 1/3 to 66 2/3% despite even the best efforts.
6. Report results. This can usually be done in five to six weeks.

SAMPLING

Sampling is a process whereby an investigator can form an accurate opinion of the characteristics of a population by examining a relatively small subset of its members.

The characteristic most commonly estimated in sampling is the *mean* of one of the attributes of the population (*i.e.* average or expected value).

The way to measure the mean of a population is to add up the attribute values of the members (*e.g.* heights of all students), then divide the sum by the number of members in the population (call it *n*).

For example, consider the following file of account balances:

1	5123	11	9395	
2	4898	12	2950	AVERAGE BALANCE = 121,333/20
3	9485	13	2532	= 6067
4	5269	14	8942	
5	4990	15	2191	
6	9140	16	9207	
7	9819	17	7642	
8	4466	18	3725	
9	3939	19	9194	
10	8282	20	144	
	TOTAL		121,333	

The value of the population mean may be estimated by computing the mean of a sample of size N where N is much less than n.

As previously mentioned, a random sample means the items to be tested are selected from a population or defined subset there to ensure that:

- Every member has an equal chance of being chosen, and
- The choice of one member does not affect the choice of another.

There are two ways to select a random sample:

1. Choose uniformly from a randomized population (*e.g.* every 10th name for a 10% sample).
   For example, take every fifth balance in our file:

1	5125	
5	4990	ESTIMATED AVERAGE
10	8282	BALANCE = 20,732/5
15	2191	= 4146
20	144	
TOTAL	20,732	

Note that this procedure results in an error of 6067–4146, or $1921.

2. Select randomly from a uniform population (*e.g.* select customer numbers with the aid of a random-number table).
   For example, let us select the numbers 9, 4, 15, 1, and 16 out of a table of random numbers:

9	3939	ESTIMATED AVERAGE
4	5269	BALANCE = 25729/5
15	2191	= 5164
1	5123	
16	9207	
TOTAL	25,729	

Note that this procedure results in an error of 6067–5146, or $921.

Sampling studies are of two general types:

- By *attributes,* which would produce an estimate of the proportion of accounts in error. For example, suppose we want to know what percentage of the balances exceed $5000. Perusing the entire file we find 11 balances over $5000. Thus the proportion of balances in excess of $5000 is 11/20 or 55%. In our random sample, three of the five balances exceed $5000. Therefore, our estimated proportion is 3/5 or 60 percent, an error of five percent.
- By *variables,* where it desired to estimate the magnitude of the average account. Here, one selects a desired level of confidence, say 5% (one in 20 chance of being wrong), and estimates an error he is willing to accept. This number will be represented by d.

Then

$$N = \left(\frac{1.96S}{d}\right)^2$$

where S is equal to

$$S = \left[\frac{n\Sigma X^2 - (\Sigma X)^2}{n(n-1)}\right]^{1/2}$$

and the X's are the balances and n is the number of entries in the file. S is called the standard deviation.

For example, we measure the standard deviation of our file as follows: First we find sum of the squares of the balances

$5123 \times 5123 = 26245129$	88266025
23990404	8702500
89965225	6411024
27762361	79959364
24900100	4800481
83539600	84768849
96412761	58400164
19945156	13875625
15515721	84529636
68591524	20736
TOTAL	906,602,385 (Sigma X^2)

Then we square the sum of the balances:

$$121333 \times 121333 = 14,721,696,899 \ (\text{Sigma X})^2$$

then

$$(20 \times 906,602,385 - 14,721,696,899)/20 \times 19 = 8,974,607$$

This intermediate result is called the variance. The answer we want is the standard deviation. It is the square root of the variance.

$$S = (8974607)^{\frac{1}{2}} = 2996$$

The standard deviation is a measure of the spread of the values of the balances. In this example, the spread is very wide.

Using our formula for sample size to find out how much confidence we can place on an estimate of average balance size made using a sample of size N = 5, we find

$$d = \frac{1.96S}{\sqrt{N}} = 1.96 \times 3898/2.25 = 2626$$

Therefore, using a sample of size 5, we can expect to get estimates of average balance anywhere between $3441 and $8693.

For audit purposes, samples can be stratified by:

1. High-value item selection, that is, viewing only the accounts having high balances. These may be debit or credit balances depending on the business.
2. Key item selection, that is, suspicious situations such as dormant accounts.
3. Value-oriented selection — in this case you would select high-value and key items. Then:
    *   Divide the population into equal material subdivisions (*e.g.* each subdivision might be chosen to represent 20% of the total dollar value of accounts).
    *   Select three, four, or six random samples from each subdivision (*i.e.* one selection for every so many dollars worth of accounts).
    *   Compute sample size as equal to:

    N = net population dollar value/materiality

    where materiality is estimated judgmentally as, say, $3,000.
    As an example of value-oriented selection, we first rearrange the file in numerical order of X

144	3939	5269	9194
2191	4466	7642	9207
2532	4898	8282	9395
2950	4990	8942	9485
3725	5123	9140	9819

Then we choose 5 subfiles each of which adds up to approximately $121,333/5 = 24,267$.

The five subfiles are:

144	4990	8282	9194	9485
2191	5123	8942	9207	9819
2532	5269	9140	9395	
2950	7642			
3725				
3939				
4466				
4898				

We wind up drawing two random samples from group 1 and one each from groups 2, 3, 4, and 5. This gives us a sample size of 6, but in this case it can't be helped.

Our sample becomes:

	2532	ESTIMATED AVERAGE
	4466	BALANCE $= 42,462/6$
	7642	$= 7077$
	8942	
	9395	
	9485	
TOTAL	42,462	

Note that this procedure results in an error of $7077-6067$ or $1010.

We can demonstrate the meaning of materiality by using a sample of size $N = 6$. In this case, materiality is quite high. It is equal to:

$$\text{materiality} = \frac{\text{net population dollar value}}{N} = 121,333/6$$
$$= 20,222$$

In dealing with a small file like this example, especially one with such a large spread (standard deviation) conservative practice would dictate that we examine every account individually.

4. Number-oriented selection. In this case:
    - Divide the population into classes on the basis of equal class limits of the attribute measure in question.
    - Select random samples from each class.
    - Determine the number of samples to be taken from each class

on the basis of one selection for every so many members of the population.

Using our file of 20 account balances as an example, we divide the file into five subfiles. Subfile one will contain account balances equal to or greater than zero and less than or equal to $2000, viz:

Class Boundaries	_Members_
1. Greater than or equal to zero less than or equal to 2000	144
2. Greater than 2000, less than or equal to 4000	2191
	2532
	2950
	3725
	3939
3. Greater than 4000 less than or equal to 6000	4466
	4898
	4990
	5123
	5269
4. Greater than 6000 less than or equal to 8000	7642
5. Greater than 8000	8282
	8942
	9140
	9194
	9207
	9395
	9485
	9819

Now we will randomly select two samples from Group 5, and one each for Groups 2 and 3 for a sample size of $N = 4$:

	3725	(group 2)	ESTIMATED
	4990	(group 3)	AVERAGE
	9140	(group 5)	BALANCE
	9485	(group 5)	$= 27340/4$
TOTAL	27,340		$= 6835$

Note that this procedure will result in an error of 6835–6044 or $768.

Another measure of the goodness of a statistical sampling procedure is called the standard error of estimate. This is defined as:

$$\text{Standard Error} = S/\sqrt{N}$$

In our sample file, using a sample of size N = 5, the standard error of estimate would be:

$$3898/2.24 = 1340$$

This means that by using our selected sample size, we could estimate the value of the average balance (which is actually 6067) as anywhere from 4727 to 7407.

Chapter 12

THREATS TO INCOME

This chapter deals with the general configuration of the sales, receipts, receivables system; the controls commonly implemented; and the various attacks that may be anticipated.

PERSPECTIVE

The activity of many firms consists of buying merchandise at wholesale prices and selling at retail. The principal expenses are cost-of-goods-sold and payroll. Inasmuch as many sales are on credit, assets reside in accounts receivable as well as inventory and cash.

The replenishment, or resupply, system consists of purchasing, receiving, and accounts payable; the delivery system consists of sales, shipping and accounts receivable. The complete accounting system is illustrated in Figure 7.2. The lower tier of this block diagram: orders, shipments and receivables, is the part of the business cycle that generates income. We will now look, in some detail, at each part of the delivery (or income) system.

THE SALES CYCLE

Sales orders must be edited to ensure that:

1. Prepaid or authorized "no-charge" orders are verified and seg-

regated for special handling. These may be gifts, samples, or represent payment-in-kind for products or service.

2.   All orders are based upon written requests.
3.   Exact type, quantity, and quality ordered are entered.

Sales orders are processed in the computer where data regarding prices, discounts, status of inventory, and credit status of customers is recalled from tables to ensure that:

1.   Customers actually exist and are credit-worthy.
2.   Inventory balance is sufficient to fill orders.
3.   Discounts for quantity or cash and price breaks are correct.

The principal output of the sales subsystem is the shipping order file. As the shipping orders file is prepared, open orders are filed in secondary storage, and exceptions, that is orders that can't be filled, are printed out for review by management.

Summary Flow—Sales

The order entry (sales) system in Figure 12.1 accepts sales orders that have been typed into on-line terminals in sales offices; punched into card files from orders received in the mail; accumulated into magnetic tape files at sales offices where traffic is dense; and retrieved from a disk-resident file of open orders (*i.e.* "send me 14 widgets on the 15th of every month until further notice"). The open-order file also contains backorders, that is, if a customer orders 100 widgets and there are only 75 in stock, the supplier will backorder 25 and ship them after they have been resupplied.

This system consults three disk-resident files: price-and-discounts, inventory, and credit. The prices-and-discounts file tells us how much to charge for so many widgets. For instance, $10 in quantities from 1 to 100; $8 in quantities from 100 to 1000; and $7 for orders of 1000 or more. These pricing rules incorporate what are known as price breaks. These price reductions of $2 and $3 are equivalent to quantity discounts.

The inventory file tells us whether we can fulfull an order or if we must backorder. Sometimes we will encounter orders for parts no longer stocked; in these cases substitutions will be suggested.

The credit file tells which customers are credit worthy and which are not. Specifically, it says for how much and for how long a particular customer can be trusted.

The order entry program prepares a magnetic tape file of shipping orders. It also amends the inventory file to place a hold (reserve) on stock

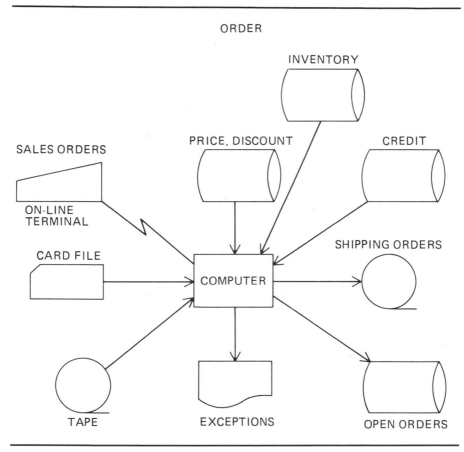

Figure 12.1. Sales system

needed to fulfill current orders and enters backorders in the open-order file. The exception report contains information regarding unreadable or otherwise unacceptable sales orders, orders that cannot be shipped because of bad credit on the part of the customer, backorders, and substitutions.

THEFT SCENARIOS

The income system is the one most prone to loss. There can be dishonesty on both sides of the counter. A leading offender among customers is the quick-change artist. The security director can help cut loss from this kind of white-collar criminal by seeing to it that sales clerks are instructed in his methods so they can be on their guard.

This drifter enters a store with a wad of "bait money" in his hand. His female counterpart, probably wearing low-cut clothing, may approach the lone male clerk with the "bait money" tucked in her brassiere. He/she will ask for a cheap article and give a twenty dollar bill in payment. The crook picks up the nineteen dollars change and places it in the wad; then, apparently acting on impulse, he lays the odd nine dollars on the counter and asks for a ten dollar bill in exchange. Many clerks will hand over the ten dollar bill before checking the money they have received.

The quick change artist now allows himself to be "caught," thereby luring the clerk into a false sense of security. Upon counting the money on the counter, the clerk discovers the one dollar shortage and this becomes the focal point of his thoughts. The offender feigns embarrassment and produces the extra one dollar to make up the ten dollars. At the same time, he lays down the clerk's ten dollar bill and asks for a twenty instead. Usually, the clerk is so relieved at finding the one dollar shortage that he hands over the twenty, and is thereby cheated out of ten dollars.

The quick-change artist also works in banks and large department stores where he may use fifty and one hundred dollar bills. These establishments are easier to cheat, presumably because of their greater volume of business.

A variation of this theme is to enter a store with a fistful of small change and ask for a small article kept on a shelf behind the cash register. Frequently, the clerk will deliver the article and open the cash register awaiting payment. While picking out the small change, the thief will, purposely, let several coins drop on the clerk's side of the counter. Following his natural reaction, the clerk stoops to pick them up while the thief reaches over the cash register and extracts a ten dollar bill from it.

Dishonest customers also cut into the profits of retail stores by piling merchandise into the bottom of shopping carts and pushing them through the check-out aisle after the clerk rings up the articles in the top compartment. They also use wheelchairs and baby carriages. Customers have been caught exchanging price tags on low-priced cuts of meat with those on higher priced ones. Other scams include the use of counterfeit discount coupons.

Computerized accounting systems make it possible for dishonest customers to operate refund fraud scams even at long distances. In 1977, a Florida man disclosed that he had falsely induced a Toronto, Canada, department store to send him a "refund" of $100,000 by capitalizing on weaknesses in its computerized accounting system. He claimed to have invested the improper loan with interest for a year, and then to have returned the money to its grateful owners, pleading that he had made an honest mistake.

Collusion between dishonest customers and back-end stockboys can result in the customer obtaining discounts and markdowns not authorized by store management. Sometimes losses such as these are incurred through negligence, by not changing price tags and shelf prices after an authorized sale is over.

In Chapter 7, we described several ways that dishonest clerks can cause loss. As a countermeasure, some stores make use of shopping teams supplied by security firms. One technique they use is to have one team member make either an exact-change or buy-back purchase while the other observes the actions of the clerk.

Lapping operations are a common source of loss. A lapping operation is one in which a dishonest clerk or cashier steals receipts and uses the money from subsequent sales to make up the loss.

In 1970, an employee of a firm of certified public accountants in San Francisco defrauded his employer of $20,000. He stole cash receipts, then manipulated input documents so the computer would print totals adjusted to cover the amount of his theft.

In 1966, a computer service bureau owner in Mansfield, California, embezzled $1 million over a six-year period from a fruit and vegetable shipping firm. He used his computer to calculate how much he could safely steal in a given period, and then did so by making offsetting charges to accounts payable and receivable.

Theft of receipts extends to dishonest deliverymen who pocket the proceeds from cash-on-delivery (C.O.D.) sales.

Agents on the street making collections sometimes keep the money they extract from debtors. Similarly, a well-situated clerk in collusion with a dishonest collection agency can see that a high percentage of accounts are turned over for collection and arrange to split the 33 percent fee, or discount, that the agency receives for servicing delinquent accounts. For this reason, an overly high success rate on collections should be viewed with suspicion.

In August 1975, two senior customer representatives pleaded guilty to swindling their employer, Consolidated Edison, New York City's electric utility, out of $25,000. They used codes designed to suppress double billing, to cancel valid obligations recorded on customer accounts. The customer paid off by giving the culprits half the amount owed. They were finally caught when checks from a customer who was paying off were, subsequently, traced to them. An inside man punched fraudulent computer input cards for the pair.

Foreign sales are sometimes made at lower prices than domestic sales. In such situations the opportunity exists for a dishonest insider to conspire with domestic customers to treat paper work on their purchases as though they related to foreign sales. This can be accomplished through mail drops or phoney foreign subsidiaries.

In retail trade, a great deal of profit slips out the back door. Sometimes it's as simple as throwing merchandise out with the trash—to be retrieved later from a compliant trash man, who splits the proceeds with the thief. Any container that is disposed of or returned to the supplier can become a temporary cover for merchandise to be smuggled out. This is why containers awaiting disposition should be broken down; and containers awaiting return should be kept open and nested.

Another way to loot a firm is to falsely produce "scrap" or "salvage" that is later sold to conspiring junkmen who resell it as the new merchandise it really is. So-called "trims" in butcher shops and produce departments can be cut so as to take in a great deal of desirable meat or vegetable, all of which can be resold.

Damaged goods, broken glassware and bottles are frequently written off as a cost of doing business. It is easy for a dishonest employee to "damage" an item he/she desires. If the employee is suitably placed, the merchandise can just be called damaged. For these reasons it is unwise to sell damaged or broken goods to employees. Furthermore, a continuous record should be kept of loss due to stock damage—½ of 1 percent is good; 2% or higher deserves a closer look.

Other sources of loss involve stales, pulls, and returns. Stales are day-old bakery products; pulls are outdated magazines; returns, in this case, are items that didn't sell. These items are returned to the vendor for credit; however, new merchandise can improperly be shipped out as stales, pulls and returns. To avoid this kind of loss, managers should keep a close count of merchandise being returned and segregate it from the receiving area. Some managers rip the cover off the first magazine in a stack of pulls to make sure they are not confused with the current issue.

SALES PROMOTION

Efforts of businessmen to promote sales can backfire when imaginative and unscrupulous persons intervene.

In June 1975, twenty-six students at the California Institute of Technology programmed the school's computer to print out 1.2 million entry blanks for a sweepstakes run by a hamburger chain. On the first draw, they won prizes worth $10,000, including a Datsun station wagon, a year's free groceries, and innumerable five-dollar gift certificates. Their computer-prepared entries made up one-third of all the entries.

In the winter of 1978, a group of promoters descended upon a small Canadian city. They were promoting something called the Golden Check Book—and golden it was—but only for the promoters. The men who put together the scheme collected more than $16,000 from local citizens. When they pulled out, two months later, they left 21 merchants with a million-dollar headache.

Salesmen canvassed the business community proposing to print a book of coupons promoting the services of local firms. It would cost nothing to participate other than the value of whatever promotional offer a firm wished to have printed in the coupon book. The promotion would also create goodwill because the books would help raise funds for the local sports club that had agreed to lend its name as "sponsor."

When printed and bound, the books were the size of a check-book and contained 140 coupons. On the cover was the emblem and name of the sports club. On the first two pages, the book stated that all certificates were "guaranteed by a signed contract" from each participating merchant, and so they were.

To sell books to local citizens, the promoters used typical "boiler room" methods. They conducted a telephone solicitation of the entire community. People were hired to man 12 phones and read the sales spiels at hourly rates, and four "runners" were paid $1.50 a book to deliver them to customers. They called telephone numbers sequentially, some as many as four and five times, over a six-to-eight week period. The books were offered at $19.95 each, but were worth more than 10 times the price in free goods and services. From these proceeds, the promoters paid $2,300 to the sports club for the use of their name.

Two months later, the participating merchants reported they were running into headaches and hassles with customers over redemption of the coupons. Each of the books sold contained coupons with a total value of $500. Multiplied by the number of books, this meant that 21 merchants were committed to honor more than one million dollars worth of free goods and services. "It could bankrupt us," said one merchant.

Safeguarding the Sales System

Precautions relevant to the sales system include the following:

1. Numerical sequence of sales slips should be checked and recorded.
2. Charges from Billing must offset credits from the Cashier.
3. Cash register totals must be checked by a bonded employee who keeps the key.
4. Get duplicate deposit slips from the bank.
5. Prove cash receipts to control totals.
6. Deposit all receipts daily.
7. Approve all discounts, markdowns, and "no-charge" transactions.
8. Record cash at time of receipt, in presence of customer, and by an automatic controllable device.
9. List all mail receipts.
10. Release no goods without a receipt.

Sales Checkpoints

Following is a list of checkpoints useful for evaluating the sales system:

1. Can payments be received and not deposited?
   - Are the cashier and receivable-ledger functions separated?
   - Are checks stamped "for deposit only" when the mail is opened?
   - Are receipts mailed directly to the cashier; and are control totals taken immediately?
   - Are deposits checked and made promptly?
   - Is control exercised over branch deposit accounts?
   - Is outgoing mail handled separately from the incoming area?
2. Can overdue accounts escape attention?
   - Are aged trial balances struck?
   - Are accounts individually followed up?
3. Can sales be invoiced but not costed?
4. Can invoicing errors occur?
   - Are pricing, quantitites, and extensions checked?
   - Is there a standard price list; are exceptions approved?
5. Can cash-sales proceeds be misappropriated?
   - Do you have a register, invoice copy, and numbered receipts?
   - Is an independent check of pre-numbered invoices made to the cash book?
   - Is control exercised over drivers' collections, C.O.D. sales, etc.?
6. Can miscellaneous receipts be missed? (*e.g.* fixed-asset sales, sales of scrap, etc.)

SHIPPING SYSTEM

The shipping system (Figure 12.2) accepts the file of shipping orders from sales as input. It produces a file of shipments as output as well as printing the documents needed to ship goods to customers such as picking and packing slips (these tell warehouse personnel where to find the goods and tell the customer what should be in the package), shipping papers to be sent to the customer so he can anticipate the arrival of his purchases, a bill of lading to be delivered with the goods to the rail or motor carrier, and a shipping order which is the document that begins the customer billing cycle. At this time the perpetual inventory file is updated to reflect the physical removal of goods. The shipping system also produces a report of errors and exceptions.

There are several opportunities for abuse in the shipping system. These

SHIPPING

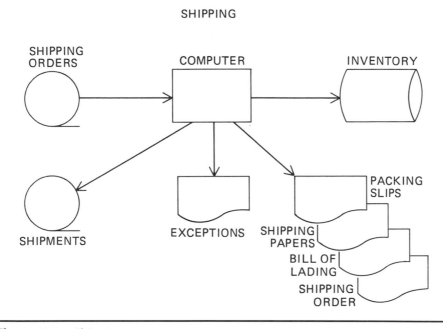

Figure 12.2. Shipping system

usually involve intercepting valuable goods before they are delivered to their lawful purchasers.

Dishonest employees can ship a lower quantity than ordered and take home the difference. They can supply an inferior brand, thereby diverting the price difference into their own pockets, or they can carry out the same scheme by shipping a lower quality item even if it bears the same brand name.

Mail order sales made on the strength of a credit card can be fraudulent if the credit card in question is misused. All that is needed is the customer's name and credit card number. In 1980, a California couple claimed that over $2000 worth of goods had been improperly charged to their credit card by thieves who had obtained the number from the credit-worthiness profile that their credit bureau kept. Organized gangs telephone individuals at random and obtain their credit card numbers under the subterfuge of making a credit inquiry. They inquire also as to credit limits. In this way, the fraudulent purchases are not stopped by a high credit check.

Department stores will sometimes deliver goods to known customers without even a credit card number. In one case, a gang moved into a well-heeled customer's home while the family was out of town and proceeded to order silverware, china, and crystal which they promptly carted away. The homeowner was unaware of the illegal entry and theft until the bills came in at the end of the month.

Another kind of theft entails giving a fraudulent high-credit rating to an impecunious customer. Of course the customer can't pay the bills but by the time the store finds out, his purchases have been turned into cash, which is split with the insider who altered his file.

In September 1976, six persons were indicted in Los Angeles for altering the credit records of 16 individuals so that persons with bad credit ratings could get favorable reports. A former clerk in the consumer relations department of TRW Credit Data altered the records. The scheme was disclosed when a man who had been approached in a bar and offered a clear credit slate for $600 contacted the FBI. Over 100 incidents may have occurred, victimizing such companies as Diners' Club, American Express, Master Charge, Bank of America, and Sears Roebuck.

Systems Safeguards: Shipping

Precautions relevant to the shipping part of the sales system include these:

1. The department originating invoices must be separated from other record keeping processes.
2. Credit terms must be approved on customer orders.
3. Invoices should be held as a control over orders awaiting shipment.
4. Goods should be released only upon receipt of a shipping order.
5. The invoice may be used as a follow-up pending release of goods from inventory.
6. Goods should be shipped only on approved orders.
7. Prices should be checked; the invoice completed, and mailed upon notification of shipment.

Internal Control: Shipping

Useful checkpoints for evaluating the internal controls over the shipping portion of the sales system are:

1. Can goods be shipped without being invoiced?
    *   Check serial continuity of shipping or sales-order numbers.
    *   Are shipping and billing segregated from cash receipts?
    *   Is access to the shipping area controlled?
2. Can goods be shipped to a bad credit risk?
    *   Is credit approval obtained prior to shipment?

RECEIVABLES

Shipments are processed against price lists, credit data, open orders and past-due orders to prepare invoices, to update the accounts-receivable ledger and to ensure that:

1. Invoices are based on shipments, which in turn are based on orders.
2. Past-due amounts are added to the bill.
3. Interest is correctly computed and applied to all customer accounts when appropriate.
4. Prices are correct, correctly extended, and uniformly applied to all customers.
5. Past-due accounts are flagged.
6. All account balances are updated.
7. Invoices are balanced to accounts receivable.
8. Bills are mailed to customers.
9. Cash received is promptly deposited and all deposits are recorded.

Summary Flow—Receivables

The receivables subsystem is shown in Figure 12.3. Entries on the shipments file trigger the billing cycle. Cash receipts from customers are entered also. First, receipts are applied against customer accounts in the accounts-receivable ledger. Next, the shipments are priced according to the disk-resident prices-and-discounts file; appropriate totals and taxes are computed; the customer invoice is printed for mailing; and the amount of the invoice is added to the customer's account.

The next steps involve monitoring customer behavior in paying their account. Periodically, say once a month, each customer's account is studied. The customer file is divided into 21 equal segments so part of it is processed every working day. Interest at our stated rate is added to all balances over 30 days old and accounts are classified by aging them, that is, under 30 days old, 31–60 days, 61–90 days, over 91 days. Statements of account are sent to customers. Warnings are given to customers whose accounts are 31–60 days old; adverse entries (*e.g.* reduction of credit limit) are made in the credit file about customers whose accounts are 61 to 90 days old. Accounts over 91 days old are printed on the exceptions report prior to being turned over to a collection agency. The open order file is analyzed and when collections are over 31 days old, the account is printed out before closing it. All actions having to do with issuance of credit warnings, entry of adverse information on the credit file, or termination of open orders are printed on the credit report.

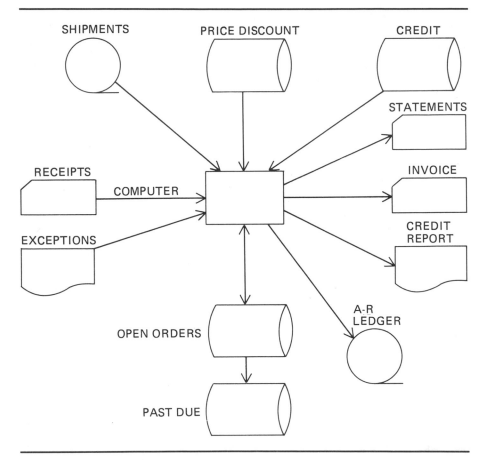

Figure 12.3. Receivables system

Altering records in the accounts receivable file can be profitable for dishonest employees working in collusion with unscrupulous customers.

In December 1977, a chemical supply company in Braintree, Massachusetts, claimed that a local service company was underbilled to the tune of half a million dollars because an employee of the chemical company falsely actuated a computer flagging code to show that the service company's receivables had been paid.

SYSTEMS SAFEGUARDS: ACCOUNTS RECEIVABLES

Precautions relevant to the ACCOUNTS RECEIVABLE system include:

1. Entry of data should be made from original documents; clerks must have no access to cash or income records.

2. Entries originating within other departments must be listed as exceptions.
3. Merchandise returned from customers should be counted independently.
4. Prenumbered memoranda should be used wherever possible; copy these numbers to permanent records.
5. Sales returns should be approved.
6. Slow-pay or doubtful accounts must be followed up.
7. Bad-debt write-offs must be approved.
8. The bad-debt file should be kept separately from accounts receivable.
9. Bad-debt entries must be confirmed.
10. Ledgers must be proved to controls.
11. Statements must be mailed to customers at regular intervals.
12. Account balances should be confirmed on a surprise basis.

Internal Controls: Accounts Receivables

The following checklist can be useful in evaluating the accounts receivable part of the sales system:

1. Can sales be invoiced but not recorded?
   - Check serial continuity of sales invoices.
   - Are shipping or sales-order numbers tied up until the documents are processed?
   - Is billing segregated from receivables?
2. Can receivables be credited improperly?
   - Is approval of prenumbered credit notes obtained independently of receivables clerks?
   - Is there proper support for credit notes?
   - Is approval required for bad-debt write-offs?
3. Is "lapping" possible?
   - Are the operations of receivable trial balancing, aging, review, and followup of the delinquent accounts done independently of posting clerks?
   - Is the checking and mailing of statements done independently of posting clerks?
   - Are customer queries followed up?

RIPPING-OFF THE SYSTEM

A dishonest employee with access to the computer based records of a firm has many strategies available to defraud it. We will now take an analytical look at the income system to try and predict possible fraud attacks.

The essential calculations of the INCOME system can be summed up concisely in these formulas:

- IF (BALANCE–DUE.GE.HIGH–CREDIT) THEN (SHIP-MENTS.EQ.0)
  In other words, "don't ship merchandise to bad credit risks"; GE means "greater than or equal to"; EQ means "equal to."
- IF ([SALES PLUS BALANCE–DUE].GE.HIGH–CREDIT) THEN (SALES.EQ.[HIGH–CREDIT MINUS BALANCE–DUE])
  Or "ship no more merchandise to a customer than his credit warrants."
- INTEREST–ADDED = BALANCE–DUE TIMES INTEREST–RATE
  Interest is to be charged on outstanding customer balances.
- BALANCE–DUE = BALANCE–DUE PLUS INTEREST–ADDED
  As time goes by, the interest is compounded.
- SALES = QUANTITY TIMES PRICE
  This is the familiar extension formula.
- NET–SALES = SALES MINUS RETURNS
  Or purchases sent back by the customer decrease the total amount owing.
- BALANCE–DUE = BALANCE–DUE PLUS NET–SALES MINUS RECEIPTS
  Receipts, that is, payments received from the customer decrease his obligation to us; additional purchases increase that obligation.

The primary attack on the sales system consists of short-circuiting receipts. Similarly, the embezzler can remove the records of an actual sale and collect from the customer personally. He can create a fictitious customer and ship merchandise to him.

A more subtle attack consists of altering files or records so as to decrease the liability of a "favored" customer or to permit that customer to acquire merchandise for which he need not pay. The favored customer may be the embezzler or a co-conspirator.

Let's assume the input file of the accounts receivable system consists of records each describing a transaction. These may be punched cards or entries on a tape or disk file. The format is:

CUSTOMER NUMBER	DATE	TRANSACTION TYPE	AMOUNT

The transaction type can be:

S =   SALE (sale of merchandise)
P =   PAYMENT (payment by customer on account)
R =   RETURN (return of merchandise by customer for credit)

An embezzler can augment the credit balance of a conspirator's account by:

- Creating the record of a fictitious RETURN
- Creating the record of a fictitious PAYMENT
- Removing the record of an actual SALE

A listing of the sorted input file with subheadings added might appear as follows:

Customer Number
01234
      Transaction Type
      Payments
            Date

	Date	Amount	
Payments	7/1/80	$21.95	sorted by
	7/15/80	$18.47	Date
Returns	7/14/80	$39.95	within
Sales			TRANSACTION
	7/3/80	$82.95	TYPE
(54321)			within
Sales	7/7/80	$ 7.55	CUSTOMER NUMBER
(78910)			
Payments	7/2/80	$ 8.40	
Returns	7/21/80	$ 1.87	
	7/31/80	$17.10	
Sales	7/9/80	$ 6.15	

The resulting monthly transaction file would reside on tape or disk and have the following format:

CUSTOMER NUMBER   MONTHLY SALES
MONTHLY PAYMENTS   MONTHLY RETURNS

An embezzler can also augment the credit balance of a conspirator's account by:

- Decreasing the MONTHLY-SALES total.
- Increasing the MONTHLY-PAYMENTS total.
- Increasing the MONTHLY-RETURNS total.

The sorted monthly transaction file is then run against last month's updated master file to produce this month's updated master file. It resides on tape or disk and has a format:

CUSTOMER NUMBER   CUSTOMER NAME
CUSTOMER ADDRESS   TELEPHONE NUMBER

DATE OPENED   DATE LAST CHANGED
DATE LAST PAYMENT   HIGH CREDIT

BALANCE DUE   OVERDUE FLAG   CREDIT-RISK FLAG

The program determines whether to set the OVERDUE-FLAG (if the balance exceeds say, $700 and no payments have been made for three months, or more); whether to set the CREDIT-RISK FLAG (BALANCE-DUE exceeds the HIGH–CREDIT limit); how much interest to add to the BALANCE-DUE (INTEREST–RATE is a program constant); and then it calculates the new BALANCE–DUE.

Another way an embezzler can augment the credit balance of a conspirator's account is by:

- Decreasing the BALANCE–DUE.
- Decreasing the interest added to BALANCE–DUE.

He could also help a conspirator by:

- Lifting the OVERDUE–FLAG from his account.
- Lifting the CREDIT–RISK–FLAG from his account.

- Inserting a current date into the DATE–LAST–PAYMENT field. (This will eventually lift the OVERDUE–FLAG)
- Raising the HIGH–CREDIT limit.

If a count of flags over the whole master file is used as a control measure, it may be necessary to cover up these actions by falsely setting flags on dormant accounts.

Similarly, if balances are taken over all accounts, it may be necessary to offset increases to, or decreases from the fields of conspirators' accounts by decreases from, or increases to the fields of dormant accounts. Thieves pick on dormant rather than active accounts because holders of active accounts are more likely to check their balances.

If, for example, you (as the embezzler) have built up a very large credit balance in an account which you control, you would want to offset it by some tactic that did not attract attention, yet kept the accounts in balance. One way to do this is to put the large debit balance into a dormant account and modify the reporting program so it zaps zeros into the balance field of the print out. This stratagem explains why customers sometimes get statements demanding they pay the sum of $000.00 and threatening dire consequences if they do not. It could be that their account is being used to cover up the machinations of an internal thief.

A thief can also:

1. Record sales by check as cash sales, thus allowing his confederate to pass bogus checks with impunity.
2. Initiate a reduction in interest-rate for favored customers.
3. Transfer payments from another customer to the account of a favored customer.
3. Cancel the deletion of an actual customer and use his account to divert merchandise.
5. Grant unearned quantity discounts to confederates.
6. Grant unearned cash discounts to co-conspirators.
7. Ship more to favored customers than shipping orders direct.
8. Ship higher quality than ordered.

Summary of Problems With Sales, Receipts and Receivables

1. C.O.D. cash sales can be diverted by drivers.
2. Direct-from-supplier sales; you may end up paying the wholesale price of the merchandise to the supplier, but never getting the retail price from the customer.

3. Incomplete or partial backorders may be overlooked losing sales and generating ill will; partial backorders may result in not billing for the part shipped.
4. Does shelf price agree with price list?
5. Are all items priced?
6. Are price lists up-to-date?
7. Do price signs and price tags agree?
8. Are special prices removed when special is off?
9. Container deposits can be misappropriated by the clerk.
10. Glass breakage; bread and pastry stales; magazine pulls; spoiled or damaged merchandise.
11. Customer rejects/returns—can be based on forged receipts or receipts retrieved from trash.
12. Coupons or trading stamps—may be forged, or retrieved if not cancelled properly.
13. Voids; overrings; underrings; failure to ring
14. Merchandise for in-house use: *e.g.* cleaning compounds, can be overstated and misappropriated for personal use.
15. Employee sales.
16. Markdowns.
17. Discounts.
18. Interstore transfers—can be used to cover up internal theft.
19. Disposal of trimmings, scrap, trash, empty containers.
20. Fixed-asset sales—don't go through normal channels; proceeds can be misappropriated.
21. Bad-debt writeoffs.
22. Consignment sales.
23. Foreign sales.
24. Outbound freight—payments by customers can be misappropriated by clerks.
25. Accounts placed for collection.

Many of these trouble spots involve transactions somewhat out of the day-to-day pattern of business; consequently, many accounting systems do not provide for them.

Chapter 13

THREATS TO LIABILITIES

This chapter deals with the general configuration of the purchasing-receiving-payables, or the resupply system; the controls that can be implemented; and the attacks that should be anticipated.

PURCHASING SYSTEM

Figure 13.1 is a systems flow chart of the resupply function. In this model, the purchase order requisition originates with the storekeeper as a result of the depletion of inventory of some item below the reorder point or upon request from some authorized company official. The request is signed by the storekeeper as well as the official concerned and then sent to the purchasing agent. If the purchase is over a stipulated amount, the purchasing agent is required to call tenders and buy from the lowest qualified bidder. In other cases, a vendor may be named on the purchase order request. When this happens, the vendor's name is run through the Dun and Bradstreet list to make sure it is not fictitious, and through their own vendor rating file to make sure they have not had bad experiences with them in the past. One copy of the purchase order request goes to accounts payable to prove that the purchase was properly authorized. Another copy remains at stores.

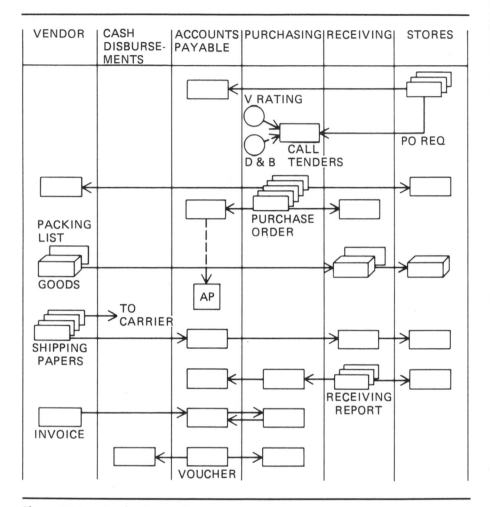

Figure 13.1. Purchasing system

Five copies are made of the purchase order. One is mailed to the vendor. The second goes to accounts payable as evidence that the purchase has been approved. The third goes to the receiving department so they can anticipate the arrival of the merchandise. The fourth goes to stores to keep them advised on the progress of the transaction. The fifth stays with the purchasing agent.

The vendor includes a packing list with the merchandise. He makes up four copies of shipping papers. One copy is sent to accounts payable to tell them what is on the way. The second copy is sent to the receiving department.

The third copy is sent to stores. The fourth copy is given to the carrier as a bill of lading.

When the goods arrive, the receiving department makes a physical count and checks it against the packing list as well as the shipping papers. Their findings are incorporated in a receiving report. One copy of it goes to stores so they know what to pick up. The second copy goes to the purchasing agent so he can tell what was ordered. A third copy goes to accounts payable.

Finally the vendor mails the bill or invoice. It is sent to accounts payable and they send a copy to the purchasing agent who makes sure that the merchandise being invoiced was really ordered.

Now accounts payable collates five documents:

- *Purchase order request* - was this purchase authorized by someone having the proper authority?
- *Shipping papers* - did the vendor ship the proper quantity and quality of product? Under the terms of sale, who pays the freight? Are shipping charges correct?
- *Receiving report* - do the items actually received correspond to those described in the shipping papers? Has there been breakage, spoilage, leakage, shortage? Where and how should claims be made?
- *Invoice* - Are prices in agreement with those on the purchase order? Have quantity discounts been taken? Has a discount been taken for cash in 30 days, if provided for? Have extensions been correctly calculated (unit price × quantity ordered)? Have sales and excise taxes and customs duties been calculated correctly? Are insurance charges, if any, correct?

If all these points check out correctly, the documents are filed together and a voucher is made out. A copy of the voucher goes to the purchasing agent. The voucher, which is a request for a check, goes to cash disbursements.

Figure 13.2 shows the cash disbursements process. This company uses the voucher system which centralizes the writing of company checks in one department, cash disbursements.

Accounts payable sends the voucher to cash disbursements. Entries are made in the voucher register and in the appropriate expense ledger, the one the check is being drawn to cover. On the strength of the voucher, cash disbursements issues a check. This action is recorded in the check register.

Cancelled checks returned from the bank are reconciled in internal audit with the bank statement, and questioned transactions can be traced, beginning with the entries in the check register and the voucher register.

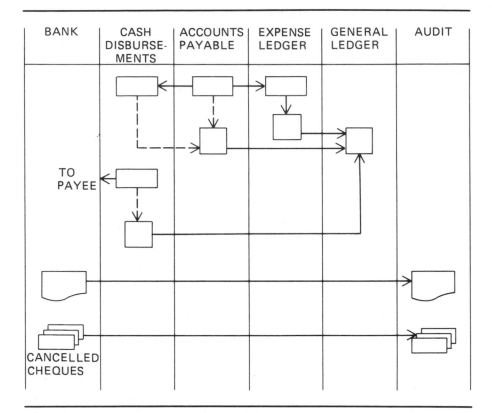

| BANK | CASH DISBURSE- MENTS | ACCOUNTS PAYABLE | EXPENSE LEDGER | GENERAL LEDGER | AUDIT |

Figure 13.2. Cash disbursements

Purchasing

Purchase requests should be verified manually, to insure they are properly authorized before entering the computer system. There, they will be checked against vendor lists and price lists. The system issues a file of purchase orders; the purchase orders are mailed directly to the vendor; and an exception report is printed.

The key points are:

1. Get authorization for purchase requests.
2. Make a record of the quantities ordered and vendors used.
3. Prepare purchase orders only when requests have been authorized.
4. Verify prices.

5. Update quantities actually ordered in a case where the requester changes his mind.
6. Use correct and current prices.

Summary Flow—Purchasing

Inventory replenishment begins with purchasing (Figure 13.3). Purchase requests are automatically generated when merchandise inventory falls below the reorder point. Requests for capital goods or expensed (expendable) items are received from officials designated to acquire them. There may also be open purchase orders (such as: "order 300 pounds of detergent on the 5th of every month"). The purchase requests are manually checked to see if they have been approved by the proper authority; then they are keyed into the

Figure 13.3. Purchasing files

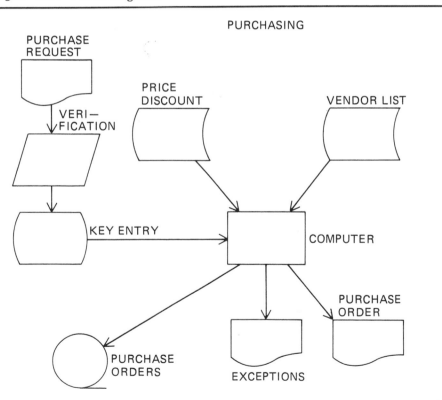

computer. The purchase order program consults two disk resident files: the list of approved vendors; and the schedule of prices we have been accustomed to paying, and the discounts we have been accustomed to receiving. The computer prepares purchase orders to be sent to the vendor and machine-readable file of purchase orders. Exceptions are printed for review. These can include prices or discount schedules notably out of line with prior experience, and orders placed with unreliable or unknown vendors.

Attacks of the Purchasing System

A hidden source of loss in the purchasing system is the kickback: a sum of money or other valuable consideration surreptitiously paid by an unscrupulous vendor to a purchasing agent, or some other person in a position to influence the choice of the supplier. The vendor generally recovers the cost of the bribe by making the customer pay an inflated price, often for inferior merchandise, short deliveries, and indifferent after-sale service.

In January 1979, the vice president of data systems for a telephone company in Texas got ten years for accepting a bribe in connection with the purchase of a $1.1 million computer. Also implicated in the conspiracy were two employees of a local equipment supplier, an employee of a finance company, a banker, and a lawyer.

In February 1977, an officer of Hartz Mountain Corp. was charged, in New York, with accepting kickbacks of $125,000 from a supplier of tabulating services and a supplier of commercial forms. An official from each of these companies was also charged.

System Safeguards—Purchasing

The following safeguards are usually implemented in a purchasing system:

1. Purchase orders should be checked by the requester.
2. Competitive bidding should be required.
3. Vendor acknowledgement should be obtained on a copy of the purchase order.

Internal Control—Purchasing

To evaluate the effectiveness of internal controls over the payables system, find out if goods can be purchased if they are not authorized. Do purchase-requisitions and purchase-orders require approval? Is purchasing segregated from receiving, accounts payable, and inventory records?

RECEIVING

The receiving report must be prepared by checking the merchandise received against the packing slip. The receiving report is in turn checked, before entry into the computer, against shipping papers mailed from the vendor.

Once in the computer, the receiving report is checked against the purchase-order file, which is then updated to reflect any discrepancies in the shipment. The perpetual inventory is updated; and exceptions are printed out for review by management.

Summary Flow—Receiving

The receiving function is diagrammed in Figure 13.4. An independent count of purchased items is made by the receiving department. This is manually compared with shipping papers received from the vendor and the results are

Figure 13.4.   Receiving system

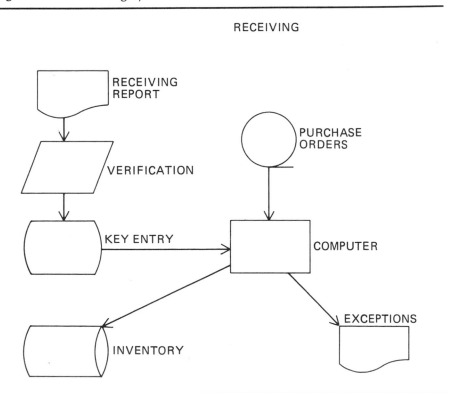

RECEIVING

keyed into the computer. The receiving reports are then compared with the entries on the purchase order file. Thus, we compare the purchase orders with shipping papers to determine whether the vendor sent what we ordered. Then we make a physical count of what we received and compare that with what the vendor says he sent.

Variances are printed on the exceptions report. This information forms the basis for claims against vendors for short shipment, claims against carriers for loss or damage in transit, and protects against theft on the unloading dock. The receiving system enters the counts of items received into the disk-resident inventory file.

The key points are:

1. Make a record of merchandise received.
2. Verify type, quantity and quality.
3. Determine that incoming quality control has indeed been exercised.
4. Check the merchandise received against the purchase order.
5. Report discrepancies, for example, short shipments.
6. Make damage claims to either the shipper or the vendor as specified in the contract of sale.

System Safeguards—Receiving

To avoid loss in the receiving part of the input cycle:

- Make an independent count of merchandise received.
- Goods received should be checked against the receiving report.

In evaluating the internal controls of the receiving subsystem, you should determine the following:

- Can payables be set up if goods have not been received?
- Is receiving segregated from accounts payable, inventory records, and purchasing?
- Is a receiving slip or other written record created?
- Is there adequate inspection, a claim made for short shipment, *etc?*
- Are invoices and receiving slips sent directly to accounts payable, not to purchasing?
- Are invoices checked against purchase orders and receiving slips?
- Are documents and duplicates cancelled to prevent re-use?
- Are unmatched documents investigated?
- Is freight checked; are freight bills matched to purchases?

ACCOUNTS PAYABLE

Invoices are verified before they are entered into the computer system. There they are checked against the purchase-order file, which, by now, has been updated to reflect the merchandise actually received. Prices and discounts are again verified and extensions checked. The computer prepares the accounts-payable ledger; maintains an open-order file on disk; mails checks directly to the vendor; and prints a record of exceptions for review by management.

The key points are:

1. Invoices are checked against the purchase-order file which has, in turn, been checked against the receiving report.
2. Prices and discounts are checked, and extensions are recomputed.
3. Report discrepancies to the vendor, and withhold payment if appropriate.
4. Issue checks only when authorized.
5. Log all checks and payment amounts.
6. Back up checks with invoices, receiving reports, and purchase orders.
7. Enter information into the computer system as it is received.
8. Confirm the existence of vendors.
9. Balance checks to invoices.
10. Mail checks directly to vendors.

Summary Flow—Payables

A system for paying bills is shown in Figure 13.5. When the invoice arrives from the vendor it is scrutinized to see whether the quantities and qualities which the requisitioner is being billed for correspond to what arrived, as evidenced by the receiving report. If the invoices appear to be correct, they are entered into the computer. They are checked off against the file of purchase orders to make sure that what has been received is what was ordered. The prices and discounts are checked against our prior experiences. Our computer recalculates the arithmetic on the vendor's invoice (i.e. extension or quantity × unit price; totals; total × tax rate, etc.). If all is correct, checks are printed out for the vendors. Otherwise, exceptions are printed for investigation. The open-order file is updated as is the accounts-payable ledger.

Fraudulent Billing Schemes

It is not uncommon for businessmen to be billed for services never received from companies that do not exist. Far too often they pay these bogus bills without question.

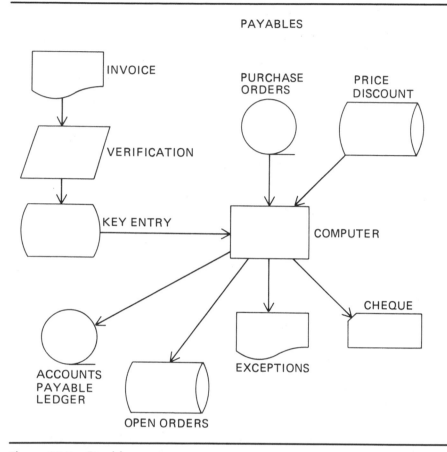

Figure 13.5. Payables system

In 1971, an official of a major auto manufacturer told me that one of their Canadian branch plants had been victimized by conspirators, including at least three clerks occupying strategic positions in different sections of the firm's accounting department. Money was stolen in the form of payments for foundry sand made to a fictitious company set up by the conspirators. The thieves created and insinuated, into the automaker's computerized accounting system, false documents including purchase requisitions, purchase orders, merchandise receipts, and invoices. These were designed to trigger both the issuance of checks and the offsetting of accounting entries to make the transactions appear legitimate to auditors.

In February 1971, it was disclosed that two men had embezzled $80,000 over a three-and-a-half year period from Forte's, Ltd., a British catering firm (now Trust House Forte). One of the thieves, an accounts clerk, infiltrated bogus invoices made out to Fountain Stores (which the pair used as a front) into the accounts payable system and made out false computer code numbers. When the invoices were processed through the computer, it issued checks for these bogus invoices and the thieves pocketed the money.

Another way to extract money from an accounts payable system is for an employee to arrange to pay a bill twice, then split the proceeds with the vendor.

In January 1979, computer expert Larry A. Glassner, the 33-year-old president of Environmental Preservation Specialists and Citation Laboratories, stood before the bar of justice in Hauppage, Long Island, and was sentenced for fraud. Shortly after, he went into the men's room and shot himself through the head with a concealed pistol. Glassner had used a Radio Shack TRS-80 microcomputer to defraud several North American municipalities out of $2 million. He billed municipalities for small quantities of herbicide and pesticide purportedly supplied by his companies. Neither the merchandise nor the companies existed, but surprisingly, most city treasurers paid the bills without question. The computer-prepared invoices appeared to be genuine. Glassner wasn't caught until a clerk in Richland Hills, Texas, became suspicious and turned a bogus invoice over to the district attorney.

Promoters have tricked thousands of careless office employees into buying listings in directories by sending out millions of solicitations which appear to be invoices for legitimate business directories. Some directories are actually published, but many have no real value to those listed in them. Many of these promotional gimmicks operate out of Los Angeles.

Recently, a law was enacted which requires that solicitations that appear to be bills must bear a conspicuous warning that it is a solicitation, and that "you are under no obligation to accept this offer." In Canada, a group continues to dupe unwary businessmen with these bogus solicitations masquerading as invoices. This happens despite the fact that they carry the disclaimer, "This is not an invoice."

On January 17, 1977, two men and a woman were sentenced in Los Angeles for mail fraud. The charges stemmed from a false billing scheme. Previously, a second woman and a third man had been acquitted. A fourth man had pleaded guilty and supplied the government with evidence. From 1971 to 1975, the gang operated an ad agency in Redondo Beach, California. Obviously, they knew they were operating outside the law because their offices were equipped with closed-circuit television, hidden microphones, electronically locked doors, vibration sensors in the hallways and stairwells, and escape hatches on the roof and at the rear of the building to prevent them from being caught offguard by law enforcement officers. Using 50 different trade names of purported minority, ethnic, or veterans' organizations in combination with numerous mail drops, the promoters sent multiple phoney invoices for non-existent advertising in fictitious publications to victim firms. If a victim paid an invoice, it would probably be billed again. An employee of one of the target firms testified he received 127 false invoices. If a firm ignored the false invoice, it would be threatened with collection action. The scheme was so sophisticated that the gang owned its own printing company which prepared the false invoices. They even used a house newspaper to prepare sheet copies of the advertisements allegedly authorized by the victim firms. This simulated the appearance that advertising had actually been placed, published, and distributed.

The agency maintained an extensive "library" of publications from which to obtain the names of victims. The names of responsible officers or employees of the victim firms were sometimes obtained by telephone solicitors, posing as representatives of a consumer research bureau, trying to warn company officials about false billing schemes. At the height of the scheme, the agency employed 75 persons. The government proved that $2.2 million found its way into four bank accounts maintained by the gang.

The employee's expense account is sometimes jocularly called the "Swindle Sheet." The name is an apt one. Many employers try to counter expense-account abuse by requiring receipts for all expenditures. However, it is all too easy for dishonest employees to find compliant innkeepers and taxi drivers to provide the documentation necessary to cover grossly inflated charges.

Among the miscellaneous gambits that help take the profit out of business is abuse of consumer warranties. Often times, the dealer, acting either on his own or in concert with greedy customers, uses the warranty to exact unearned money from the manufacturer he represents.

In May 1975, in the Boston area, an investigation touched off speculation that Chevrolet had lost hundreds of thousands of dollars because of warranty fraud by dealers who had learned how to use false serial numbers to deceive the company's computers. It led to dismissal of 43 employees in the New York and New England area. In what was probably a related incident, the body of a Chevrolet service representative was found floating in the Charles River in January, 1974. Computer-related crime is not always without its violent side.

System Safeguards—Accounts-Payable

The accounts-payable system can be the locus of substantial financial loss. For this reason:

Terms of sale must be reviewed.

- Invoice, purchase order, purchase request, receiving report, and accounting distribution (charges made to internal accounts) must all be verified.

When it comes to paying for purchases, the following safeguards are frequently implemented in the case of cash disbursements:

1. Bank statements and cancelled checks must be reconciled.
2. Supporting documents are checked during check or voucher preparation.
3. Cash payments will be made only on an approved voucher.
4. Supporting documents must be cancelled before a check is signed.
6. Checks must be mailed by the signer.

Internal Controls—Accounts-Payable

In evaluating controls over the accounts-payable system, examine the following points.:

1. Can payments be made if not properly supported?
   - Are discounts taken?
   - Is a check made of extensions, additions, discounts?
   - Are there two check-signing officers who are independent of purchasing, receiving, accounts payable, and check preparation?
   - Does the first signing officer examine the documents presented to support payment, and approve for completeness?
   - Does the second signing officer scrutinize these supporting documents for validity?
   - Are checks "protected" by a perforating printer before signature; is control exercised over signature plates in cases where checks are not signed manually?
   - Are checks mailed out directly?
   - Are payables trial-balanced monthly?
   - Is there independent reconciliation of checks? These should be returned directly from the bank.
   - Are prenumbered checks used? Is continuity accounted for? Is there control over unused checks?
   - Are bank transfers controlled?
   - Can bearer or "cash" checks be produced?
2. Can payments for non-routine purchases (*e.g.* for services such as

typewriter repair) be made if they are not authorized or properly supported?

3. Can liabilities be incurred, but not recorded?
   - Are suppliers' statements of money owing or credits on account reconciled?
4. Can charges be distributed to improper accounts?
   - Are the distributions of purchase orders and vouchers, among internal accounts, reviewed?
5. Can petty cash be misappropriated?
   - Do you use imprest funds in reasonable amounts?
   - Are approvals and vouchers cancelled?
   - Do you make periodic counts of the petty cash?
6. Can fixed assets be acquired, or disposed of, without proper authorization and recording?
   - Are approved work-orders required for construction or major repairs?
   - Is approval required for cost over-runs?
   - Is there a check on reporting of scrappings and disposals?
   - Is there a detailed fixed-asset ledger; is it periodically inspected?

SYSTEM RIP-OFFS

We will now take a systematic look at how a dishonest employee with access to computer-based files could defraud a company. The following formulas implement the arithmetic operations involved in maintaining an accounts-payable file:

IF (VENDOR–RATING.EQ. FALSE) THEN (PURCHASES.EQ.∅)

in other words, if the vendor's name is flagged as being unreliable, don't buy from him.

PAYMENTS.LE.BALANCE–DUE

LE means "less than or equal to" – (*i.e.* no prepayment).

INTEREST–ADDED (on our delinquent accounts with vendors) = BALANCE–DUE TIMES INTEREST–RATE (as stated in the contract of sale)
BALANCE–DUE = BALANCE–DUE PLUS INTEREST–ADDED
NET–PURCHASES = PURCHASES MINUS CREDITS (for merchandise returned to vendor)
BALANCE–DUE = BALANCE–DUE PLUS NET–PURCHASES MINUS PAYMENTS (made by us to vendors)

Employee attacks on the payables system sometimes entail collusion with dishonest vendors. The objective is to increase, fraudulently, the obligation of the victimied firm to that vendor. Following are some possible attacks on a payables system:

1. Create a fictitious vendor.
2. Stop deletion of a vendor and use this account to defraud the firm.
3. Neglect a quantity discount.
4. Ignore price-breaks.
5. Neglect a cash discount.
6. Pay for more merchandise than received.
7. Pay for higher quality merchandise than received.
8. Pay excessive interest on overdue bills.
9. Pay current bills as if they were overdue.
10. Insert fraudulent invoices.
11. Insert forged purchase orders.

Following is a discussion of how a dishonest programmer can fraudulently manipulate an accounts-payable system. Let's assume the input file consists of records describing each transaction. These may be punched cards or entries on a tape or disk file. The format is:

VENDOR NUMBER DATE TRANSACTION TYPE AMOUNT

The transaction type can be:

O = ORDER (purchase of merchandise)
P = PAYMENT (payment by us on account)
C = CREDIT (return of merchandise by us for credit)

An embezzler can augment the debit balance of our account with a conspiring supplier by:

1. Creating the record of fictitious ORDER.
2. Removing the record of an actual PAYMENT.
3. Removing the record of an actual CREDIT.

The input file is sorted by date, transaction type, and vendor number; its total produces the monthly transaction file for the current month. It resides on tape or disk. Its format is:

**VENDOR NUMBER MONTHLY ORDERS MONTHLY PAYMENTS
MONTHLY CREDITS**

An embezzler can augment the debit balance he has with a conspiring vendor by:

1. Increasing the MONTHLY-ORDERS total.
2. Decreasing the MONTHLY-PAYMENTS total.
3. Decreasing the MONTHLY-CREDITS total.

The sorted monthly transaction file is then run against last month's updated master file to produce that month's updated master file. It resides on tape or disk. Its format is:

VENDOR NUMBER VENDOR NAME VENDOR ADDRESS TELEPHONE NUMBER

DATE OPENED DATE LAST CHANGED DATE LAST PAYMENT PURCHASE LIMIT

OVERDUE FLAG

The program determines whether to set the OVERDUE-FLAG (by consulting a TERMS-OF-SALE table that resides on disk. This table is entered by VENDOR-NUMBER and by taking into account the entry in the DATE-LAST-PAYMENT field); whether to set the HOLD-NEW-ORDERS-FLAG (this is done if the BALANCE-DUE exceeds PUR-CHASE-LIMIT); whether to raise the VENDOR-RATING-FLAG (by consulting a VENDOR-RATING table that resides on disk and is entered by VENDOR-NUMBER). It also determines how much interest to add to BALANCE-DUE (INTEREST-RATE is found on the TERMS-OF-SALE table) and calculates the new BALANCE-DUE.

An embezzler can augment the debit balance he has with a conspiring vendor by:

1. Increasing the BALANCE-DUE.
2. Increasing the interest added to BALANCE-DUE.

He could, on the other hand, help a conspirator by:

1. Lifting the VENDOR-RATING-FLAG.
2. Lifting the HOLD-NEW-ORDERS-FLAG.
3. Setting the OVERDUE-FLAG.

4. Inserting a prior date into the DATE-LAST-PAYMENT field. This will have the effect of eventually setting the OVERDUE-FLAG.
5. Raising the PURCHASE-LIMIT. This will have the effect of lifting or withholding the HOLD-NEW-ORDERS-FLAG.

If a count of flags is made over the entire master file as a control measure, it may be necessary to, falsely, raise (*i.e.* set) or lift (*i.e.* reset) flags on dormant accounts in order to cover up defalcations.

Similarly, if balances are taken over all accounts in the master file, it may be necessary to offset increases in debits or decreases in credits from the fields of our account with conspiring vendors by making fraudulent decreases from, or increases to, corresponding fields in dormant accounts. Furthermore, if an embezzler could penetrate the terms-of-sale table, he could alter its entries to make the terms-of-sale more favorable to the vendor with whom he is conspiring. Similarly, if he could penetrate the vendor-rating table, he could erase a "black mark" posted against his confederate because of some unhappy business experience with them.

SUMMARY OF SPECIAL PROBLEMS WITH THE RESUPPLY SYSTEM

1. Removing or tampering with trailer seals.
2. Unsealed cartons from which merchandise can be looted.
3. Short shipments.
4. Re-use of receiving documents to cover up theft of inbound freight.
5. Inbound freight—is its point of origin accurate?
6. Are quantity discounts taken?
7. Are discounts taken for payment made in cash?
8. Service vendors (*e.g.* linen supply) may inflate bills.
9. Partial shipments—they may never be filled completely.
10. Nonexistent vendors.
11. Price-breaks, (*i.e.* price reductions for buying more than a stated number of items).
12. Advertising billing. Agencies may bill for space when the ad is prepared and again when it is printed—sometimes the agency is phoney.

Chapter 14

THREATS TO INVENTORY AND PAYROLL

This chapter covers the general configuration of payroll and inventory systems, the safeguards that can be implemented, and the attacks that may be anticipated.

INVENTORY SYSTEM

The inventory file is updated from the receiving system to show additions, and from the shipping system to show deletions. In addition, the computerized system features a visual display for those persons whose work requires this information, and it produces shelf cards that are used to keep a manual, perpetual inventory.

For every commodity there is an *economic order quantity* (EOQ), or batch size, from which it is ordered. It is selected to achieve the most economical balance between the cost of placing an order and the cost of holding an item in stock.

There is also a *reorder point* (ROP) which equals expected demand during the time required for delivery of new stock. Whenever the amount-available declines to the ROP, the computer automatically places an order for the EOQ.

The *reserved stock* is a quantity of goods set aside for some imminent contingency. *Goods issued* are those shipped to customers; and *orders-placed* are goods ordered from vendors.

Summary Flow—Inventory

The inventory system (Figure 14.1) consists of a single file, the perpetual inventory, so called because it just goes on and on with additions and withdrawals being recorded as they occur. Its outputs consist of a video display so that warehouse personnel can quickly tell whether or not a current order can be filled. The shelf cards which the system produces are kept in storage bins; they are replaced when a product is replenished or depleted so they always show current status. The *exceptions report* lists items whose stock has fallen below the ROP.

Figure 14.1. Inventory system

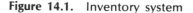

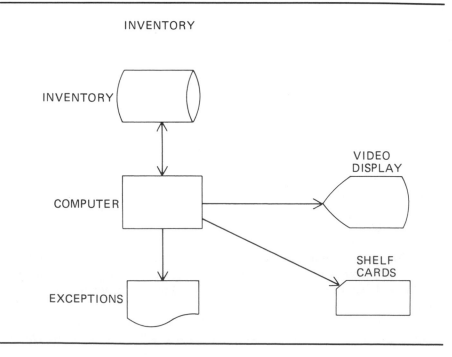

Inventory Rip-Offs

We will now hypothesize several ways a dishonest employee with access to a computer-based inventory system could defraud a firm.

The appropriate control equations are:

- GOODS-ISSUED.LE.RESERVED-STOCK
- GOODS-RESERVED.LE.AMOUNT-AVAILABLE
- IF (AMOUNT-AVAILABLE.LE.RE-ORDER-POINT) THEN (ORDERS-PLACED.EQ.ECONOMIC-ORDER-QUANTITY)
- GOODS-RECEIVED.LE.ORDERS-PLACED
- GOODS-RETURNED.LE.GOODS-ISSUED
- AMOUNT-AVAILABLE EQUALS BALANCE-ON-HAND PLUS AMOUNT-ON-ORDER MINUS RESERVED-STOCK

$$AA = BOH + 00 - RS$$

<u>ORDER</u>   (0)

$$AA + 0 = BOH + (00 + 0) - RS$$

<u>RECEIPT</u>   (S)

$$AA = (BOH + S) + (00 - S) - RS$$

<u>RESERVE</u>   (R)

$$AA - R = BOH + 00 - (RS + R)$$

<u>ISSUE</u>   (I)

$$AA = (BOH - I) + 00 - (RS - I)$$

<u>RETURN</u>   (N)

$$AA = (BOH + N) + 00 - (RS + N)$$

$$\underline{AA} \quad = AMOUNT\ AVAILABLE$$
$$\underline{BOH} = BALANCE\text{-}ON\text{-}HAND$$
$$\underline{OO} \quad = ON\text{-}ORDER$$
$$\underline{RS} \quad = RESERVED\ STOCK$$

A likely strategy of attack on an inventory involves getting the victim, unknowingly, into an oversupply situation in some attractive commodity, to allow the criminal to steal it without risk of detection, or to help a "favored" vendor.

Specific attacks possible on an inventory system are:

- Add an item to inventory
- Stop deletion of an item

- Initiate an item addition
- Falsify incoming Quality Control data
- Falsify receiving count

Let's assume the *input file* consists of records each describing a transaction. These may be punched cards or entries on tape or disk. The format is:

STOCK NUMBER   DATE   TRANSACTION TYPE   QUANTITY

The transaction type can be:

I	=	goods issued
O	=	goods ordered
R	=	goods reserved
N	=	goods returned to stock
S	=	goods received

In the ordering cycle a thief can cover up theft by:

1. Increasing the count of goods ordered or creating unauthorized orders. These orders will be placed with the suppliers, but will not be reflected in inventory.
2. Decreasing the count of goods returned to stock or destroying the records of actual returns.
3. Decreasing the count of goods received or destroying the records of actual receipts.
4. Increasing the count of goods issued or creating unauthorized issues.
5. Increasing the count of goods placed in reserve stock or creating unauthorized reservations. Of course, these reserved items will never be required by the shop because they were initiated by the thief, and not in response to manufacturing needs.

The input file is sorted by date, transaction type, and stock number; this is totalled to produce the transaction file for the current day. It resides on disk. It's format is:

STOCK NUMBER   DAILY ISSUES   DAILY ORDERS
DAILY RESERVES

DAILY RECEIPTS   DAILY RETURNS

A thief can cover up theft from inventory by:

1. Decreasing the DAILY-ORDERS total to cover up the unauthorized orders placed.
2. Decreasing the DAILY-RECEIPTS total.
3. Decreasing the DAILY-RETURNS total.
4. Increasing the DAILY-RESERVES total.
5. Increasing the DAILY-ISSUES total.

The sorted daily transaction file is run against the master file to produce an updated master file, sometimes called the "perpetual inventory" inasmuch as it is continually updated. It resides on tape or disk and has the following format:

STOCK-NUMBER   ITEM-NAME   REORDER-POINT
ECONOMIC-ORDER-QUANTITY

SHELF-LOCATION   BALANCE-ON-HAND
AMOUNT-AVAILABLE   RESERVED-STOCK

AMOUNT-ON-ORDER

Summary of Problems with Inventory

Thieves attack inventory files by:

1. Placing unauthorized orders with suppliers, seeing to it that these unauthorized orders are not reflected in the perpetual inventory records either as amount-on-order, or balance-on-hand (merchandise received).
2. Increasing the count of parts issued, or by decreasing the count of parts returned, to stock; thus, making it appear that the shortages are due to abnormal use on the shop floor. Both of these actions tend to reduce reserved-stock.
3. Seeming to put the missing parts aside into reserved-stock. An alternative to this ploy would be to change the shelf-location to some remote or hard-to-get-to place.
4. Crooked managers can rip off inventory by getting into an overstock position in a commodity that can be disposed of as surplus with personal gain accruing to them. They can get into an overstock

position by reducing the amount available (which triggers the reorder cycle). Decreasing balance-on-hand, increasing reserve-stock, or decreasing amount-on-order triggers the reorder cycle. Decreasing the reorder-point has the same effect; while increasing the economic-order-quantity increases the size of the reorder.

Attacks on Inventory Systems

With the price of nearly every commodity literally skyrocketing, a firm's inventory becomes an even more tempting target for a variety of grafters and grifters. The classic literature of white-collar crime is replete with ingenious ways to steal from inventory and cover up the theft.

In the early 1960's, a speculator named Tino di Angelis got in debt, over his head, by trying to corner the world market for salad oil. When a speculator tries to corner the market on any commodity, he buys as much as he possibly can, then he gets loans, using his inventory as collateral, to buy up all the contracts he can for future deliveries. The idea is that the shortage he has created of this commodity will cause the price of it to rise, whereupon the speculator quickly and quietly unloads both his inventory and his portfolio of future contracts at substantial profits.

It takes a great deal of money to pull off a successful corner. Even Bunker Hunt, with his vast fortune, failed in his attempt to corner the silver market. Di Angelis, who was nowhere near Hunt's league, felt the pinch early on; so he turned to inventory fraud. He had been storing his inventory of salad oil in a former petroleum tank farm in Bayonne, New Jersey. He turned the tank farm over to the highly respected American Express Field Warehousing Co. as collateral for loans. The tanks contained water, not salad oil. The only salad oil was in a narrow cylinder directly below the opening where the AEFW inspectors stuck their dip sticks to measure the height of liquid in the tanks.

In the 1930's, F. Donald Koster (real name Philip Musica) and his three brothers used an inventory scam to loot the old line drug firm of McKesson and Robbins after they had acquired control of it. They claimed to be reinvesting company profits in building up an inventory of crude drugs. These drugs were supposed to be warehoused by a company in Montreal. In fact, the profits were going to the crooks; and the warehousing company in Montreal didn't exist—except as a mail drop.

Both of these cases demonstrate the wisdom of taking careful physical inventories and not relying on documentary evidence or what other people say. In many ways, the advent of the computer has made it easier than ever to steal, and get away with it. There are two reasons for this: first, people find it more convenient to believe in an "omniscient" computer than to go out to the warehouse and count physical items, especially today when warehouses are very large and there are a great many of them, many at distant places; second, once a thief can get into a computer system the records he forges to cover up his theft will be completely indistinguishable from the real thing. There is a court case on record where a person charged with transporting a forged check interstate got off when a federal judge ruled that the check, which had been printed by computer, was perfectly good; it was the program that instructed the computer to print it that was fraudulent.

What has become a classic case in the annals of computer crime was settled in November 1975 when Jerry Neil Schneider, who had been convicted five years earlier of swindling the Pacific Telephone and Telegraph Co. out of $250,000 and subsequently served 40 days in jail, settled a civil suit growing out of the incident by agreeing to pay the phone company $141.50 a month for five years. At the age of 19, Schneider was president of his own company, Creative Systems Enterprises of Los Angeles. By using discarded telephone company documents and interviewing employees while posing as a journalist, Schneider was able to discern the workings of the phone company's computerized on-line outside-plant supply system. He was then able to use a pushbutton phone to instruct the computer to order supplies of wire, cable and such to be delivered to convenient locations where he would pick them up and, subsequently, resell them as surplus merchandise. He also entered additional false information which caused the computer to erase traces of transactions. The scheme was discovered when Schneider's truck driver exposed him as a result of wage dispute. Schneider is now a computer security consultant.

In August 1977, Lieutenant Colonel Lindsay L. Baird, Jr., (USA-ret.), told a Senate subcommittee that while he was provost-marshal of the U.S. Second Division, Korean criminals, military people, politicians and police conspired with U.S. Army enlisted men to manipulate the Army's inventory of supplies in Taegu. The thefts occurred in the early 1970's; they involved Schneider-like deception and cost the U.S. Government $28 million a year.

In March 1976, 12 employees of a furniture store chain outlet in Pennsylvania, including the warehouse foreman, dock workmen, and truck drivers, were arrested for theft of merchandise over an 18-month period. The thefts were covered up by keying into a local terminal, on-line to company headquarters in Chicago, data indicating that various items of furniture were stored in locations different from where they actually were. Whenever a stolen item was requested through a terminal, the computer would indicate that it had been "misplaced." After another item had been substituted for it, the misplaced item would be shown to have been "found," but only on paper. The scheme was discovered when the wife of an employee saw furniture on the loading dock being handled in what she perceived to be a suspicious manner and called the store manager.

The equipment-rental business presents many opportunities for inventory theft. In one case, 10 executives rented out two of the earthmoving machines that their firm manufactured, one machine to Company A and one to Company B. However, they recorded the transaction as being the rental of two machines, on a rotational basis, by Company A so wear would be even on each machine. The proceeds from the unrecorded rental of a machine to Company B were distributed among the executives. Next, they sold a machine to a third company and recorded it as having been cannibalized for parts to repair other machines, a not-uncommon practice with heavy equipment. Again, the profit was divided equally.

When uncovered, the fraud had cost the company $250,000. When asked by police why such a loss went unnoticed, top management admitted they did not understand the information provided by the computer.

A simpler scheme took place in a medium-sized city. Whenever crooked management personnel in the City Engineer's department coveted city-owned automobiles or earth-moving equipment, they declared them surplus and bought them at a salvage sale. To avoid conflict-of-interest situations, it is a good idea to exclude employees from these sales of surplus assets; try to conduct such sales as well-advertised public auctions. It may also be worthwhile to call on an outside consultant who will determine whether equipment regarded as salvage has, in fact, reached the end of its useful life. Be alert for attempts to accelerate wear and tear on capital equipment to pave the way for disposal of items where such disposal would benefit the employees involved. Employees too squeamish to turn back odometers have been known to pile-up miles by running government cars for hours in the parking lot with their rear ends jacked up on blocks.

Internal Controls

The following checklist may be used to evaluate internal controls over inventory:

1. Can inventory items be lost or pilfered?
   - Are storekeepers responsible? Is there security fencing of stores where appropriate?
   - Are detailed, perpetual records segregated from stock?
   - Is there trial balancing of records and periodic counts?
   - Does the storekeeper independently advise stock records about receipts from receiving?
   - Are written requisitions required?
   - Is there control over items expensed, but physically on hand?
2. Can inventory in production be consumed or wasted without being recorded?
   - Is there control of excess material requisitions?
   - Are there hidden allowances for inventory shrinkage, etc.?

- Are receiving counts reconciled?
- Is a scrap report required prior to scrap disposal?
- Is scrap weighed and sales proceeds checked?
- Is reporting of obsolescence slow, or too rapid?
3. Can work-in-process be charged with items and never relieved?
- Have all proper variances been developed?
4. Is information produced by the cost system adequate for proper control?
- Are reliable and up-to-date standards used?
- Is variance analysis considered?
- Are overhead and other cost allowances reliable?
- Are budgetary controls checked?

Special Problems with Inventory

1. Standing purchase orders that are not reviewed periodically.
2. Updating costs to reflect current market value.
3. Slow-moving items that can be stolen without being missed.
4. New or discontinued items not listed in inventory.
5. Expensed items still on hand—such as paint brushes that are considered to be expendable, or fully depreciated capital assets?
6. Material requisitions in excess of shop requirements.
7. Material stores off premises in rented overflow warehouses.
8. Deceptive arrangement of stock—piled high in front, pilfered in the rear.

PAYROLL SYSTEM

The configuration of a typical payroll system has been covered in earlier chapters, therefore, no diagram will be shown here.

Some of the main points of control are:

1. Job-time tickets should be checked to clock cards.
2. Amounts charged to the payroll clearing account should be cleared by a labor-distribution entry.
3. Payroll should be computed at rates and hours determined by independent departments.
4. Supporting documents should be verified and a voucher drawn on general funds.
5. Occasional payoffs can be made by a bonded and specially designated individual upon positive identification.
6. One check should be drawn on general funds for net payroll. This check should be deposited in an imprest payroll account.

System Rip-Offs

We will now examine the payroll system and determine how a dishonest employee with access to computer-based files could defraud a company.

The formulas used in payroll calculations are:

- STRAIGHT-TIME-HOURS.LE.40
- IF (STRAIGHT-TIME-HOURS.LE.40) THEN (OVERTIME-HOURS.EQ.0)
- STRAIGHT-TIME-PAY EQUALS STRAIGHT-TIME-HOURS TIMES HOURLY-WAGE-RATE
- OVERTIME-PAY EQUALS OVERTIME-HOURS TIMES OVERTIME-WAGE-RATE
- GROSS-PAY EQUALS STRAIGHT-TIME-PAY PLUS OVER-TIME-PAY
- WITHHOLDING-AMOUNT EQUALS GROSS-PAY TIMES WITHHOLDING-RATE
- DEDUCTIONS-AMOUNT EQUALS GROSS-PAY TIMES DE-DUCTIONS-RATE
- NET-PAY EQUALS GROSS-PAY MINUS WITHHOLDING-AMOUNT MINUS DEDUCTIONS-AMOUNT

The strategy behind an attack on the payroll system is to get unearned income for the embezzler or a co-conspirator. Here are some possible attacks on a payroll system:

1. Add fictitious names to payroll.
2. Stop a termination (keep paying ex-employees).
3. Transfer funds from other NET-PAY accounts.
4. Transfer funds from other WITHHOLDING-AMOUNT accounts.
5. Transfer funds from other DEDUCTION-AMOUNT accounts.
6. Treat STRAIGHT-TIME-HOURS as OVERTIME-HOURS for computation.
7. Transfer breakage of computations to WITHHOLDING-AMOUNT.
8. Initiate a hire.
9. Print multiple paychecks.

Let's assume the input file consists of records of hourly work done. These can be punched cards, or tape or disk entries. The format could be:

EMPLOYEE NUMBER   START DATE   END DATE
STRAIGHT-TIME HOURS   OVERTIME HOURS

At this point an embezzler can inflate the hours worked by co-conspirators.

The input file is sorted by employee number to produce the weekly transaction file. It resides on tape or disk and has the same format as the input file.

The transaction file is run against the master file to produce the payroll and an updated master file. Its format might be:

EMPLOYEE-NUMBER   EMPLOYEE-NAME
EMPLOYEE-ADDRESS   TELEPHONE-NUMBER

TAX-EXEMPTION-CODE   VOLUNTARY-DEDUCTION
YEAR-TO-DATE-WITHHOLDING-TAX

YEAR-TO-DATE-UNEMPLOYMENT-INSURANCE
YEAR-TO-DATE-PENSION-CONTRIBUTION

YEAR-TO-DATE-MISC-DEDUCTIONS

YEAR-TO-DATE-NET-PAY   STRAIGHT-TIME-PAY
OVERTIME-PAY   GROSS-PAY

TAX-WITHHELD   UNEMPLOYMENT-INSURANCE
PENSION-CONTRIBUTION

MISC-DEDUCTIONS   NET-PAY   EMPLOYMENT-DATE
DATE-LAST-CHANGE

STRAIGHT-TIME-RATE

Many of these fields can be the target of a fraud attack. An embezzler can misappropriate money for himself or a confederate by:

1. Lowering the TAX-EXEMPTION-CODE.
2. Using the VOLUNTARY-DEDUCTION field as a repository for "salami" shaved off other workers' pay checks.
3. Using the YEAR-TO-DATE-WITHHOLDING-TAX field as a repository for "salami."
4. Increasing STRAIGHT-TIME-PAY or OVERTIME-PAY.

5. Increasing GROSS-PAY or NET-PAY.
6. Using TAX-WITHHELD as a repository for "salami." The crook gets the money from this or other repositories in the form of an improper tax refund.
7. Increasing YEAR-TO-DATE-MISC-DEDUCTIONS or using this field as a repository if it is to be applied toward purchase of securities such as company stock of government savings bonds.
8. Increasing the STRAIGHT-TIME-RATE. (Overtime rate is usually just 1.5 times straight-time rate, and is seldom subject to attack.)

Attacks on the Payroll System

Payroll is one of the largest expense items in almost every business. It is replete with opportunities for theft.

A frequently used scam is to enter fictitious names on the payroll and cash their checks. These fictitious persons are called "horses" because of one English gentleman who did, in fact, enter the names of his horses on the payroll of a firm he controlled. He could then cash their paychecks, and thereby increase his return from the enterprise—all without any argument from his board of directors. Sometimes the names belong to real people, sometimes shirt-tail relatives of the boss who do no work.

Unclaimed paychecks lying around the pay office present a temptation to some dishonest employees. These checks should be kept under secure conditions. Sometimes the internal auditor is charged with making these and other irregular payments, personally.

The practice of employees punching out the time cards of their absent buddies is one of the most common violations of industrial discipline, and a very real source of loss to a great many firms. A photoelectric counter that records the number of employees punching out can be used to guard against it. The number recorded automatically should correspond with the number of time cards punched. The Identimat scanner has also been used in this application. It scans the geometry of the palm of each worker and compares it with the palm geometry described in a code punched into the time card itself.

Between 1959 and 1963, the manager of data processing for a New York brokerage house was reported to have stolen $81,150 by having the computer print checks payable to fictitious employees. The unforeseen return of a check betrayed the scheme.

In 1969, an employee running the payroll for a medium-sized manufacturing company created duplicate pay cards and instructed the computer to omit the detail data entry of every other check (that is, the fraudulent ones) while including their amount in the total.

During the first nine months of 1968, New York City's Human

Resources Administration, an anti-poverty agency, was defrauded of $1,750,000 by a gang of youths it employed in its computer center. They processed fraudulent Youth Corps payroll checks at the rate of 102 a week. They were said to have been caught when a policeman discovered a batch of checks while investigating an illegally parked car. Really, there was an informer.

In January 1976, a Michigan court issued a warrant charging the head of a computer payroll accounting service with larceny. An investigator revealed that bad checks, totalling $1 to $1.5 million, had been issued by the firm. Also unaccounted for were several hundred thousand dollars in income tax withholdings and social security payments. The firm served an estimated 500 to 600 clients. At the time the warrant was issued, neither the named man nor his family could be found.

Internal Controls

The following checklist can be used to evaluate internal control over a payroll system:

1. Can a payroll be inflated in any way?
    - Is payroll segregated from personnel?
    - Are calculations checked; is there division and rotation of duties?
    - Are totals reconciled independently with previous or "standard" payroll?
    - Is check signing segregated from preparation and distribution?
    - Are foremen and payroll segregated from pay distribution?
    - Are employees identified when pay is distributed?
    - Is there control of unclaimed pay?
    - Is there an independent reconciliation of the bank account or a test of payroll receipts for cash against payroll?
    - Is there budgetary control and analysis of labor variances?
2. Can employees be paid for work not done?
    - Are clock cards used?
    - Do foremen approve job, work, or time sheets?
    - Are piece-work tickets approved by foremen?
    - Are piece-work counts reconciled with production records or are counts spot checked?
    - Is there control over pay for spoiled items or other "overbooking" possibilities?
    - Are salesmen's commissions checked to sales records?
3. Can other errors occur in payroll calculations?
    - Are rates and rate changes in personnel records authorized?

- Is payroll notified in writing of additions, terminations, or rate changes?
- Are calculations checked by a second employee or a computer program?
- Is there a system of payroll approvals and distribution review?
- Is an imprest bank account used?
- Are proper authorizations required for payroll deductions?

SUMMARY OF PROBLEMS WITH PAYROLL

1. "Horses" (fictitious employees) on payroll.
2. Unauthorized rate changes.
3. Unauthorized hires; terminations not entered.
4. Changes of address to address where checks can be intercepted by the thief.
5. False clock cards; "punching-out" by friends.
6. Inflated piece-work tickets.
7. Pay claimed for spoiled work.
8. Inflated sales commissions.
9. Fraudulent expense accounts (expense-account reports should sometimes end in 5 or 0, fraudulent entries are seldom rounded off).
10. Contracts for services (made with employees).
11. Checks not picked up; these are subject to theft.
12. An improper payroll algorithm may be used.
13. Overtime claimed by exempt employees.
14. Salesmen's bonuses may not have been approved.
15. Unapproved overtime.

BIBLIOGRAPHY

Analytical Auditing, R.M. Skinner and R.J. Anderson, Pitman, 1968.

Assets Protection (magazine), Vol 3, No. 3, Fall 1978.

Auditing With Test Decks, J.F. Kuong, Management Advisory Publications, 1975.

The Bank Inspector Fraud, Insp. T.D. MacLeod, Ontario Police College, 1979.

Computer Abuse: Perpetrators and Vulnerabilities of Computer Systems, Donn B. Parker, SRI Inc, 1975.

Computer Audit Guidelines, Canadian Institute of Chartered Accountants, 1975.

Computer Control and Audit: A Total Systems Approach, John G. Burch, Jr., and Joseph L. Sardinas, Jr., Wiley, 1978.

Computer Control Guidelines, Canadian Institute of Chartered Accountants, 1970.

Computers: Auditing and Control, Elise Jancura and Arnold Berger, Auerbach, 1973.

Computer Security, John M. Carroll, Butterworths, 1978.

Credit Card Fraud and Legislation in Canada, Garry Saunders, *RCMP Gazette,* June 1970.

Crimes Against Business, U.S. Dept. of Commerce, 1976.

Do You Sincerely Want to be Rich? Charles Row, Bruce Page, and Godfrey Hodgen, Viking, 1971.

Electronic Data Processing and Auditing, Felix Kaufmann, The Ronald Press, 1964.

The External Audit I, R.J. Anderson, Pitman, 1977.

The External Audit II, R.J. Anderson, Pitman, 1977.

Finders-Keepers, Sgt. A. Falconer and Sgt. F. Cam, Metro Toronto Police, 1979.

Fraud and False Pretences, Sgt. R.W. Rivers, RCM Police, 1973.

Fraudulent Home Repairs, Peel Regional Police, Ontario Police College, 1979.

Fraud Investigation, J.A. Driver, Ontario Police College, 1979.

Foozles & Frauds, Harold F. Russell, Institute of Internal Auditors, 1977.

Great Business Disasters, Isadore Barmarsh, Ballantine, 1972.

Memoirs of a Scam Man, Patsy Anthony Lepera and Walter Goodman; Ferrar, Straus and Giroux, 1974.

The Oklahoma Offer, Windsor Star, March 22, 1977.

An Overview of Fraud, Ontario Police College, January 1978.

Scoundrels and Scalawags, Readers Digest, 1968.

The 100 Million Dollar Conspiracy Case, Joseph S. Williams, Amethyst, 1968.

The Swiss Bank Connection, Leslie Waller, New American Library, 1972.

Vesco, Robert A. Hutchinson, Praeger, 1974.

Welfare Frauds, Ontario Police College, Feb. 1978.

INDEX